FOOTBALL LIBRARY

TITLE
Rejected FC Vol. 1

AUTHOR/EDITOR
Dave Twydell

PUBLISHER
Yore Publications

DATE 1992.

RECEIVED Aug 92

SOURCE
Soccer Bookshelf

CATEGORY D NO. 065

REJECTED F.C.
Volume 1.

Histories
of the Ex–Football League Clubs.

By: Dave Twydell.

Published by:
Yore Publications
12, The Furrows,
Harefield, Middx.
UB9 6AT.

Published by:
Yore Publications,
12 The Furrows,
Harefield
Middx.
UB9 6AT

British Library Cataloguing–in–Publication Data
A catalogue record for this book is
available from the British Library.

ISBN 1 874427 00 3 (2nd Edition. Re–set, plus minor
revisions and additions)

(ISBN 0 9513321 0 4 1st Edition)

Printed by:
BPCC Wheatons Ltd.,
Hennock Road,
Marsh Barton,
Exeter. EX2 8RP.

The time you won your town the race
We chaired you through the market—place;
Man and boy stood cheering by.
And home we bought you shoulder—high.

To—day, the road all runners come,
Shoulder—high we bring you home,
And set you at your threshold down,
Townsman of a stiller town.

Smart lad, to slip betimes away
From fields where glory does not stay
And early though the laurel grows
It withers quicker than the rose.

Now you will not swell the rout
Of lads that wore their honours out,
Runners whom renown outran
And the name died before the man.

So set, before it's echoes fade,
The fleet foot on the sill of shade,
And hold to the low lintel up
The still defended Challenge Cup.

And round that early—laurelled head
Will flock to gaze the strengthless dead,
And find unwithered on it's curls
The garland briefer than a girl's.
....

(From: 'To An Athlete Dying Young'
By: A.E. Housman. 1859—1936.)

Acknowledgements:

My grateful thanks are given to many people throughout the Country, particularly those connected with, and those with an interest in, the Clubs themselves. The list below represents the help I received for Volume 1 of 'Rejected F.C', without which this book would never have been possible. There are many others, who have helped with the occasional fact or statistic, who have not been named, but to whom I collectively offer my gratitude.

The Staff, and particularly the Local Historians, of the following Public Libraries: Aberdare, Ashington, Bootle, Bradford, Burton, Colne, Gateshead, Glossop, Loughborough, Nelson, South Shields, Stalybridge and Workington.
The Staff and facilities provided by the British Library in respect of the Newspaper Library in Colindale and the Map Library in London.
The Glossop Heritage Centre.
Aerofilms Limited.

The following individuals (Random order): Steve Durham, Bryan Horsnell, Richard Wells, David Kirkby, Mike Jay, David Ellis, E.P.(Ted) Smith, Louis Burgess, Jon Weaver, Malcolm Hartley, Graham Gorman, Ray Spiller. Arthur Appleton, Patrick Conway, Dr.John Rowlands, Mark Herron, Colin Davis.
(In addition for this edition: Trans Video Productions and Brian Tabner – the latter for the average attendances given).

References have been principally obtained from countless local Newspapers – both past and present.
Other Publications to which reference was made:
Reports of the Association of Football Statisticians.
'Requiem for Redheugh' by Goff Esther.
'Non League Directory' (Various years) by Tony Williams.
'Non League' by Bob Barton.
'Encyclopedia of British Football' by Phil Soar and Martin Tyler.
'Great Soccer Clubs of the North East' by Anton Rippon.
'Workington A.F.C. 1884–1984' by Steve Durham.
'The Book of Football' (Published 1905)
'The Story of The Football League' Published by the Football League.(1938)
'The Official History of the F.A.Cup' by Geoffrey Green.'
'Asociation Football and English Society 1863–1915' by Tony Mason.
'Hot Bed of Soccer' by Arthur Appleton.
'A History of Bradford Park Avenue' by Malcolm Hartley.
'The Official History of the F.A.Cup' by Geoffrey Green.
All of the above can be recommended for further reading.

Every effort has been made to acknowledge – where applicable – the source of specific items and to ensure that copyright has not been infringed.

CONTENTS:

Introduction... or... 'A Guide to this Book'!

(As given for the First Edition)

A book of this nature requires a few words of explanation, or in this case more than just a few!

I have adopted a certain approach and highlighted certain aspects which may – I hope to only a small minority – be considered shortcomings. Having no prior knowledge or specific interest in any of these Ex-League Clubs, it may seem an impertinence for an 'outsider' to chronicle their histories. But a 'one club' devotee is liable to become dogmatic and wish to include every fact and figure – an objective that this book does not set out to do, nor has the space to include; I would stress that, in stating this, it is not meant in a derogatory manner, since I owe much of my material to several such experts. There is without doubt a place for such historians to fully record the facts and figures, and I fully applaud their efforts. I do not consider 'my' histories that follow, in any way compete with the full Club details that were, are, or will be available, but rather complement same; if one or more particular Clubs are of sufficient interest, then where available buy a copy, and read on. But significantly in the majority of cases no such fully detailed books exist, at the time of writing, and in some cases are unlikely to in the future. Whilst not complete, I hope a significant part of the gaps are filled.

My aim was simple; a passion to dig out the main facts and relate them as I would wish to read them – in a simple style. Written as it is, with enthusiasm and from the heart, then I hope I have achieved my goal, and hopefully fulfilled the expectations of you the reader.

The following paragraphs are not meant as excuses for any shortcomings but short explanations on how I approached the subject, and the factual interpretation:

This is not a Football Book!
It is a history book about Football Clubs.

1. The Beginning. An area often glossed over, from which errors are stated and easily become established fact. I have delved as far as is reasonable, and come up with what I consider are the true facts, as well as being interesting and necessary points that help to establish each Club within the framework of the game at that time.

2. Football League Days. The essence of this book, and the area where information is fairly easily – in a statistical form – obtainable elsewhere. A long list giving details of week to week matches, goalscorers, attendances etc., I believe makes boring reading! This is a 'reading book, therefore such events have in general been glossed over ... except ... those Clubs whose Football League careers were limited. In such cases I have deliberately elaborated on their brief existence. In these instances, one Club History, may be on the face of it, out of proportion in detail compared to others; this was deliberate for in these cases, little, can be read elsewhere – therefore it's here!

3. After The League. This has been tackled in a somewhat cursory manner. In

most cases the Clubs still exist and/or the historical period is relatively recent. And so once again the information is more readily available.

4. The Ground(s). In one respect perhaps the most important item. Very little information on the majority of these Clubs Grounds is generally available elsewhere, and yet as the decades roll by, and the supporter watches his team, what remains unchanged ? The Ground! The Players, the Managers, the Directors and even the Supporters are replaced and often forgotten – but the two prominent and constant factors are the name (admittedly sometimes with changes) and the Ground – again with some exceptions. 'The Ground' however must be taken in it's right context. In the late 19th Century, the home venues throughout were generally little more than a fenced field with perhaps some banked earth terraces and a small wooden seated covered area; dressing rooms were nothing more – no running water – or non–existent; the local Publican often offered his facilities with the expectation of increased custom. With a large number of Clubs emanating from Cricket Clubs, the latter's terminology remained; a 'Pavilion' was – at the football ground – the covered seated area; what we would now call the 'Stand'. To add to the confusion, what was frequently and originally titled a 'Stand' was very often an uncovered – terraced in timber – seated or standing area!

As the start of the 20th Century loomed, then passed, the slopes became concreted, the Pavilions became Grandstands, and the standing areas often became covered. With imagination (and this book), the inquisitive can find the exact locations of these Grounds, and where little or nothing remains, conjure up in their own minds, perhaps, a picture of those former days

5. The People. With many notable exceptions these have been ignored! Who should be referred to, and who cannot – due to space – be included? This is a job for the expert of each Club, where there is one, and for the statistical publications.

6. Attendances. A great fascination for many, particularly when comparisons can be considered within the long time span encompassed here. Whilst it is interesting to make these comparisons, the figures given must be taken in their right context. Crowd figures given before the Second World War were more often estimated. A 'round' thousand stated, usually relates to the estimate given at the time by a News–paper Reporter or Club Official, and therefore can only be approximate. 'Gates' invariably related to the cash receipts taken, and therefore with the knowledge of the entrance charges, a reasonably true attendance can be calculated. Conversely, precise attendances can be considered as accurate and official.

7. The Leagues: For simplicity and clarity, in all cases the original, and revised, titles of the various Leagues prior to any prefixed or new titles due to Sponsorship have been referred to.

(Additional notes regarding this edition)
Minor amendments have been made including the (relatively few) factual errors contained in the first edition, that were discovered and/or advised. Information has also been updated in respect of the careers of Clubs since the first edition.

Geographical Locations of the ex-League Clubs

Clubs featured in:
- ● Volume 1.
- ○ Volume 2.

ABERDARE ATHLETIC:	1921 – 1927.	GATESHEAD:	1930 – 1960.
ASHINGTON:	1921 – 1929.	GLOSSOP:	1898 – 1915.
BOOTLE:	1892 – 1893.	LOUGHBOROUGH:	1895 – 1900.
BRADFORD (PARK AVENUE)	1908 – 1970.	NELSON:	1921 – 1931.
BURTON SWIFTS	1892 – 1901.	SOUTH SHIELDS:	1919 – 1930.
BURTON WANDERERS	1894 – 1897.	STALYBRIDGE CELTIC:	1921 – 1923.
BURTON UNITED	1901 – 1907.	WORKINGTON:	1951 – 1977.

¤ THE LIFETIMES OF THE EX-LEAGUE CLUBS ¤

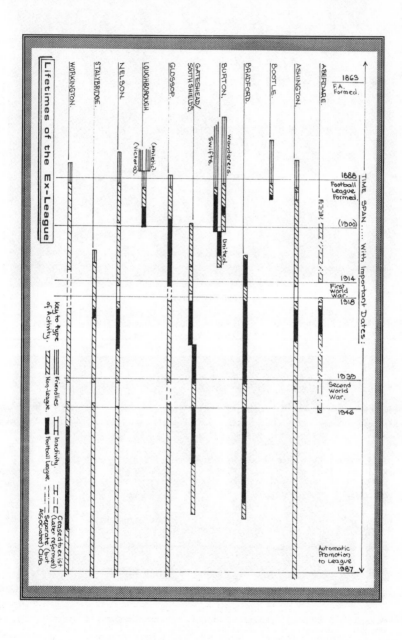

9

ABERDARE ATHLETIC

1890 Team Group:
(Players) (Rear): J.Thomas, H.Jones, J.Cook, A.Davies, J.Deans (Trainer)
(Middle): F.Caldicott (Hon.Sec.), S.Parker, S.Jones, G.Shenton, H.Williams, L.Budd.
(Front): G.Davies, W.Jones, A.Jones.

(Rear):   W.Clancy (Trainer). J.Harwood. J.Walsh. A.Brown. T.Brophy.
(Front): F.Sheldon. J.Miller. A.Nichol. J.Martin. J.Smith. D.James. B.Taylor.
         S.Beaumont (Manager). George Hall M.P. R.Hurt (Director).

The 1924 team – outside the Houses of Parliament

ABERDARE ATHLETIC

Football League:1921/22 - 1926/27.

1893 - 1914. Original 'Aberdare Town'.
1919 - 1920. Reformed as 'Aberdare Amateurs'.
1920 - 1926. Reformed as 'Aberdare Athletic'.
1926 - 1928. Changed name to 'Aberdare and Aberaman'.
1934 - 1939. Reformed as 'Aberdare Town'.
1945 - 1947. Reformed as 'Aberaman and Aberdare'.
1947 -1948. Club split into 'Aberdare' and 'Aberaman'.

****

1893 - 1896/97.	Friendly Matches.
1897/98 - 1906/07.	South Wales League.
1907/08	Western League.
1908/09 - 1913/14.	Southern League Div. 2.
1919/20	Welsh League Div. 2
1920/21	Southern (Div.2) and Welsh (Div.1) Leagues.
1921/22 - 1926/27.	**Football League Div.3 South.**
1927/28.	Southern League.
1934/35 - 1938/39.	Welsh League Div.1.
1939/40 - 1945/46.	Ceased Activity.
1945/46 - 1947/48.	Welsh League Div.1.

(((((((((((((+)))))))))))))

Football League Record:

	Played	W.	D.	L.	F.	A.	Pts.	Posn.
1921/22.	42	17	10	15	57	51	44	8th.
1922/23.	42	9	11	22	42	70	29	21st.

Successfully re-elected.

	Played	W.	D.	L.	F.	A.	Pts.	Posn.
1923/24.	42	12	14	16	45	58	38	12th.
1924/25.	42	14	9	19	54	67	37	18th.
1925/26.	42	17	8	17	74	66	42	9th.
1926/27.	42	9	7	26	62	101	25	22nd.

Unsuccessful re-election application 1927.

Summary of Facts.

Grounds:	c.1893:	Aberdare Park.
	from c.1893:	Athletic Ground. (Also referred to as Ynys Stadium)
	1934 - 1939:	Plasdraw Park.
	1945 - 1948:	Ynys Stadium.

Nickname: 'Darians' or 'Dare'

Colours: Football League: Blue and Gold Striped Shirts, White Shorts.
(Maroon shirts with white cuffs and pocket to 1898.
from 1898/99 Dark Blue and Gold Striped Shirts)

First League Game: August 27th 1921.(Home) Versus Portsmouth. (0-0 draw)
Attendance: 10,000.
Last League Game: May 7th 1927. (Home) Versus Brighton. (0-0 draw)

Record Attendance: (Claimed Capacity: 40,000).
Ground: 22,584. Wales v. Scotland Schoolboys. 14th May 1921.
Club: 16,350 (Receipts £864) Versus Bristol City (3rd Division South). 2nd April 1923.
Football League average attendances: 1st season 9,525. Last season 2,499.

Programmes: Believe to have been issued throughout from re-formation in 1920.
....

Main Achievements:
Best League Match Win -   8-1 v. Watford. (Home) 1925/26.
Worst League Match Defeat - 0-7 v. Q.P.R. (Home) 1926/27.
Total Number of Football League matches played: 252.

International Players (Wales):   W.Jones (1900/01). H.Jones (1901/02).
T.Jones (1907/08). A.Brown (1925/26). L.Evans (1926/27).

F.A.Cup: (Modern day equivalent, 3rd Round)
Reached 1st Round: 1922/23. 1923/24. 1925/26.
(As Non-League Club)   First Round: 1927/28.
Southern League (Welsh Section):   Runners-up 1920/21.
Welsh League Champions: Div.1 1920/21.
Div.2 1919/20.

South Wales League Champions: 1899/1900.
League Cup Winners: 1901/02.
Welsh Senior Cup Runners-up: 1903/04. 1904/05. 1922/23.

THE CENTRE OF THE STAND
Showing Extensions in course of construction on the North End.

There can be few Football Clubs who have consistently bounced back following financial adversities that have caused the earlier collapse of a local team; it is perhaps a tribute to the enthusiasts in the area who fought so gamely to ensure the representation of a Football ('round ball') Club in an area which was becoming a Rugby Union stronghold. Whilst a Senior Football team in Aberdare no longer exists it is now an historical fact that the town shares a distinction shared only by a hundred or so other towns, in that for a period the population has been able to enjoy full Football League status.

The full facts concerning the actual formation of a Football Club in Aberdare are now, as is so often the case, lost in the mists of time. The one inescapable fact remains that a Football Club was first formed in the town during 1893, representing one of the earliest - if not the first - in Southern Wales. North Wales adopted the game around ten years earlier, and it was not until the 1890's that Football recognition in the South was fully appreciated with the final accolade of appearances in the Welsh Senior Cup Final, by Aberaman in 1903, followed by Aberdare the following two years.

The actual formation of Aberdare Town F.C. has been attributed to a few men from the Midlands who had moved to the Welsh Coal Mining area for employment; more conclusively was the involvement of Mr. J.E.Newton, who, in 1893, became the Club's first Secretary. Initially the Club played their home matches in unenclosed Aberdare Park, but within a short time moved to Ynys Meadow. The Ynys consisted (as it still does to this day) of a large grassed area to the South-East of the town, for which an initial annual rent for the Club's part use was £5-00. That the playing pitch was at least partially fenced in during these early days is evidenced by the entrance charge of 3d. (just over 1p), but free to ladies. No record of the first ever match has been traced, but the attendance was ten!

With few local opponents and a lack of an organised regional competition, the Club had to rely on playing friendly games until their entry into the first local League - the South Wales League - for the 1897/98 season. The popularity of the game was shown by the 'large crowds' that were reported, including a stated attendance of 1,500 for the friendly match visit of Llandiloes over Christmas 1897. The constitution of the 8 club league at this time was: Aberdare, Barry District, Ebbw Vale, Rogerstone, Porth, Nelson, St.Margarets, and Cardiff Teachers.

By 1898, Aberdare had become one of the undisputed top Clubs in South Wales and prestigious friendly games were played. Two notable matches were the visit of Sheffield United in the 1898/99 season (F.A.Cup Winners) when the ability of the Welsh team was noted with their 2-1 victory, (the

13

Aberdare goals were scored by the new Secretary – Fred Caldicott), plus the appearance next season of Aston Villa (Football League Champions). The Villa game resulted in a 1–6 reverse for the Non–leaguers, but was watched by a record attendance of approximately 8,000, who paid £120 for the privilege. The Club had by now entered their most successful period and proceeded to win the Leominster Cup in seasons 1899/1900 and 1901/02 plus the South Wales League Championship and League Cup. Also appearances in the finals of the Welsh Senior Cup and the winning of the South Wales Cup were made during this time. In 1900 the legendary Billy ('Fatty') Wedlock, later to move on to Bristol City, signed for the Club. The Chairman of the Welsh League since 1901 – T.D.Jones – became the Club's new Secretary in 1903.

Aberdare Town's relative prosperity was demonstrated with the erection of a moveable Grandstand (complaints were made that it had been erected facing the sun) in 1900, which overlooked the pitch during the football season. Other improvements to the Club's Ground and facilities were also made. The last match in the 1898/99 season – a single goal victory at Swansea – clinched the League Championship, and the homecoming was celebrated with a wagonette procession of the team, headed by a brass band, through large cheering crowds. The Club's books showed some interesting expenditures: Ground rent – £5, Fencing to field – £11, Police – £8–12–6d, Players travelling expenses – £46, plus Players Expenses of £34. The latter item moving a Mr.J.Davies to allege that:
" The Club had not carried out its Amateur status." (!)

Season ticket prices for the 1899/1900 season were 3/6d. (17.5p.) and the Club's supporters were able to see their team progress the furthest to date in the Welsh Cup. Home victories were recorded over Barry Unionists and Rogerstone (each game before 800 home 'gates') before bowing out at Rhyl in the 3rd round. Christmas victories were achieved in home friendlies versus near neighbours Aberaman – 7–0 (goalless first half) and Crewe Alexandria – 6–1. Aberaman, who were linked to Aberdare so frequently during the ensuing years, were a South Wales League Division 2 team at this time but became 1st Division Champions three years later in their only season ever as a professional Club.

For a few years Aberdare endured a slump period but were revitalised, with the appointment of W.Cas.Jones as Secretary during the 1906/07 season, and who assisted in no small way towards the team's further progress. This revitalisation resulted in the Club's entry in the 1907/08 season, into the Western League Division 2 – along with the likes of the reserve teams of Bristol Rovers and City – as well as the Glamorganshire League (later to become the Welsh League).

Two years later another upward step was made with the team's invited entry into the Southern League Division 2 with the unusual guarantee (which appears to have been unfulfilled) that providing the Club remained with the League for two consecutive seasons they would be automatically promoted to the 1st Division! In addition, and in view of the long travelling distances involved (amazingly Burton United and Stoke helped to form the six Club, section 'A' division), Aberdare – together with Merthyr and Ton Pentre – were allowed to select referees and linesmen from their own localities!

The anticipated 'huge' gates at matches did not materialise, aided in no small way by the Club finishing in bottom position (although their fixtures were not completed), and with high travelling costs finance became a very real problem. The Club's first match in the Southern League was on the 6th of September 1909, when Ton Pentre were beaten by two goals (one in each half), with Bradbury scoring the first. No other wins were achieved in the seven games that were played. However the Ynys had undoubtably become one of the best grounds in Wales, and the Club had been honoured with the staging of a full International match in 1908 (0–1 defeat to Ireland), and an Amateur game versus England one year later.

Few successes were achieved in the years leading up to the First World War, and the wisdom of the Club's 16 Directors to remain in the Southern League was questioned as finances reached a critical level. Even anticipated 'money spinner' friendly matches – with the single goal victory over Aberaman Athletic on the 30th of April 1914 and a 3–1 win over Cardiff (a gate of £35) seven days later – failed to attract large support. The last Southern League match resulted in a 2–2 draw at Caerphilly, and shortly afterwards the Club folded, blaming lack of support and poor management as the causes for the demise of the *'Oldest Soccer Club in South Wales'*.

Soon after the end of the hostilities, a new Club was born in the town, that of Aberdare Amateurs, who managed no small success by becoming the Welsh League Division 2 Champions in their first, and only season (1919/20). However a large body of football followers in the area decided that a 'new' Aberdare should be formed on a professional level. A meeting on the 13th of April 1920 at Mile's Restaurant was convened by the local Chamber of Commerce and was attended by all sections of the community. The meeting captured the imagination of the local populace with such a large and enthusiastic gathering that many were shut out. The initiative had already been taken by the hitherto non–football minded Mr.W.M.Llewellyn M.E., with his announcement that he had purchased the Ynys Field for the purpose of staging football there. It was acknowledged that in the past there had been lack of capital and security of tenure at the ground, and along with Mr.F.W.Mander J.P., Illtyd G.Williams (one time Chairman of the former

Club) and Cas.Jones (the former club's Secretary), Mr.Llewellyn outlined the ambitious plans that had been made for the new Club.

A limited Company with a share capital of £10,000 was proposed with the intention that 50% should be available by subscription via 5/- (25p) shares; four individuals had already indicated their willingness to each purchase £250 of shares. Such a confident move would: *"Invariably produce a Football team worthy of the Football League, would encourage Business and healthy recreation in the town (and draw men away from the Pubs), and attract enormous crowds to the team's matches ..... it was galling for many of those present to see the rise and success of Cardiff City and Swansea Town F.C."*

It was with a feeling of euphoria that those assembled were told that it was the Club's intention to enter both the Welsh and Southern Division 2 Leagues (uncertainty was expressed over the best route towards the Football League!), and for the Ynys to be converted into an impressive football ground, with a grandstand and embankments to all four sides.

Officials from Aberdare Amateurs F.C. – a club started by just a few enthusiasts and little money – who could now feel proud of being £50 in credit, were present at the meeting, and Mr.Shelby James (Secretary) was offered the chance for the team to throw in their lot with the new ambitious Club. Despite their initial, not unreasonable, reluctance and 'upstaging' experience, the Amateurs eventually disbanded. Many players subsequently played for Aberdare Athletic, most of them appearing as amateurs in the Welsh League Division 2 reserve team.

Despite the earlier promises and £250 raised at the April meeting, only 19 shareholders had come forward by mid–July. However, not discouraged, Mr.Bowen – who had been appointed as Secretary of *'The movement to retain Football in Aberdare'* – pursued his task and by the start of the 1920/21 football season an impressive set–up had been accomplished – albeit with reduced financial participation from the public. £4,000 had been spent on laying out the field, £600 paid on summer wages and although work had commenced on the impressive Grandstand, £6,000 in total would eventually be spent on the completion of it.

On the 16th of August the Club's first trial match was played before an attendance of around 2,000, with many ex–Football and Southern League personalities on view; Leahy and Bradshaw (Southend), Jones, Kelso and Hughes (the latter a Welsh International) from Manchester City, Hudson (Manchester United), Thompson (Norwich), Turner (Sunderland), Taylor

(Wolves), Rogers and Spottiswoode (Crystal Palace), Henderson (Brighton), Tomkinson (Stoke), Sheldon (Swansea) and Hyam from Bristol Rovers. It is doubtful if any Club formed in such a short period had ever commenced a season with such an impressive array of talent.

Aberdare Athletic F.C. played their first competitive match on August the 28th at Porth in the Welsh league Division 1, and the 1,000 'Darian' supporters cheered their team on to a resounding 4–0 win, with goals by Bradshaw, Rogers, Sheldon and Player/Manager Cas.Jones. However the Porth ground must have come as a shock to most of the players since it consisted of nothing more than a levelled out ash tip! The first home game on September the 2nd, versus Bargoed, was attended by some 4,000 spectators each paying 8d.(3.5p) admission. A 10,000 crowd was anticipated, but the reduced numbers were happy with the 2–0 victory.

With regular victories following, the attendances rose – September the 4th, 5,245 (versus Porth)... over 5,000 for the visit of Treherbert... 7,500 versus Pontypridd, and 8,000 (£458 receipts) for the local Welsh League derby with Aberaman on New Year's Day. After 8 games the team were 5 points clear at the top of the Welsh League and finished the season as Champions.

Games started later in the Southern League with the first being played at Pontypridd on the 11th of October (a one goal defeat) and the first home encounter on November the 1st versus Mid–Rhonda. Life in this company was harder, but nonetheless a final Runners–up position was achieved in the 11 team league. The first ever F.A.Cup match in Aberdare attracted a 6,000 gate to see the 2–0 win over Barry; but further progress was halted at Bath City following a home drawn game.

The fame of this new Club was spreading, for even the reserves were proving to be an attraction both at home and away; the visit to Abercynon produced a new record attendance in South Wales Junior football with a £100 – around 5,000 – gate. Robert Spottiswoode, who had been expected to become a favourite with the crowds, found his time in Aberdare come to an abrupt end in November following a dispute with the Club.

Meanwhile the Ground was rapidly developing with the completion of the Grandstand (although the anticipated extensions scheduled for Easter 1921 had to be postponed in January with £3,000 still required), and the new dressing Rooms by Christmas. On May the 14th 1921 an all time record attendance was established at the Ynys when an astounding 20,000 crowd attended the Wales versus Scotland Schoolboy International, with Aberdare providing three players, for the 0–3 defeat.

– Aberdare Athletic –

The new Club's first programme and Cardiff City offer their support for Aberdare's League application.

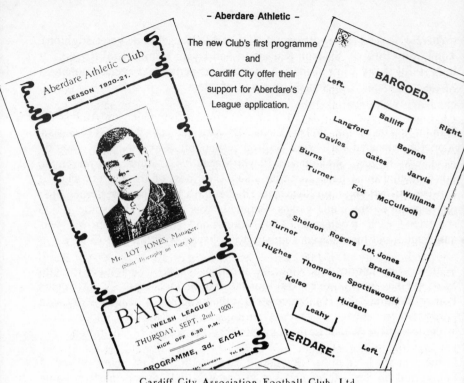

Aberdare Athletic Club
SEASON 1920-21.

Mr. LOT JONES, Manager.
(Short Biography on Page 3).

BARGOED
(WELSH LEAGUE)
THURSDAY, SEPT. 2nd, 1920.
KICK OFF 6.30 P.M.
PROGRAMME, 3d. EACH.

BARGOED.

Left.   Right.
        Langford   Balliff
    Davies   Beynon
  Burns   Gates
    Turner   Jarvis
            Fox   Williams
                McCulloch
            O
        Sheldon Rogers Lot Jones
    Turner   Bradshaw
  Hughes Thompson Spottiswoode
      Kelso   Hudson
          Leahy

ERDARE.   Left.

Cardiff City Association Football Club, Ltd.

52 Partridge Road,

Cardiff,

May 17th, 1920.

To the Aberdare Athletic Club.

    On behalf of Cardiff City Football Club I have great pleasure in wishing you success in your efforts to secure admission to the Third Division of the League. You have a splendid ground in the midst of a big sporting population, and are ensured of the support necessary to run a League Club successfully. Your application has the whole-hearted support of my Directors, and we shall be glad to do anything to help on your cause.

        Yours faithfully,

Fred Stewart.

The formation of the 3rd Division North of the Football League during the Summer of 1921 resulted in a change of divisions for Grimsby Town, and with the promotion of Crystal Palace, the way was left clear for the election of two new clubs to the Southern section of the 3rd Division. A vigorous campaign was undertaken by the 'Darians' led by the indominatable young Chairman, W.M.Llewellyn. Although all the other Clubs seeking election could point to a longer history, none could present a better case than Aberdare for potential. With a local population of 75,000 and a claimed catchment area encompassing some half million, good support was thought inevitable. The past season appeared to proved the point with attendances rising to five figures, and crowds of 15 to 18,000 in the Third Division were confidently anticipated.

The Club owned the freehold of the six acre Ynys, and could now boast of a ground capacity of 35,000 (with a hoped for increase to 65,000), a Stand seating 1,000 (4,000 with extensions that were underway) complete with modern Dressing Rooms, Offices etc. The Club were on a reasonably sound financial footing and had by now 1,500 shareholders from the general public.

On May the 30th a telegram was sent by Llewellyn to the Club:
" Kingsway, London.
Aberdare top of Poll. Charlton second".

With 38 votes from a possible 45 the Club had gained the confidence of the Football League members; other (unsuccessful) Welsh applicants were, Barry, Aberaman, Abertillery, Bridgend and Pontypridd. Llewellyn's return to Aberdare was greeted with that normally reserved for a returning hero, with thousands of people and the brass band assembled in Victoria Square.

The pre–season trial game on August the 20th was seen by over 6,000 spectators, and one week later the first game in the 3rd Division South was played. Portsmouth were the visitors to the Ynys and a crowd of 10,000 witnessed an evenly matched scoreless draw. On the 3rd of September the first away game produced a 2–1 win at Swansea, followed two days later by a 4–1 (0–1 at half time) victory in the return match – a 15,000 crowd was present for the all Welsh game. On September the 24th, following the home win over Watford attended by 10,000, the Club was top of the League. The euphoria created by the team's incredible start was quelled by a run of mediocre games, and by the end of November the warning bells were already sounding with home attendances dropping to less than the 10,000 required to break even. Football, after the initial boost experienced following the end of the War, had already started a general downturn with Lincoln City and Charlton Athletic in serious financial trouble.

EMBANKMENT AT ONE END OF FIELD
During progress of a Match

ANOTHER VIEW OF FIELD

Extract from the Club's Football League application brochure.

By Christmas Aberdare lay in 6th position in the League, although the enthusiasm was still present, albeit at a lower level than that hoped for, whilst the reserves were regularly attracting four figure crowds. A record attendance was expected for the local derby match with Merthyr Town on January the 21st, but the special trainloads of away supporters were disappointed when the match was postponed due to a waterlogged pitch; the game was finally played on April the 10th, when a 14,000 crowd witnessed a drab scoreless draw. The best–of–season score, 6–1, was achieved with the visit of Gillingham on the 8th of April. No honours were won in cup Competitions – the first round of the F.A. Cup was not reached, and in the Welsh competition a 2–3 home defeat to Swansea in the second round resulted. However a measure of the popularity of the game at this time could be judged by the 9,000 attendance at the Ground who saw the Southern League beat the Welsh League by 3–1 in a representative match.

A final League placing of 8th was hardly a disaster, but gate receipts were down on that anticipated, and plans were put in hand to make collections for the Club's benefit, at the local Collieries. Mr. Llewellyn, who had acquired the status of a local 'Folk Hero', was also known as the *'Coal King'* in his position as Manager of Bwllfa Collieries.

The first game of the 1922/23 season started well enough with a 3–1 win over Exeter City, but this type of result was to be only rarely repeated. As the defeats followed, then inevitably so did the attendances drop, and worries were frequently expressed. The Supporters Club which had been formed in January 1922 showed natural concern over the deteriorating state of the Club's finances, which was countered by the Football Club's warning them not to interfere with the financial aspects of the organisation! This led to a threatened boycott of matches by the supporters – which was not carried out – and by the end of the season the two 'clubs' had patched up their differences. Conversely a good run was made in the F.A.Cup. In the 5th qualifying round Newport County were finally disposed of at Cardiff, after two drawn matches, followed by a 2–1 replay win at Carlisle. The first round proper provided the Club with the most glamorous match in the Club's history when the mighty Preston North End visited Wales. The attendance of over 16,000 on January the 13th represented a club match record to that date, with the remark that although the ground was *'black with people'*, so spacious was the enclosure that there was still plenty of room for more!

> *Leahy, Price, Brooks, Saunderson, Anderson, Archibald, Tompkinson, Brown, Martin, Rogers and James....*
> formed the home team's line–up.

The Darians put up a spirited fight, despite the visitors rather flattering 3–1 win.

Poor results in the League continued and the gates remained disappointing. Both matches with 'high–flying' Swansea were lost with the home game producing:

> *"Probably the worst game ever seen at the Ynys Enclosure."*

Despite being a local 'derby' the attendance was well under 9,000. Something of a recovery was made during February and March, including surprise away victories over Norwich (4-1) and Brentford. This form encouraged the crowds and for the visit of table-topping Bristol City (aided by a large contingent from over the Severn) an all time Club record crowd of 16,350 (£864 receipts) was present. At the final count it was a dismal season in the League and with a final bottom but one placing, a re-election submission had to be made, with the Club being retained with maximum votes. The final of the Welsh Cup was surprisingly reached, the deciding game producing a defeat to Cardiff at Swansea before an 8,000 crowd.

With a Supporters Club membership of 4,000 and the appointment of a new team Manager - ex-England International Frank Bradshawe - it was hoped that the previous year would only be a temporary setback. On the playing front this optimism was justified, for a big improvement to a final placing of midway (12th) in the League resulted. Despite reaching the 1st round proper of the F.A.Cup again, the Club were unceremoniously knocked out with five unopposed goals at First Division West Ham. However the new Manager's stay was a short one for he left the Club in April 1924. On the financial front things were far from rosy, with fears expressed as to the Club's future being voiced in May. This led to a public meeting and a pledge by the true supporters to make 3d (1p) weekly donations to the Club.

The 1924/25 season gave little cause for celebration as a slide down the table to a final 18th position resulted, with little progress in the two major Cup Competitions. In the financial circumstances - which was aggravated by the mounting unemployment in the area - it was somewhat surprising, and perhaps foolhardy, that further money was spent to complete the long awaited extensions to the Grandstand. The Club's entry to the Football League five years earlier was hoped to attract at least 15,000 home gates; however anything like this number was only very rarely reached, and by the 1925/26 season a norm of approximately 8,000 had to be budgeted for. On November the 9th tragedy hit the Club, when a fire completely gutted the Wooden Grandstand - plus the Offices and Dressing Rooms below - that the Club were justifiably so proud of. Whilst the Club received £10,000 in insurance money, it was a blow to morale for those connected with the Club. On the playing front it turned out to be a season of mixed fortunes.

Whilst heavy defeats were experienced, including five goal defeats at Brighton and Norwich, the Club's record win was also achieved - 8-0 at home to Watford on January the 2nd before one of the smallest gates of the season. The F.A.Cup brought its own rewards with victories over non-league Torquay (following a scoreless draw in Devon, before 6,000 fans including 500 from Aberdare), Reading and Walsall.

The latter match was played at the Ynys due to a suspension of home matches for the Midlands Club. The first round proper was lost at Newcastle by 1–4, but only after Taylor had equalised for the Welshmen in the second half, following an eighth minute Newcastle goal. When all things were considered it was a fairly successful season, with a final 9th placing in the League – Aberdare topped a group of three teams (on goal average), each with 42 points from 42 games. The Club's A.G.M. in August showed that the takings at the gate were encouragingly up on a year earlier – producing a total of £7710 – whilst player transfers showed a credit of £510, and profits from programme sales brought in £36. An additional stand had been erected at one end of the ground in addition to the replacement main stand, and with a number of new signings producing a 'strong on paper' defense, the future looked generally fairly bright.

A somewhat unusual step was taken, with Aberdare Athletic amalgamating with their very close rivals – Welsh League team Aberaman. The playing arrangements agreed were probably unique since it was agreed that whilst the Football League team would retain the name of *'Aberdare Athletic'* – and continue playing at the Ynys – the reserve Welsh League team would play at Aberaman Park, under the name of *'Aberdare and Aberaman'*! It was hoped that the combined teams would add 2,000 to home gates and relieve the financial burden that the Football League Club still bore. Although this would appear to have been a sensible arrangement, all were not in favour of this major change and three Aberdare Directors resigned in protest.

The new season started badly for the team with frequent defeats which inevitably produced low attendances, and despite a slight recovery in October, by the following month the Club were bottom of the League table. The local Press where somewhat critical of the referee who officiated at the 1–2 home defeat to Norwich, when he was referred to *" The Autocratic little Knight of the whistle."*

With an early F.A.Cup exit at Exeter, things were far from healthy, and a prolonged industrial dispute in the coalmines led to a further reduction in attendances. The Club's fortunes slipped further and a worst ever home defeat, by 0–7 to Bristol City, sent most of the 5,000 crowd home disgusted; the return match with the Champions–elect resulted in a narrow 1–2 defeat before 25,000 fans. By April, the team was firmly entrenched at the bottom of the League, and with finances reaching a critical state players had to be released. In the last ever League match for the Club – on May the 7th – Aberdare scored very late in the game to record a 2–2 draw with Brighton. But this result was of little consequence as the team, by finishing bottom, were seven points below their nearest rivals, and had conceded 101 goals.

Re-election was not considered a formality, but in view of their overall past performances, confidence was high in the Welsh Club's camp. It therefore came as a severe shock when the Club were voted out in favour of Torquay United. The voting on the 29th of May 1927, produced an unbelievably close result. It was understood that overall the other Clubs in the Third Division would opt for Aberdare, but in the vote the Darians tied with new aspirants Torquay, each gaining 21 votes. (Watford were re-elected with 44, whilst Kettering and Yeovil managed only one each and Ebbw Vale nil). A second vote was required and on this occasion Aberdare lost out to Torquay 19 votes to 20. Unsubstantiated accusations were made that the scrutineer had favoured Torquay, but these were overruled. And so after six seasons the Club were forced to leave the elite, and the Aberdare public were again provided with (Western Section) Southern League football entertainment.

Initially results and attendances were encouraging, but both began to fade, particularly the latter, so much so that the F.A.Cup home tie versus Exeter was reversed and played in Devon - and ended with a humiliating 1-9 defeat. As the crowds turned away from the Club - aided by spells of particularly bad weather - accusations began to fly:

"Is there any truth that a prominent committee man of the Supporters Club visited Merthyr on monday in preference to watching his own club at the Ynys ? "

(The audacity of it !!)

The Club finished the season around mid-table in the Southern League, and the last ever game played by the team was the 5-1 home win over Weymouth; on paper a good result, but in reality it was a tired Dorset eleven who were playing their second Southern League match on the same day! By now the Ynys was heavily mortgaged and talks were held regarding the holding of Greyhound Racing (which was eventually introduced) at the Stadium to bring in extra money. A determined effort was also promised to regain the Club's Football League status, helped by the forlorn hope of raising funds from the townspeople. But with the Club in debt and showing a £400 loss on the season - attendances were seldom above 2,000 - a late notice withdrawing their original application for renewed Football League status was made on the 8th of June 1928. Cash was not forthcoming and the Aberaman faction decided to split from Aberdare. This move was justified on the grounds that the Club Manager had not even visited the Reserve Team ground, and the Welsh League side had rarely played home games in Aberaman - resulting in them not completing their fixtures. The Aberdare Club were forced to sell the Ynys and folded. The most devastated fan was surely Mr. Llewellyn who had to a large degree created and financially supported the Club.

The local population was openly criticised for their dwindling support – it was on one occasion reported that:

"The gates at the Ynys have fallen below zero" (!)

But the fact remained that with a prolonged coal stoppage coupled with ever increasing unemployment even many that wanted to watch the football could not afford to do so.

Back as a separate Club, Aberaman was elected to the Welsh League Division 1 for the 1928/29 season. Seven years were to pass before a reformation of the Aberdare Club took place, this time under the name of *'Aberdare Town'*. Although entry into the Welsh League Division 1 was obtained, the Reserve Team, playing in the Aberdare Valley League, folded before Christmas. At the start of the 1934/35 Campaign, the Club played once again at the Ynys, but this time only as tenants. However work and fundraising had quickly begun in earnest for the new Club to have its own new Ground. A suitable site close to the Ynys but on the other side of the railway line was found and converted. On the 9th of February, Plasdraw Park was opened and a fitting first game played there versus Aberaman in the 5th round of the Welsh Cup. A most encouraging crowd of 3,000 was present, but the result was hardly wanted, a 0–5 thrashing. Facilities initially at Plasdraw were non–existent, for the local drill hall nearby had to be used as dressing rooms, but at least the Ground was enclosed by fences and had one raised bank. The support was initially evident, for a Supporters Club was once again formed, and some excellent home attendances recorded – 4,000 (versus Lovell's Athletic), 3,000 for Ebbw Vale's visit, 5,000 for the 7–0 win over Cardiff Reserves and 5,000 when leaders Swansea Reserves came to Aberdare. The start of the next season saw improvements at the Club's headquarters, and within a few months Dressing Rooms, a Pavilion, a Press Box and a Covered Terrace had been added.

It was the Club's firm intention to regain the town Club's former glory, with an entry into the Southern League as a first priority. Crowds of 4 and 5,000 were not uncommon, and even the newly formed Reserve Team could attract 1,500 at home. But by the advent of the second world war in 1939, no honours had been won, and support had once again dwindled. The Club ceased playing during hostilities and on resuming again in 1945 combined yet again with Aberaman, presumably with the memories of some 16 years earlier forgotten. But this time there was a difference as the Club were now known as *Aberaman and Aberdare*. The first post–war season (1945/46) in the Welsh League was successful with the Club – now once again playing at the Ynys – finishing in 5th position in the 19 team table; in 36 league matches, 110 goals had been scored. This happy state of affairs did not continue, for the 1946/47 season resulted in a poor period with a distinct lack of success. The Club, still nicknamed 'The Darians' – as in the distant past – were once again struggling and by 1948 they were fortunate if they were able to record 1,000 home gates – at a time when football was generally at an all time 'high' – and despite the reformation of a Supporters Club. With the main influence coming from Aberaman, the 1947/48 season saw two separate clubs once again. But the Aberdare team lasted for just one season, and from the 1948/49 season it was left to Aberaman F.C. to provide the football entertainment in the area. But by the mid–1980's this team had gradually lost their status, playing at the unenclosed Aberaman Welfare Ground, in the lower division of the Welsh League.

YNYS STADIUM.

For the memory to *'Aberdare Athletic'*, little remains. The 'Ynys' as such still exists as a large expanse of sports fields, a leisure centre, and a Rugby pitch complete with wooden Grandstand – but virtually nothing of the former football Club, since the original stadium disappeared during the 1960's. When the first Grandstand was built in the 1920's the Club were justifiably proud of their neat wooden structure which contained below it both Dressing Rooms and Offices. The Stand was later extended towards the West. The large soil embankments and wide flat area on the railway side provided the ground with its very large (claimed) capacity – albeit but from an uncomfortable position for the majority in wet weather!

The new Sports Centre is located partially on the site of the former Football Ground, with an adjoining all weather pitch located over the remaining area of the earlier grass pitch. The North–west boundary of this centre is grass banked, and this is the sole remaining feature of Aberdare's Athletic's Football Ground. As for the Plasdraw Park football ground, the exact location is not obvious, for no evidence remains. Meanwhile, a short way along the road lies Aberaman, where this Football Club's Ground is situated. Facilities for spectators are now non–existent – probably as they were during the war years and when the Ground was used as Aberdare's reserve pitch.

In 1921, the Club had proudly announced its ease of accessibility – the railways at that time being the principal means of travel – but now the town is somewhat off the beaten track, having been ignored by the Motorway era, whilst the population, so necessary for support, has shrunk during the 60 plus years from 75,000 to less than half this number.

PROGRAMMES:

It is most unlikely that pre–1920 programmes were produced. However, from the first trial game, they were issued and probably continued until the 'Athletic's' demise. It is possible that from the new Club's formation, these may have been issued once again, and at least for the one post–Second World War season, programmes were once again produced. In any event, any remaining pre–War copies can be considered very rare.

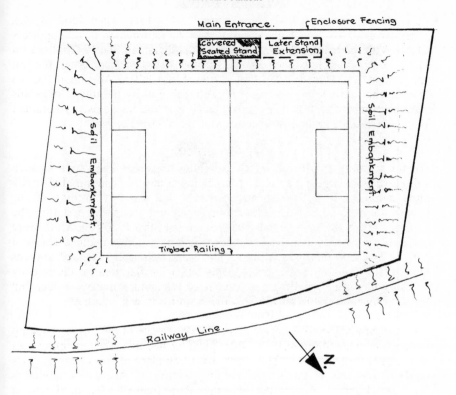

The Ynys Stadium (c.1920)

Location Plan of the Grounds

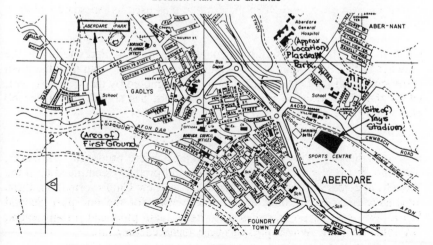

27

ASHINGTON

Team Group c.1929.
(Rear): J.Price, ? ? ? G.Thompson, F.Chipperfield, ?
(Front): J.Alexander, W.Harris, G.Johnson, J.Charlton, Richardson.

The Captains approach for the toss–up.
Aston Villa F.A.Cup match 1923/24 season.

ASHINGTON

Football League: 1921/22-1928/29.

****

1883 - 1892.	Friendlies
1892/93.	Northern Alliance.
1893/94 – 1894/95.	Ceased Activities.
1895/96 – 1901/02	East Northumberland League.
1902/03 – 1913/14.	Northern Alliance.
1914/15.	North Eastern League.
1915/16 – 1918/19.	Ceased Activities.
1919/20 – 1920/21.	North Eastern League.
1921/22 – 1928/29.	**Football League. Div. 3 North.**
1929/30.	North Eastern League Div.2.
1930/31 – 1934/35.	North Eastern League Div.1.
1935/36 – 1939/40.	North Eastern League.
1940/41 –	Northumberland & Durham War Lge.
1941/42 – 1943/44.	Ceased Activities.
1944/45 – 1957/58.	North Eastern League.
1958/59 – 1959/60.	Midland League.
1960/61 – 1961/62.	Northern Counties League.
1962/63 – 1963/64.	North eastern League.
1964/65.	Wearside League.
1965/66 – 1967/68.	North Regional League.
1968/69.	Northern Premier League.
1969/70.	Northern Alliance.
1970/71 – 1981/82.	Northern League.
1982/83 – 1983/84.	Northern League Div.1.
1984/85 to date.	Northern League Div.2.

....

Football League Record:

	Played	W.	D.	L.	F.	A.	Pts.	Posn.
1921/22.	38	17	4	17	59	66	38	10th
1922/23.	38	11	8	19	51	77	30	19th
Successfully Re-elected.								
1923/24.	42	18	8	16	59	61	44	8th
1924/25.	42	16	10	16	68	76	42	10th
1925/26.	42	16	11	15	70	62	43	9th
1926/27.	42	12	12	18	60	90	36	16th
1927/28.	42	11	11	20	77	103	33	18th
1928/29.	42	8	7	27	45	115	23	22nd
Failed to gain Re-election.								

....

- Ashington -

Summary of Facts:

Grounds: 1883 – 1908:   Ashington Recreation Ground, Ashington,
                1908/09:   Station Road Ground.
                1909/10 to date: Portland Park. (Originally named Station Road)

Nickname: Colliers.
Colours:(Football League)   Black and White Striped Shirts, Blue Shorts.

First League Game: 27th August 1921. Versus Grimsby Town (Home) Won 1–0.
                        Attendance approx. 9,000.
Last League Game: 27th April 1929. Versus Halifax Town (Home) Lost 0–3.
                        (Attendance less than 1,000)
Record Attendances: All time: 13,199 (Receipts £655) versus Rochdale,
                        F.A.Cup 2nd round. 9th December 1950.
                        Football League Days: 11,837 (Receipts £806) v. Aston Villa,
                        F.A.Cup 1st round. 12th January 1924. Main Achievements:
Football League average attendances: First season 5,050. Last season 1,666.

Main Achievements:

Northern Alliance Champs.:   1913/14.
Cup Winners: 1947/48 (Reserves).
North-Eastern League   'Non-reserve' Medal Winners: 1957/58.
                                League Cup Winners: 1933/34 (joint), 1939/40.
Midland League Runners-up: 1958/59.
East Northumberland League Champs.:   1897/98.
Northumberland Senior Cup Winners: 1920/21, 1932/33, 1938/39, 1949/50,
                                1955/56, 1956/57, 1961/62, 1966/67, 1979/80.
Northumberland Challenge Bowl Winners: 1912/13, 1921/22, 1922/23, 1923/24,
                                1925/26, 1933/34.
Northumberland Minor Cup Winners: 1896/97. 1897/98. 1898/99.

F.A.Cup: (Pre-1926 1st round equivalent to modern 3rd round)
1st Round: 1921/22. 1923/24.
3rd Round: 1926/27.
2nd Round: 1950/51.
1st Round: 1929/30. 1952/53. 1961/62.

F.A.Amateur Cup Semi-finalists: 1973/74.

Number of Football League matches played: 328.

Best League Wins: 1923/24 – 5–0 v. New Brighton (Home).
                        1924/25 – 6–1 v. Walsall (Home).
                        1925/26 – 6–1 v. Doncaster (Home).
Worst League Defeats: 1926/27 – 0–7 v. Stoke (Away).
                        1928/29 – 0–7 v. Crewe (Away) and
                                  2–8 v. Bradford C.(Home)

For the first two decades of the existence of Ashington F.C. the Club's role was only in a minor capacity, but in line with the increase in population within the town, a slow rise to Football League status was eventually achieved.

Until 1851 Ashington was little more than a village tucked away between the boundaries of the Tyne and the Scottish border, however with the rapid increase in coal mining in the area the number of inhabitants increased accordingly. Two separate eras, each of two decades, marked this population growth. By 1871 the town was 'on the map', but with football still in its infancy, for the newly emerging sport had barely reached this North-eastern outpost of England. From 1891 to 1911 the population again rose rapidly, and it was during this second period that the sport started to really make its mark in the town. Football gained support from two principal sources in addition to the natural nationwide rise in interest. The mine owners, in common with most large employers of the time provided the limited leisure facilities for the short period in a hard working week when the workforce had time for such pursuits; and that same workforce consisted of many migrants from Scotland who were able to bring with them the skills and background of Football where the game had taken on an early popularity. The circumstances however were hardly conducive for providing a healthy and fit football team, for the housing that was rapidly erected for the workers in the former years, was cramped, boringly the same and desperately of an insanitary nature!

Until the turn of the century the sport was played at a minor level in the town, and hence references to the local team were for nearly twenty years, rarely reported upon. Ashington F.C. were formed in 1883, and despite their minor status entry into the F.A.Cup competition was reported as early as 1887. Whilst Mickley F.C. has been referred to as the oldest Club in Northumberland – being also formed in 1883 – therefore the time distance between the birth of the two must have been months or weeks! These early years of Cup competitions produced many long forgotten names, and this first reference to Ashington's involvement recorded that in a qualifying round the team were matched against Weetslade.

The Club played their home matches at Ashington Recreation Ground, a sporting area that still exists, to the West of present-day Ashington, and immediately adjacent to, and provided by, the town's Colliery. The venue it can be assumed was completely lacking in facilities, save for a (probable) roped off pitch, although it was credited with hosting one of the first long distance cycle races, of 100 miles. These initial seasons were no doubt a struggle for survival, with a limited number of clubs with whom friendly matches could be arranged, and support for the team itself was such that on occasions even a full eleven could not always be guaranteed to appear. A local sports writer though was moved to write in September 1888 that:

> *"This Club has made great improvements in*
> *its play, and should provide a better showing*
> *during the coming season".*

It would appear that such improvement did not occur since the neighbourhood sports writers of the day continued to favour nearby Blyth in their reporting!

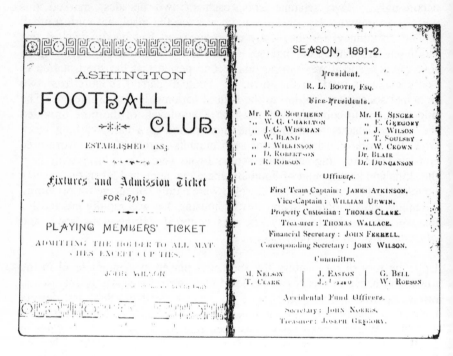

By the 1891/92 season Ashington F.C. were running a reserve side, although the first team had yet to reach a high enough level for which entry into a league was possible. One point of note occurred in January 1892 when the team beat the reserves of Northern Alliance Club, Rendel, (*Rendel Swifts*) – the latter eleven's first defeat for two seasons. The next season saw matches against clubs of a higher status, notably Blyth (the first game in late September), Sunderland Albion – a short–lived offshoot of the current Roker Park club, Shankhouse (in the Northumberland Senior Cup) and Hebburn Argyle. Consistent support from within the Club was often difficult, for in the latter match – at Hebburn – the Colliery Club lost by seven goals, handicapped as they were by the presence of only a ten man team, which was reduced to nine during the game due to injury! The team were also crushed at Sunderland by the same score which led to the comment:

"What's wrong with Ashington?"

The local Association did however use the Ashington player, Waldock, in a trial game for the County side.

A bold attempt to increase their status was made for the 1892/93 season, when an entry into the three year old Northern Alliance was made. Alongside the likes of Newcastle United's and Sunderland's second strings, the season finished with no honours – although fellow newcomers Blyth finished as runners–up. A period of disinterest followed, and for two seasons the Club ceased their activities. But on the 31st of May 1895, an appeal was made by the existing committee, to actively reform the team.

> *"A large and representative meeting was held in the football cabin at the recreation grounds, when an invitation was extended to all persons interested in football as a healthy exercise for the youth of the Colliery, and those wishful to have a Club worthy of Ashington."*

The meeting was a great success and a large Committee was voted in. The first competitive game for the Club, in the East Northumberland League was played at Cambois, at the venue of the local Flower Show, that was in progress at the time! A *'large gathering'* of spectators witnessed a 3–3 draw, which Ashington were winning by two nil at half–time.

For seven years, starting with the 1895/96 season, the Club continued in a non–prominent level, but brought its own rewards with the East Northumberland League Championship in 1897/98 and three consecutive wins in the Northumberland Minor Cup. However these successes contrasted sharply with a disastrous last season in this league when a 3rd from bottom at Christmas 1901 was not improved upon by the end of the campaign. Overall it was a dismal season which was emphasised by a lack of interest within the team when a Northumberland Senior Cup game was played at Shankhouse.

The match kicked off with only six Ashington men representing the Club! Fortunately two more players turned up in the first half, but this could not prevent the visitors from going in six goals down at half–time. The second half turned into a farce with a strong wind and torrential rain, and after 15 minutes of the second period Ashington's eight exhausted players refused to continue; by now they were ten goals down, and this score was allowed to stand!

The Colliers – by now the nickname of the Club – were joined in league competition with locals Blyth Spartans and the unlikely sounding New York United! Ashington F.C. had experienced a history of success and failure, particularly the latter during this last season, and a complete re–organisation of the Club led to acceptance once again into the Northern Alliance for the 1902/03 campaign. The first game in this competition was played away to the railway team of Gateshead N.E.R., on the 6th of September, but ended in a 1–2 defeat. However as the population of the town had increased enormously, and with the Club now strongly represented – the players included Harvey the ex–Bristol Rovers man – so had interest in football within the district and a large number of spectators lined the ropes for the team's first league match at the Recreation Ground. This first home game provided the first points when Hebburn were beaten by a first half goal. An encouraging start however did not continue, and by Christmas the team were placed bottom in the league, not helped by the deduction of two points due to having played an ineligible player.

Until the Colliers re–appearance in the Northern Alliance, the honours were regularly taken by the reserves of Newcastle United and Sunderland, until the two transferred their allegiances into the Northern League. This left the Non–league teams to fight out the Championship, although it was not until the end of the 1905/06 season that Ashington made their presence felt when they were runners–up to Willington Athletic. As the population of the town increased, it was considered preferable to move to a more central location and in 1908 the Club re–located to the Station Road Ground. The move had entailed a great deal of hard work for the Committee, but at least they had the satisfaction of having their own Ground.

The 1908/09 season had its high spots, and by the turn of the year the Colliers were handily place in third spot in the league, but the final season result was a somewhat disappointing fifth; during the season Bumphrey left the Club to join Birmingham City. However, by now the Club had further ambitions, and a further and final move was made during the Summer of 1909 to – later named – Portland Park. Although it was to be three years before the ambition was fulfilled, the Club's Officials vowed to undertake their biggest ever venture, with the provision of a Grandstand.

The 1909/10 season was much the same story for Ashington F.C. as that of a year earlier, and they still had to prove themselves in the F.A.Cup which was regularly entered for – on this occasion defeat in a local derby at Bedlington.
However a major achievement came their way again, in the 1910/11 season, when runners–up in the league was once again achieved. But strikes in the area caused attendances to drop and a £47 loss on the season was made.

This loss would have been double the sum had it not been for the £50 the Club received from Hull, for the transfer of Joseph Potts. A decision was taken that Gatemen would be paid in future, since Committeemen objected to missing part of each game! One year later the League runners–up spot was retained.

After so many years in the backwaters of football, the Colliery team were at last making an impression in the region, but always with strong competition from near neighbours Blyth Spartans. The Club's dream of a Grandstand (holding 1,000 and at a cost of £340) was at last realised, and on the 16th of September, Newcastle spoilt the opening party with a single goal win. The Club was honoured with a Schoolboys representative game at the Ground, and a 700 gate. On their travels the team won 8–2 at Blaydon Haughs, but lost at Blyth – before an £80 record gate – in the F.A.Cup. Overall things were looking up as the season saw the Club capture the Northumberland Challenge Bowl for the first time and when May 1914 arrived, the Colliers could look back on their best ever season, having taken the Championship of the league.

The Club's 'arrival' on the football scene was unfortunately ill–timed for war clouds were looming over Europe, and there was to be little opportunity for the team to prove itself in a higher competition. The Club's entry was accepted into the highly rated North–Eastern league, when they replaced Seaham Harbour, but the following months proved to be a difficult financial struggle. With many of the men from the town conscripted, low gates were the order of the day, and they were not helped by a poor home record. Fortunately good results were achieved on the Club's travels and by the turn of the year, following a good run of two wins and two drawn games, seventh in the league was achieved. Although a satisfactory final place in the table of ninth (of twenty Clubs) was the eventual outcome – with 15 victories, 11 draws and 12 defeats – the season was a financial disaster. By February, when Dinnington were in opposition at Portland Park, for the Aged Miners Cup, a 9–1 victory was achieved, but the attendance was the lowest of the season – less than 100!

The North–Eastern league initially intended to carry on for the 1915/16 season, but with only seven Clubs, and with professional football frowned upon by the Country as a whole during the wartime years, a localised Tyneside League was created for the few teams in the area that were able to struggle on. Ashington were not amongst this small band, and they ceased activities until the resumption of normal football in September 1919.

With the Great War over, the Colliers carried on where they left off as members of the North–Eastern League.

But with major changes afoot in the set-up of the Football league, the opportunity was soon to present itself that would have been unthinkable just a few years earlier when they were only members of the Northern Alliance.

The 1919/20 season passed by in a satisfactory manner with a final placing of seventh of eighteen teams in the league. In the F.A.Cup, the Club were knocked out in the second qualifying round in a home local derby with Blyth Spartans. Aided by many visitors, a new record attendance of 8,000 was present to see the Colliers beaten by three unopposed goals.

Meanwhile, down South, the whole Southern League was retitled to become the new Third Division, an honour that its member Clubs had earned over the years. There were also plans to create a Third Division North a year later (with the original new League retitled to become the Third Division *South*) presenting the opportunity for Ashington, and other progressive Non-league Clubs, to jump on the band waggon. However, things did not go entirely to plan, for the 1920/21 season finished with the Club in a disappointing ninth place of twenty teams, with 14 wins, 13 draws and 11 defeats.

But with a Football League status carrot being offered to the Club, work was put in hand to bring the Ground upto the necessary standard in April, such that several of the last few games of the campaign were played away from home. By January the 22nd a 'low' was reached when the home game with Wallsend was lost – the visitors first victory of the season! A gradual improvement followed, and by mid-February the team lay in 12th position. The last home game played on the 30th of April was won with Parsons scoring – and also missing a penalty – and the return at Carlisle was drawn 1-1, Dickinson being the marksman.

With confirmation of the Club's election to the new Third Division North division, confirmed as early as March the 10th, the incentive was there for all those connected with the Club to work hard on this rise in status. The Ground was transformed from a typical Non-league venue containing no more than a simple seated and covered stand, to a stadium designed for 20,000. The pitch was re-laid, the Pavilion reconstructed, a Tea Room and a large Press Box added, and high terraces built around the pitch.

Having sorted out the Ground, thoughts turned to the playing staff with the intention of having 18 to 20 professionals for the opening of the 1921/22 season; nine players re-signed whilst amongst the newcomers, Knowles from Manchester United, Thompson from Leeds and Foster (ex-Sunderland) were added to the payroll. In the other direction, Carter departed for Wolverhampton.

For the North–Eastern league teams, the election was not nearly so easy as a year earlier for the ex–Southern league teams, or for those of the North–West based Central League (most of whose teams were elected). Along with the Colliers, just Darlington, Durham City and Hartlepools United were the accepted lucky ones whilst West Stanley were one of the unfortunate Clubs left out.

Concern was however expressed for the Club's reserve team, for they queried whether the North–Eastern league would provide a sufficiently high standard – with the existing Football League Clubs having pulled out their own reserves – and with the introduction of theoretically inferior teams to replace the 'deserters'. Eventually they decided to settle on the North–Eastern, after having stirred things up and threatening to form a new league if their own second string were not re–admitted at this level. But the Club was not elected, and much to their embarrassment, and with insufficient time to organise an alternative competition, the 'stiffs' were finally accepted into the lower Northern Alliance!

The Club's entry into the Football League was heralded at Portland Park with the opening ceremony conducted by Mr Ridley Warham, appropriately the Managing Director of the town's main employer – the Ashington Coal Company – on August the 27th. The attendance for this first game was hardly poor, at between 9 and 10,000, but the remodelled arena was not even packed. The team for the opening fixture consisted of:

> Davidson, Bradford, Buxton, Miller,
> O'Connell, Featherstone, Foster, Thompson,
> Dickinson, Mc.Gill and Brayson.

A second half dropping shot by Dickinson, after the Grimsby Town goalkeeper had first punched out a centre from the wing, settled the issue and gave the Colliers a one goal win.

This victory was not repeated in the return match one week later when the Colliers were humbled by the Mariners by 6–1, after only a single goal reverse at half–time. Seven days later the Club's high hopes took a further dip when they were beaten by two unopposed goals at Wrexham. The situation looked more hopeful when the Welshmen came to Portland Park on September the 17th and the homesters took a comfortable two goal half–time lead, but the final result was a 2–2 draw. This dismal start continued when the Colliers were then beaten at nearby Durham by one goal to nil. However, their hopes were reinforced on the first day of October with a reversed scoreline against the same opposition. The most reassuring aspects was the attendance of 6,500 and the fact that it was the Cathedral City Club's first Football League defeat; the single goal was scored after thirty seconds!

As the weeks progressed, results continued in a dismal vain; a two goal defeat before a 7,000 crowd at Barrow and the same goal loss in a poor home return. On October the 22nd the first away win was recorded, at Crewe, to relieve the gloom, but this dark cloud returned when the Railwaymen stole the points with a single goal at Ashington. By the time Lincoln came to Northumberland on November the 12th several forward changes had been made (having also lost 1–4 at Lincoln a week earlier), and they produced the desired effect with a 4–2 win; the locals remained reasonably loyal with a 5,000 crowd being present. By Christmas, the Colliers were placed 6th from bottom, but a reasonable recovery was then made until the end of the season (apart from the embarrassment of 0–5 and 2–6 defeats at Darlington and Walsall respectively), to give a tenth final position with 17 victories and defeats plus just four drawn games. The F.A.Cup produced three home ties. On the 17th of November Close Works were easily overcome by six unopposed goals (before the smallest gate of the season – 2,767), followed by a narrow 3–2 victory over Leadgate Park – watched by 3,670 spectators. Defeat came in the final qualifying round to Stalybridge Celtic, which produced receipts of £280 from the 5,785 gate.

After an awful start to the 1922/23 season when the Colliers were beaten 1–6 at Wigan Borough, a good recovery was made which saw the team win all three home games, a draw at Darlington and only one defeat at Hartlepools – all in September. By the end of October a reasonable twelve points from twenty possible had been taken, but then a terrible string of defeats followed during the next three months including a 2–6 hammering at home by Barrow on December the 23rd. By now the public had certainly become disillusioned and for the New Years Day visit of Durham, 3,500 turned up (little more than half of that of a year earlier) to see a drab scoreless draw. Worst was to follow, on two fronts! For the defeats continued with alarming regularity, and on February the 10th a pathetic attendance of only 1,500 was present to see six goals – four scored by opponents Crewe. A vast improvement occurred one week later when the team ran out 7–4 winners. Early in the first half the homesters were trailing 1–3, but pulled back well, to be sharing the six goals by half–time. The second half was a thriller, for with just 15 minutes remaining the Colliers trailed 3–4, but scored four times in the remaining time; just 2,000 were present for the spectacle.

A Shareholders meeting was held a few days later, to discuss ways in which the Club could improve the financial situation caused by poor home gates, which was not helped by the equally poor weather. An offer was made for the supporters to buy shares in the Club on a weekly payment scheme which initially produced a good number of applicants.

Whilst the League position did not improve, the support – in line with the weather – did, and 3,500 were present for the 2-5 defeat to Accrington Stanley, and 4,646 for Walsall's appearance; the latter match saw the debut of Price from Nelson, in a best of season 3-0 victory. By the end of the season only one away victory had been obtained, by 3-1 back in October at – of all places – Nelson, the eventual League Champions! But it was to the other end of the table that Ashington had to look, for they finished just two points and one position above their near rivals Durham City in bottom place. Re-election had therefore to be applied for.

Ashington topped the poll with 45 points, along with newcomers Doncaster Rovers and New Brighton (the league having been extended), and finally Durham. Nuneaton and Wallasey received not one vote of support. The reserves in the Northern Alliance, with a runners-up position gave cause for optimism; even the support was good, with the match at home to Hexham – some 2,000 – exceeding at least one of the first team's fixtures!

August the 25th, 1923, heralded the start of another campaign and another wretched start for the Colliers – 0-4 at Wrexham, before a 4,000 rain soaked crowd. The Welshmen completed the double seven days later, but before an excellent attendance of 6,300. It began to look as if the team were going to have a desperate struggle on the field again though. Even the reserve team were finding things hard for they lost at Ashington in September to Spen Black and White, in a Northern Alliance fixture before a 2,500 crowd, yet the previous season they had remained unbeaten at home. Things began to look better when a run of victories ensued. Firstly Durham were beaten 3-2 after a two goal lead at half-time before an attendance of 5,800, followed by both home and away wins against Crewe.

On November the 10th following an impressive four goal defeat of Halifax, the Colliers had gone ten League games undefeated, but this joy was shortlived for seven days later a 0-3 defeat was sustained to the same team at The Shay. With a 1-2 defeat at home to Rotherham (attendance 5,358) things once again did not look so rosy. However the F.A.Cup trail had by now commenced and a relief from League struggles.

The fourth qualifying round was won by 2-0, when Bishop Auckland – complete with a special train and 'motor Parties' of supporters visited Portland Park. Carlisle were the next easy victims – before a 4,753 gate, followed by the third home tie when Hartlepools United provided far more stiffer opposition. This was only the second time in the Club's history that victory had been achieved over their neighbours– 6,540 were there to see it.

The draw for the first round proper set the town buzzing when it was announced that the next opponents, at home, would be the mighty Aston Villa. With the town now having a population of around 35,000 the informed sports writers of the day showed their ignorance when they described Ashington as a *'little mining village'* in their pre-match build-up for this 'David and Goliath' clash. One week before the 'big one', and before a season's best attendance of 8,824, the Colliers were thrashed 1–7 by Champions–elect Wolverhampton Wanderers, although a twenty minute injury to Henderson had virtually reduced the homesters to ten men.

An all time record attendance of approximately 20,000 was forecast for the Cup game, and work was put in hand to ensure that the spectators could view the game suitably. Crush barriers were installed on the terracing and with the level areas at the top, a capacity crowd of around 28,000 was considered possible.

Aston Villa dominated most of the play, but the Colliers – in the stripes – managed a second half consolation goal at the railway end.

On the match day ten special trains arrived from the Alnwick area in the North, whilst there were thirty constables, plus mounted police on duty as opposed to the normal six officers. Heavy snow had fallen during the week and therefore a distinct possibility of a postponement, but with a thaw on the day, the pitch had become muddy but playable. Crowds started gathering at the ground before midday, and there was an air of intense excitement for this, the Colliers biggest game.

At the final count, the attendance was a very disappointing 11,837 (receipts of £807), but nonetheless a record figure that was to remain throughout the Club's Football League career. Many local pit workers did not go to work that afternoon, whilst others came straight from the coalface to the match, and most of the locals displayed their favours with their black and white rosettes. Villa soon took the lead, but this goal was equalised by Robertson amidst a *'loud outburst of cheering'*. But level terms with their lofty opponents was shortlived, and handicapped by an early injury to the home player, Price, the minnows were eventually overwhelmed with the final tally of 1–5.

Although the rest of season was played out with an undefeated home record, attendances once again took a tumble; 5,400 two weeks after the Villa game, only 3,500 when Southport were the visitors, 5,800 for the local derby with Darlington and 4,100 for another local match this time versus Hartlepools United. A poor away record was terminated with the last game of the season, a two goal defeat at Chesterfield. With a final finish of eighth, it was a vast improvement on twelve months earlier, but with attendances overall only a little better, the Directors still had problems.

A surprisingly good start was made to the 1924/25 season, resulting in the Colliers as early leaders, but some terrible defeats on their travels – 3–7 at Doncaster, plus three, four and five goal defeats without reply at Southport, Nelson and Doncaster respectively – despite a good home record – saw the Club slump to 14th place by mid–October. The F.A.Cup produced a local home tie with Hartlepools on November the 15th – which only attracted £230 at the gate – but a draw required a midweek replay, resulting in defeat by 0–2. Three days later the Colliers lost 0–3 at home – to Hartlepools! With this latter poor run, the gates inevitably started falling. There were 5,800 fans present when Darlington – leaders and eventual Champions – were surprisingly beaten by 4–2, but a record low gate of only 1,311 two weeks later for Wrexham's visit, confirming that the Ashington support had reached a low ebb. Perhaps the exceptionally low attendance could have been due to the just pre–Christmas date for the game, as the visit of Nelson in the New Year attracted a reasonable 4,245.

By now, despite the end–of–year lapses, and a high number of goals against in away games, the team were actually placed in a better League position than one year earlier! Two further away wins, (to add to the Christmas Day victory at Rotherham County) aided an indifferent home record to the end of the season, and a final tenth place in the League, two positions lower than a year earlier. Finance was still a problem, if not a serious one yet, for attendances were again generally poor; later figures included 3,380 for Lincoln's visit (although this was no doubt affected by the late working of the Pits that day) and 3,200 when Grimsby visited, and won, in March. However, low attendances were not only a problem for the Colliers for the visit to high flying Rochdale only attracted some 4,000.

A good start was made to the 1925/26 season, but results on the field were not matched with good crowds, and for Crewe's visit a gate of 4,589 was well down on previous early season figures. The away record was boosted with two points at Rochdale on the 17th of October with a 3–1 victory, although the locals felt somewhat cheated as the Colliers last two goals came in the final five minutes! The 28th of November was F.A.Cup day, but the match against fellow North–Easterners Durham City, at the Cathedral City, was postponed for four days.

The Colliers were somewhat apprehensive about their visit having never won at Durham, but with a goal lead at half–time it looked as if the homesters may at last lose their record. However an equaliser – that so pleased the scorer that he embraced a nearby policeman – was followed by two more goals, and so cut short any hopes of a Cup run for the Ashington men. By May 1926 another mediocre season had been completed, reflected in the apathy shown by the April gate of only 2,700, despite the fine weather, when Rotherham were the visitors. The season's end came to a sour conclusion with a last game 1–6 defeat at Chesterfield.

As the 1926/27 season was about to commence, local events were in progress that were to hit the Club financially. Disharmony was being expressed at the Coalmines, and with the vast majority of the Football team's support coming from this direction, the strike that followed was to have serious effects on the home gates.

> *"League football commences on Saturday under the shadow of a great Industrial crisis, and the consequences will be felt by all the local football clubs."*

A scribe of the day wrote on August the 26th.

Due to this unrest the first home game scheduled for the first day in September against Nelson was postponed. The trial games had attracted attendances of two, three and four thousand, but admission prices for these were low. With the workforce on strike, Council house rents unpaid, and families dependant on free food handouts there was little money for football games. The first home game was eventually played on September the 4th (two goals shared with Wrexham), and the official attendance was a paltry 1,823. Despite a small but enthusiastic following (the Club by now had a Supporters Club) who wished to see their favourites, crowd trouble ensued when a section of supporters climbed the walls and opened the South side gates, letting in an estimated 1,500 free entrants.

A similar incident ensued at the Doncaster game two weeks later, on which occasion there were several minor casualties, as around 2,000 spectators broke into the ground to add to the 1,500 who had paid for their admission. The fixture two days later with Walsall was postponed in order to avoid a repeat occurrence.

On October the 2nd, the home fixture with Rotherham was played, and apart from a repeat of only a small (paid) attendance, the game was trouble free. Those present however had their moneysworth, for the Colliers were four goals in arrears after only 18 minutes, but the final result was an incredible 4–4 draw, and the consensus of opinion was that should the game have continued longer Ashington would have won. However this sort of fighting spirit had not been evident in other games, for, no doubt influenced by the general unrest in the area, the team had made an awful start to the season. This result was the third draw in the three home games played, whilst away the six games had produced just one win – at Wigan Borough – whilst four had been lost, not least a seven goal hammering at Stoke City.

The first home win was achieved against Tranmere Rovers in late October, once again without incident, but before a lamentably small attendance. Fortunately results generally improved upto the New Year, including away wins at Hartlepools and Durham, and saw the Colliers in 14th place in the League.

The F.A.Cup campaign at least provided some urgently needed funds. The first round, produced a poor quality game but a 3–2 win to Ashington at Stockton's Victoria Ground, followed by a home draw in the next round. A healthy attendance of 5,265 – three times more than any other gate to that time that season were present – and included many from the visitors, Nelson. The crowd witnessed a match of many missed chances but an odd goal in three victory to the homesters.

The Directors of the Club were overjoyed when the third round draw was made for it had paired them with a home tie versus Nottingham Forest. In view of the financial problems prevalent in the town as a whole, due to the Industrial situation, there was no question of a new record attendance at Portland Park. However, with heavy rain on the matchday, coupled with many who didn't turn up as they expected the gates to be shut before the kick–off time, the final attendance was reduced even further. The Cup–tie admission costs were one and two shillings (5p and 10p) for the South side open stand, 2 shillings and sixpence for the Paddock and three shillings and sixpence for the main covered stand. The second lowest Cup crowd of the day, 9,242, paid £513 to see their favourites rather unluckily lose by two unopposed goals.

The home defence played well, but the Forest produced quality football, to go in at half-time one goal ahead. An injury had reduced the Colliers to only ten fit men, and with the rain coming down in torrents, the Second Division team sealed the match with a brilliant header after 17 minutes play in the second period.

Early December had seen the signing on of a player with a 'pedigree', (a rare event for the Colliers) that of Centre Forward Frank Walls, who with his previous Club, Larne – in Ireland – had scored 26 goals in 22 games and had also played in the Irish League side. Placed fourteenth in the League on January the 1st, there was plenty of room for improvement, but by late March after generally poor results the Club were fifth from bottom, and dangerously near the re-election zone. They eventually finished in 16th place, in view of all the turmoil that had gone before them, a reasonable position. One rare bright spot was the reserve team who won promotion in the North-Eastern league and hence regained their place in the first division.

Just one new player was signed on for the coming season, Hopper from Coventry City, but in fact a former Colliers man. The first match was played at home versus Bradford City, who provided a sharp contrast with the thousands of pounds spent on the Yorkshire team compared to the, by now, near impoverished Colliery team. Four goals were shared in this match, and overall a bad start was made to the campaign. The first victory did not arrive until November the 12th, when Tranmere were defeated by three goals, with an attendance of less than 2,000. Previously heavy away defeats had been received at Bradford (0–5 before an 8,000 crowd), Darlington and Wrexham (1–5), Halifax (1–6) and a six goal crash at New Brighton. This encouraging win was not repeated seven days later when another defeat was sustained before a 7,000 crowd at Stockport.

With the Club now languishing in the bottom reaches of the table, it was hoped that the F.A.Cup could lift the morale. The first round brought Crewe Alexandra as opposition at home. £246 was taken at the gate from the reasonable attendance of 4,793, where the team played well and were denied a winning goal, which was first allowed and the decision then reversed by the referee. The replay was lost, and so the team were left to concentrate on lifting themselves from their desperate position in the League.

An amazing 5–1 victory at Nelson (before only 1,500) lifted the Club's hopes, but such a result was not to be repeated. By the New Year, attendances had settled to a crippling low of only 1,500 (from the early Football League days average of four to five thousand) and an announcement was made of the serious financial difficulties that the Club was in, and expressing the hope that in future there would be a considerable increase; at the next home match (a good 5–1 victory over Rochdale), there was gathering of 1,200 – 300 less than the previous Portland Park match! At home to high–flying Bradford Park Avenue in early March, the home team were denied a penalty that was greeted with boos and hisses from their supporters, but this award would have had little effect as the Colliers went down by three goals to nil. Fortunately some improvement was made as the season came to a close, ending in an amazing six goal home win over Rotherham – and a safe but far from healthy 18th place in the League resulted. The series of heavy defeats produced a goal difference of 77–103.

After a 1–2 close defeat at Southport on the 25th August 1929 before an attendance of 3,244, home victories were achieved over Darlington and Rochdale to give the Club some degree of optimism for the future. But such successes became rare events as the season wore on. An away win at Accrington in October by a single goal was soon after followed with an embarrassing 2–8 home defeat to Champions–elect Bradford City, and by Christmas things were in a desperate state both on the field – the team holding up the rest of the League – and financially within the Club. With the continuance of the Industrial situation that had caused low employment in the area, the home gates continued at a disastrously low level. The F.A.Cup produced nothing in either prestige or cash as the team bowed out at Wigan by 0–2, following a 1–5 League defeat one week earlier at the same venue in front of 5,000.

A scheme was suggested whereby the Mineworkers would agree to donate one penny per week from their wages in return for a greater say in running the Club; the suggestion was not a popular one with the Ashington F.C. Directors! As the Club were heading for a re–election application, the Chairman – John Craigs Junior – announced that some Directors were willing to stand down in favour of any individuals willing to put money into the Club – 1,947 shares at £1 each were still available – to which there was little if any interest shown.

A seven goal defeat at Crewe on April the 6th virtually sealed the team's fate, (they had lost the earlier encounter 0–5 before a miserable gate of 1,100) and three weeks later, came the Club's last League match. Even a victory would not avoid the bottom position in the League. The Club had come to the conclusion that they would receive little support from the other League Clubs in their re–election bid, for nearby Durham City had bid their farewells just 12 months earlier, and the North–East did not prove a popular venue for travelling teams; they could not even expect the financial reward in terms of a good gate at either of the Clubs.

"Probably the Colliers final appearance in
League Football.... Efforts still being made to
persuade the League Clubs to revise their
attitude towards them (viz. Ashington)."

It was reported in the press prior to the home game with Halifax.

On a rainy day the team took the field before less than 1,000 spectators, and after holding the visitors to a goalless half–time score finally succumbed 0–3, hindered as they were by an injury to Robson. The team consisted of:

Latimer. Robson. Stephenson. Wilson.
Price. Chipperfield. Alexander. Harris.
Johnson. Carlton. Richardson.

Re–election was applied for on June the 3rd, but with only 14 votes they were ten short of York City's successful bid. Ashington F.C. found to their cost that they had few friends in the Football League. Although looked at realistically should they have been successful in their bid, where was the financial support to maintain a League team to come from? After eight seasons in the Football League, and only their second re–election application – the first six years earlier – they were rejected back into the Non–league world.

A further rejection was then experienced when it was found that there was no room in the North–Eastern League Division 1, the most senior level option that the Club would reasonably have been expected to be welcomed into. The reserves had just been relegated to division 2 of the league and this was the only one realistic position that could be taken up by the first team. Ashington F.C. were now faced with the ludicrous position of playing in a league lower than that which their reserve team had played in just a few weeks earlier!

It was generally assumed that against such 'unheard' of opposition – such as White–le–Head Rangers, Bedlington United and St.Peter's Albion to name but three – promotion would be a mere formality. The first game on August the 31st was played at home with Crawcrook Albion, and within a few minutes the Colliers were two goals in arrears! The final result was in fact a 5–3 win to the homesters, and other frequent victories were forthcoming. By the end of September the team were heading the table, and although promotion to the first division was achieved it was not the walkover that was expected. The Club were in a desperate situation at the season's end, when only two teams were promoted, and they finished third! Still running as a professional team, the Colliers were on the brink of extinction through trying to continue with home crowds that could be counted in handfuls.

However, luck turned their way, for second placed White–le–Head declined the move up, and Ashington were allowed to take their place.

On another, but brighter, note the F.A.Cup run had proceeded through to the 1st round proper after Stockton were beaten 4–2 at home in the 4th qualifying round. A nostalgic visit had then been made to Rotherham – Football League opponents one year earlier – and despite their very much reduced status, the game was much closer than the 0–3 scoreline suggested; a crowd of 6,537 was present.

Until 1935, the North–Eastern league (Division 1) was almost totally dominated by the reserve teams of Middlesbrough, Newcastle and Sunderland, leaving few honours for the Non–league contingent. However, even in the few years leading upto the second World War, when the way was open to the 'Non Reserve' teams, Ashington led an undistinguished life on the field without ever getting amongst the honours, save for the winning of the League Cup – jointly with Sunderland in 1934, and solely in 1940. The league was reduced to only ten teams for the 1939/40 season, due to resignations, as the War commenced in earnest. On November the 25th a five goal hammering of West Stanley was followed by six games when a total of only one point was obtained! This put the Club in 8th position in the league and by the season's end rose just one place; victories included a 9–1 home victory over Spennymoor – in which the forwards were criticised for missed chances!

A number of local Clubs formed the Northumberland and Durham (Wartime) league, in which there were initially ten competing Clubs, as diverse as Newcastle reserves and Holiday's Sports Club, but East Cranlington resigned in February. With so few Clubs the season was in effect split into two separate halves, and in the second series the Colliers finished in third place. The total gates for the season produced a pathetic sum of only £333, and with a loss on the season of £200, the Club decided to call it a day until the hostilities had finished. In all these latter years the first round of the F.A.Cup was never again reached.

The early post–war years produced little for the Colliers fans to enthuse over, and the end of the 1949/50 season saw the Club languishing near the bottom of the table, in a final 15th position. However the next campaign at least brought its excitement in the F.A.Cup competition.

The second qualifying round produced a poor contest when the Colliers were held to a scoreless home draw with Hexham Hearts, but they won the replay by six unopposed goals. By the date of the next Cup match the team held an unbeaten run of fourteen games, which was then increased when Cramlington Welfare were beaten 3–1. Cup fever was by now beginning to grip the town, and the largest attendance for many years, 6,700, was present at Portland Park to see the local team dismiss Farsley Celtic in the final qualifying round of the Cup. After an absence of nearly twenty years, the club graced the first round proper, and then proceeded to make National headlines, when they were the victors over league team Halifax at The Shay. £530 was taken at the gate, and amongst the 7,440 crowd, 1,500 were from Ashington.

The Club's first ever entry into the second round of the National Cup produced unprecedented interest in the town, and an all time record attendance of 13,199 (£656 gate receipts) were present for Rochdale's visit. Ashington played the first half somewhat in awe of the Football league team, and went in for the break 1-2 in arrears. A storming second half, which included 14 Ashington corners in the last 15 minutes failed to produce an equaliser.

In view of their performances, exemptions for the 1952/53 season F.A.Cup gave them another appearance in the first round proper, but on this occasion they were overwhelmed at Tranmere Rovers scoring just one of the nine goals! Another five years passed by in the North-Eastern League without honours, until something of a crisis occurred at the end of the 1957/58 season. A most encouraging third place had been attained, but Ashington and others were most unhappy to discover that the 'glamour teams', the Reserves of the Football League Clubs, were resigning to join the newly formed North Regional league, and intending to enter their third team in the North-Eastern league. The quality of the competition would have undoubtably been devalued and this suggestion was turned down. However replacements for the 'defectors', of a suitably senior status, were not found and the League after nearly sixty years existence, closed down.

This left many Clubs leagueless, and the remnants of the former league joined forces with the somewhat geographically unsuitable Midland League. There were rumours at this time that the Club were seeking to join the Scottish League, but this was firmly denied by the Directors. The move 'South' proved a good one – at least on the field – and the next two seasons were to be arguably their best ever. The League was a quality Competition, and contained nineteen – mainly unknown to Ashington – teams. However this was the era of the redoubtable Peterborough United, who, sweeping all before them, dominated the League. The first game in the Competition, was a daunting one for Ashington – away to Peterborough! Before a 10,000 crowd, the Colliers crashed by 1-6. The balance was somewhat redressed with the 7-0 demolition of Skegness Town a few days later before a 5,000 Portland Park crowd. More victories continued, and by Christmas the team was in the second place slot, with the same number of points as the inevitable leaders Peterborough.

By the season's end, the Club's expectations were exceeded when the runners–up place was held. The goal difference in the League, was a staggering 125 for and 40 against.

One year later things were nearly as good, with a third placing behind Peterborough (seven points ahead) and South Shields who had four points more. Despite these two fruitful seasons, the travelling costs were proving to be a crippling liability, and along with the five other ex–North–East contingent, they all resigned to help form a new Northern Counties league. These resignations had unfortunate repercussions for the rest of the Midland league, for they in turn now had insufficient teams, and this league suspended operations for one season.

The Northern Counties league was a shortlived competition that lasted just two seasons, uneventful at least for Ashington, although the latter – the 1961/62 campaign – saw the Colliers once more through to the first round proper of the F.A.Cup. On this occasion there was to be no giant–killing, and they were easily overcome at Chester by four goals to one.

The 1962/63 season saw a return, after several seasons of inactivity, of the North–Eastern league. Ashington, along with most of the other Clubs who had tried both the Midland and Northern Counties leagues, were pleased to join forces in the regional competition after four somewhat nomadic years. But the revival of the league was shortlived and after two seasons, without honours for Ashington, it was time once again to seek pastures new. For just one year Ashington joined the Wearside league – somewhat of a climbdown from three years earlier when they were on equal terms with Peterborough United who by now were competing in the Third Division of the Football League! However with the North East of the country in something of a football turmoil, Ashington then found themselves admitted to the North Regional league (for two seasons), a competition that had been reserved almost exclusively for the Reserve elevens of the local Football League teams.

At last the 1968/69 season saw the first serious attempt to group together the ambitious Clubs of the North, and along with fellow North regional leaguers Gateshead and South Shields, the Colliers were accepted into the fold; on the senior status ladder, another move upwards from the yo–yo ability existence that they had found themselves in. Yet again the Club were to find the unsuitability of their situation, and as in the Midland league the amount of travel to most games became a severe strain on the purse strings, so yet another move was made. This time the choice was for the Northern Alliance, an organisation that was last encountered some fifty five years earlier by the Club's first team.

However the fact that the Colliers reserves were playing in the league just one season before, illustrates how difficult the Club were finding it to reach a suitable level for their abilities. Fourteen seasons earlier, the reserves became Champions, and one year either side they were the runners–up, but such was the fortunes of these nomads among the leagues, that no such honours came the way of the first team, and so yet another move was made.

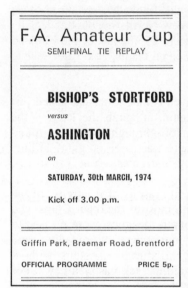

F.A. Amateur Cup
SEMI-FINAL TIE REPLAY

BISHOP'S STORTFORD
versus
ASHINGTON

on

SATURDAY, 30th MARCH, 1974

Kick off 3.00 p.m.

Griffin Park, Braemar Road, Brentford

OFFICIAL PROGRAMME   PRICE 5p.

The Club's entry into the Northern league was in effect an upward move in status, and competing with such quality teams as Spennymoor United, Blyth Spartans and Bishop Auckland was eventually to prove too difficult for the Colliers. From 1970 to the end of the 1983/84 season they competed without any real success, at which time one of the low spots occurred in the long history of the Club. The years in the Northern league had produced mixed fortunes, but this, their unlucky thirteenth, was the worst, and by finishing in bottom but one position in the league – seven points adrift of the next club, Ferryhill – they were relegated to the two year old second division.

Although this plunge in the team's playing ability would appear to be so removed from those earlier days in company with the likes of Grimsby, Rotherham, Stoke and Bradford City, such are the fortunes of football that the Colliers in a relative backwater of the game once again would rub shoulders with the likes of Durham City, Willington and Stockton – Clubs also with a past history that have seen the higher life.

One achievement that cannot be ignored, is that achieved in 1974, when the Club – by that time having reverted to Amateur status – reached the semi–finals of the F.A.Amateur Cup. The Colliers came so close to reaching Wembley Stadium, but could only manage a scoreless draw with Bishop Stortford at Sunderland, and in the replay at Brentford they bowed out of the competition with a three goal defeat. Ashington are unique as an ex–Football League team in almost reaching the peak at the Amateur level, and this achievement can never be equalled or improved upon, for this was the last ever F.A.Amateur Cup tournament!

PORTLAND PARK.

Prior to 1909, Ashington's football was principally played at the Recreation Ground, located about three-quarters of a mile to the East of Portland Park. Just as the formulative days of the Colliers history are lost in time so are early references to the home venue. However since the creation of the team was very much due to the influx of workers that were required to work in the Coalmines, then the main Employer, The Ashington Coal Company, were involved too. They provided a suitable field, located adjacent to the Colliery, and it is most likely that this venue was the Headquarters of the Football Club from their founding. The facilities were no doubt limited to a laid out pitch, roped around (at least in the latter days), with perhaps rudimentary changing rooms. Football (and Rugby now) is still played at the Recreation Ground.

For the 1908/09 season a move for one year was made to the Station Road Ground – located where the present park adjacent to the Library is situated – an unenclosed Ground rented from the Co-op! On being asked for double the rent for the next season, the Club decided to seek new pastures.

As Ashington F.C. rose in football status, so did the town increase in size. It was considered necessary to stay close to the centre, and a local Farmer, Mr. Nixon, was persuaded to sub-let a field to the Club. For a few years the new home venue was also named the Station Road Ground, but around 1914 it was re-named Portland Park in deference to the Duke of Portland who owned the land. Initially, in 1909, the Ground was sparsely developed. But as the years passed, the Grandstand was proudly built, and finally seated 1,000 spectators, with changing rooms, boilerhouse, and other facilities contained under. Natural boundaries already existed on two sides, formed by the cuttings for the main Railway line and a smaller Wagonway (the latter no longer there). Boundary fences, on the other two sides, had by now no doubt already been introduced to provide a fully enclosed Ground. On the Club's election into the Football League in 1921, 2,000 shares were issued to help finance improvements to the Ground, which finally totalled some £6,000. Concrete terracing was installed to three sides of the pitch whilst other improvements were made including a reconstructed Pavilion (Grandstand), and the provision of a Tea Room and a large Press Box. The terracing finished at below pitch level, and a shallow brick perimeter wall capped the field's boundary. By this time there were three entrances into the ground, including one at the South-west corner which by way of a narrow alley led out into Station Road. In 1924, safety crush barriers were installed on the terracing, prior to the F.A.Cup match with Aston Villa. At this time, there were no covered areas for standing spectators, and in view of the Club's limited period in the Football League and its impoverished existence for much of this time, this situation remained until after the 2nd World War. With the introduction of Greyhound Racing in the early 1940's, the Ground layout was completely changed.

The pitch was moved some distance Northwards, various buildings on the North side disappeared, and the arena area was transformed into the required oval shape, which necessitated the removal of the end terracing. By now the reduced pitch size, required the removal of the greyhound rail to temporarily enlarge it for Cup–ties! The Grandstand was either moved or more likely replaced with another, but now flanked on each side with covered terraced sections, the whole stretching almost the entire length of the pitch. On the opposite side to the Grandstand a flat raised concrete standing area was provided, which was roofed over at a later date. The use of the Ground then reverted back to solely Football for a while, and the oval arena became a familiar rectangle once again; by now a Clubhouse/Headquarters building had been added in the South West corner of the ground. The Greyhounds that moved out in 1964, were later replaced with Speedway and Stock Car Racing at Portland Park, but following a meeting of the latter in the Autumn of 1971, the Grandstand was destroyed by fire.

On the site of the original small Grandstand, a modern Cantilevered roof style Concrete structure was built (to seat just over 300). Floodlights were installed in 1980, and by 1984, Greyhound Racing had once again returned to the Ground. The Grandstand, Clubhouse, Covered standing Area, shallow banking, turnstile entrances off Station Road, and enclosure walls remain today, but after so many changes it is now difficult to imagine that Football League matches were ever held here, with a claimed capacity of 28,000!

Portland Park in 1987.

PROGRAMMES.

Football programmes in the early years of the Century do not appear to have been a popular feature with most Clubs in the North–East of the Country, and it is more than likely that Ashington were no exception. However with the Club's entry into the Football League, match programmes were definitely issued, at least for the seasons 1923/24 and 1924/25. However, surviving copies – if there are any – would be extremely rare, and the matchday publication may well have soon stopped until the post–2nd World War days.

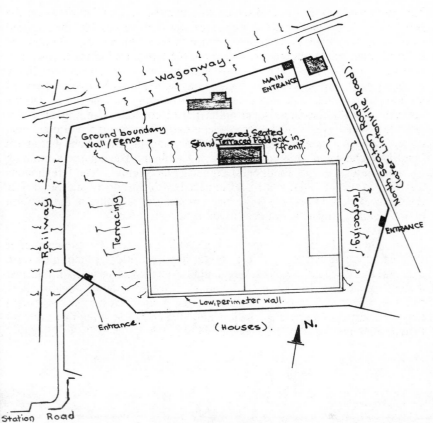

Portland Park c. 1921

Location of the Grounds

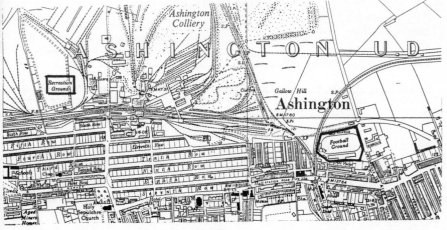

BOOTLE

(Rear): W.Hastings, D.Jardine, R.Anderson (Umpire).
(Middle – players): J.Woods, F.Woods, J.Jackson, R.McFarlane, W.Campbell, A.Allsop.
(Front): H.Heard(Sec.), T.Morris, H.Galbraith, R.Jamieson (Capt.), J.Jones, J.Kilner, J.Prescott (Treasurer)

Pre–League days Team Group – taken outside the Hawthorn Road Pavilion.

BOOTLE

Founded: 1878. As Bootle St.John's.
1880. Changed name to 'Bootle'

Football League: 1892/93.
****

1878 – 1889	Friendlies.	
1889/90 – 1891/92	Football Alliance.	
1892/93	**Football League Div.2.**	

<<<<<<<<<<<<<>>>>>>>>>>>>>

Football League Complete Record: Season 1892/93.

September	3rd	Ardwick	(Away)	0–7.
	10th	Sheffield United	(Home)	2–0.
	17th	Burslem Port Vale	(Home)	1–1.
	24th	Burton Swifts	(Away)	1–2.
October	1st	Northwich Victoria	(Away)	2–3.
	8th	Grimsby Town	(Away)	0–3.
	22nd	Darwen	(Away)	0–3.
November	5th	Small Heath	(Home)	1–4.
	12th	Burslem Port Vale	(Away)	0–0.
	26th	Sheffield United	(Away)	3–8.
December	3rd	Northwich Victoria	(Home)	2–5.
	17th	Grimsby Town	(Home)	3–1.
	24th	Walsall Town Swifts	(Away)	4–4.
	31st	Darwen	(Home)	5–1.
January	7th	Crewe Alexandra	(Away)	1–2.
	21st	Ardwick	(Home)	5–3.
February	18th	Small Heath	(Away)	2–6.
	25th	Burton Swifts	(Home)	3–2.
March	18th	Walsall Town Swifts	(Home)	7–1.
	25th	Crewe Alexandra	(Home)	2–1.
April	1st	Lincoln City	(Away)	1–5.
	15th	Lincoln City	(Home)	4–1.

Played.	W.	D.	L.	F.	A.	Pts.	Posn.
22	8	3	11	49	63	19	8th.

Summary of Facts.

Grounds:

1878 – 1884 :	Bibbey's Lane : Marsh Lane : Cricket Ground, Irlam Road.
1884 – 1893 :	Hawthorne Road (Cricket Ground).

Colours (Football League):   *Blue and White Shirts, Blue Shorts.*

Record Attendance (Probable):
Approx. 20,000. 26th December 1889. Versus Everton (Friendly) Lost 0–3.
Average attendance (Football League season): 2,000.

Main Achievements:

F.A.Cup: Quarter Finals: 1889/90.
1st Round, 2nd series (Modern equivalent 5th round) 1887/88.
1st Round (Modern equivalent 4th round) 1888/89. 1891/92.
2nd Round (Modern equivalent 3rd round) 1881/82.

Liverpool Challenge Cup Winners: 1882/83. 1887/88. 1888/89.

****

Later principal 'Bootle' Clubs. (Not decended from the original).

Bootle: *Founded 1947.*

1947 – 1951:	*Bootle Stadium.*
1951 – 1953:	*Bootle Greyhound Stadium.*

Disbanded during 1953/54 season.

1947 – 1948:	*Friendlies.*
1948/49 –	*Lancs. Combination Div.2.*
1949/50 – 1953/54:	*Lancs. Combination Div.1.*

Langton: *Founded 1952.*
Changed name to Bootle: *1973.*

Grounds: Orrell Mount Park : Bucks Park, Northern Perimeter Road, Netherton.

1952/53 – 1963/64	*Liverpool Shipping League.*
1964/65 – 1973/74	*Liverpool County Football Comb.*
1974/75 – 1977/78	*Lancs. Combination.*
1978/79 –	*Cheshire County League Div.2.*
1979/80 – 1981/82	*Cheshire County League Div.1.*
1982/83 to date	*North–West Counties League Div.1.*

The few historical football references found regarding Bootle F.C. give the Club's formation year as 1880. However, a detailed investigation indicates that this occurred in 1878.

In the 1870's, Bootle, on the Northern outskirts of Liverpool, was not the most salubrious of areas. The economy of the area based as it was – principally on Shipping – attracted a cosmopolitan population, both permanent and temporary, from the many nationalities that frequented the Docks area. As the Docks developed, housing for the workers was needed quickly, and the quality of the accommodation was of secondary consideration! Ironically, the name 'Bootle' was derived from 'Botelai' (as referred to in the Domesday Book), meaning 'House or Dwelling place'. By the 1890's the area was full of primitive dwellings that were both overcrowded and unhygienic; Cholera, Typhoid and Smallpox were endemic. Behind this grim backcloth, football quickly became a release valve for the local male population, and as the sport rapidly developed towards the late 19th Century, Lancashire was to the fore, and Bootle was not left out.

'Football', as such, began to gain popularity in the area in the late 1870's, and the Rugby version appeared to have initially captured the imagination of the populace. Even into the 1880's, most references in the local press referred to the non-round ball sport. *Liverpool Wanderers* (who played at Bootle Cricket Field, Irlam Road) appeared to be the principal team in the locality, and close behind were *Bootle Wasps* who played at Marsh Lane, which was to be later jointly used by *Bootle F.C.* Early soccer club references in the town favoured *St. John's Bootle* – although information on this Club was, even so, sketchy – and *Everton United Church*. As with the majority of Clubs at this time in the Midlands and North of England, football interests were channelled through the Churches – the pursuit of a healthy, competitive sport – and were very often coupled with the local Cricket Clubs. There are two facts to confirm that St.John's Bootle was one and the same as **the** Bootle F.C., that went on to enter the Football League.

A report in the local press in 1880 stated with regard to a match with Everton on February the 7th, that:
> *"Bootle St.John (were) a Club with a formidable reputation, re–named as Bootle...."*

Another Newspaper report referring to the same match, names the Club as *St.John Bootle* – therefore it would appear that the name change had not filtered through to all of the local press, and it would seem that 1880 was the year when the Club's title was changed.

As reasonably conclusive proof, a book entitled 'Football Records' (published in 1881), lists amongst the 59 members of the Lancashire Association – which had been formed three years earlier – just one 'Bootle' Football Club, and gives their formation year as 1878; the Ground was stated as Bibbey's Lane. The Bootle F.C. fixture list detailed in the Bootle Times for the 1880/81 season also refers to this venue. One fact to cloud the issue, was the occasional references to a *'St.John's Bootle'* Club – at least up until 1888 – who played at Hawthorne Road; since by this time, this was also the home venue for 'Bootle', it would not be unreasonable to assume that 'old habits die hard', and just as in modern times a Club is often referred to by its former name even several years after any such change!

The formation of the Club and rise to prominence was due in no small part to an already experienced player, R.E.Lythgoe. Lythgoe moved to Bootle in 1877, where he found that Rugby had taken a hold in the area, and was determined to change this state of affairs. He had previously played in goal and at outside right, for the Welsh Club – The Druids – a team who were to become early and frequent winners of the Welsh Cup. He became the Secretary of Bootle F.C., a position he had held at the Druids, and his enthusiasm and influence was to have a large effect on the Club. Lythgoe eventually rose in this sport to become a Council Member of the Football Association.

One of the earliest matches reported on the Bootle Club was a game on the 6th of December 1879, when the team were victors, at home, over Birkenhead by 3–1. Everton United Church were another prominent Club around this period, and who played their home games at Stanley Park. Within a short period of time, amongst the myriad of Football Clubs that quickly sprung up in Liverpool and its suburbs during the late 1870's, two Clubs were to evolve as the 'top dogs' – Everton and Bootle.

Although the two teams had played each other from the earliest times, one of the first to be reported, was that for the game held on the 7th of February 1880, which resulted in a two goal win by Bootle at their opponents Ground, the football pitch in Stanley Park. Bootle's team that day consisted of:

E.R.Keely, S.Keely, Gosson, Rev.Chapman, Woods, W.Allsopp, Skillicorn, Betts, C.Allsop, Masheder and the Rev.A.W.Keely.

With two Churchman in the team (not withstanding the three brothers), this provides another pointer towards the Club's Christian origins. A return game was played with Everton two weeks later, but at the same venue. On this occasion the Bootle team were victorious by four unopposed goals. Between times, on February the 13th, there was another away game, at Newsham Park; this time Liverpool Association (not 'the' Liverpool) were the hosts. The match appeared to have had its arguments, since the result was recorded as a victory to Bootle by five (one disputed) goals to two (one disputed) goals! The local scribe reported that:

"The success which has marked the career of the Bootle Club throughout the season, followed them on Saturday..."

Obviously the Club's prowess was rapidly increasing. In the return game with the Liverpool Club, an even more emphatic victory was achieved, this time by 7-0. Bootle's opponents were somewhat understrength for they had to use two players who were only used to Rugby rules; *"this may have accounted for their wild play..."* was the wry comment from the reporter! At this game there were 'a considerable number of spectators present'.

The proposed fixture list for the 1880/81 season included games against, Chester, Everton, Liverpool Association, Birkenhead and Middlewich. Inevitably games were added too or cancelled – often for trivial reasons. The game at Chester on October the 9th, was a poor opener of the season for Bootle. With five of the regular first team missing, and the players in great need of practise – as evidenced by the wild kicks of the forwards – the Merseysiders went down by 0-2. (Bootle had a goal disallowed) In this game the team were represented by:

E.Keeley (Captain), Bruce, Gosson, Aske, C.Allsopp, Smith, Betts, A.Allsopp, Sloane, Masheder, and Jones.

Probably the first ever Cup match was played on October the 23rd, when the first round of the Lancashire Cup was played at home. The Club's opponents were the strangely named *'Accrington Num Nook'* team! The fixture intrigued the locals, who turned up in large numbers to view the 'new' game. The town had been dominated by Rugby until this time, and was for the majority of the crowd, a novelty and undoubtably their first ever Football match. The Accrington team were, however, vastly superior to the homesters and ran out easy winners.

Shortly after the Cup game, a local derby with Everton was played. Bootle dominated the first half, and changed over two goals up and another one was added in the second half. A further two weeks passed before the next match, a home game with the Liverpool team. This resulted in a poor match, but a vast improvement was made in the return at Newsham Park, where Bootle triumphed 3-0.

On November the 20th an easy home win over Birkenhead was obtained with a 6–0 scoreline, but the later match at Middlewich was cancelled for the simple reason that the Bootle team didn't turn up! In early December the 'no show' was turned on Bootle, when their opponents, The Wanderers of Chester, failed to put in an appearance.

At this time it was usual for the Club to field the first team against their opponents first eleven, whilst the reserves of each Club played another game on the same day; one game at home and one away for each Club. On December the 11th, the home match featured St.Peter's Athletic in opposition. Bootle's opponents were dismayed to find, that it was only the Bootle reserves; Lythgoe was to make a rare appearance in this match. Meanwhile on the same day the Bootle first team were thrashing Shrewsbury School 6–1, in Stanley Park. One week later the Club received its first representative honours, when two of the Keeley brothers were selected to play for Lancashire in a game versus Birmingham. The casual approach towards matches can be appreciated, when, in the 'match of the day', Bootle were three players short, and cajoled from the spectators, volunteers to make up the number! The match was a single goal defeat to Everton. Blackburn Olympic who were also founded in 1878, and were later to achieve fame in the F.A.Cup, were entertained at Marsh Lane on April the 16th, but Bootle fielding a weak team lost the game. For the first time, the season had been a full one in respect of matches played.

For the 1881/82 season, 29 first team matches were scheduled between the 1st of October and the end of April, with the reserves having a similar number of games arranged. In fact the first match took place on September the 24th at Liverpool Association's new ground at Wavertree, but the home team had no cause for celebration as they lost by a single goal. Early season visitors to Bootle included Birkenhead (beaten 4–1) and the rapidly rising to prominence, Bolton Wanderers; the latter game in particular, *attracted considerable attention'*.

The Merseysiders status by now was shown with their entry not only into the Lancashire Cup (which was lost to Preston North End), but also their first venture into the F.A.Cup Competition – both played on the same day! The first game, the F.A.Cup match, was played at home to Blackburn Law. Despite having the most of the play, Bootle went in at half–time in arrears – a lucky goal by the visitors. But the homesters made amends in the second half and ran out as 2–1 winners. After a short interval, Preston provided the opposition in a game that ended in a 1–1 draw; extra time should have been played, but was not possible due to fading light.

Preston protested Bootles's decision to kick–off so late (due to their first game), but in any event, in the replay the Bootle team lost 1–2. The first efforts in the F.A.Cup took the Club through to the 2nd round, but they met their match when losing 0–4 to the strong Turton Club.

The first major honour came Bootle's way when they won the Liverpool Cup Competition – which had been inaugurated by Mr.Lythgoe – in the 1882/83 season – and two seasons later they were losing finalists – to Everton. By now, both Bootle and Everton were commanding respect, and were rapidly developing as the two quality teams in this area of Lancashire. In January 1882, at Marsh Lane, a crowd of some 500 attended one of the many games between the two, but within four years, the fierce partisanship had reached a peak, and Everton had emerged as the more successful Club.

On the 26th of March 1882, Bootle were honoured with a visit from the Corinthians Football Club. This London based Club were founded in October 1882, from ex–Public Schools players, and were to become a highly respected team, truly amateur in name – but not in the quality of their play. The match at Bootle was the third game in their Easter tour, and resulted in a 2–0 win to the homesters. The other Clubs that Corinthians played in this series were Accrington, Church and Stoke. In November 1882, the match against Everton was won 2–1, and in this game the Club Secretary, Mr.Lythgoe, persuaded Williams of The Druids, Britten – a Brentwood Player – and Ashton from Darwen to 'guest' for Bootle. Whilst it was hoped that with the winning of the Liverpool Cup the Club would grow strongly – and hopefully win some of Everton's support – but the reverse happened. For nearly two seasons Bootle lost the edge, and as they struggled, Everton prospered.

An interesting tour was made around the start of 1884, when a visit was made to play Glasgow (Possil Park) and to the Irish Cup–holders Cliftonville. Later in the season the Club entertained the all conquering Scottish team, Queens Park. The result, a 1–9 defeat, was perhaps no surprise, but the attendance of only 400 was surprisingly small. This was the Scots third visit to Bootle, and they won on each occasion. The Liverpool Cup run ended in disaster when before another 400 attendance, a 0–4 defeat at home to Earlstown resulted.

The start of the next season, the 1884/85, was not very encouraging, and the team hoped for a return of support, which was gradually slipping away to Everton. Their cause was not helped, when, on October the 4th, Bootle lost at Darwen before a crowd in excess of 1,000, to a score of 1–9; although an injury and retirement from the field of David Williams, reduced the visitors to only ten men. Shortly after this Lancashire Cup game, Bootle lost 1–2 at home to Wrexham Olympic, which gave cause for the local press comment: *"How the mighty have fallen"*. Further defeats followed before a draw with Southport halted the slide. Another match was played at Hawthorne Road against Everton, which by all accounts was a rough affair; Bootle lost 0–2. The Bootle Times were dismayed to find that the names of the Bootle players were not given before the match, and led to a suggestion that perhaps the Club were importing players – at this time, the use of players not living in the area of the Club had still to be resolved between the Clubs and the Football Association. At the end of the season a return match was played with Cliftonville, and won 6–1. Bootle were, perhaps, on the way back!

By now, Everton had graduated to their own enclosure at Anfield (the later Liverpool F.C. Ground). It was opportune that their first opponents at this venue should be Bootle, in a local Cup–tie. In 1886, interest in Football on Merseyside, and particularly towards Everton, had reached a peak, as can be seen from a game played at Bootle. The attendance at Bootle's (by now) Hawthorne Road Ground was estimated as a record 10,000 when the two teams met. The Crowd was so large, that many bypassed the one Official entrance and entered free of charge by way of the hoardings enclosing the Ground! The size of the crowd was unprecedented for a game in the Liverpool area, and the loud cheers that greeted the two teams entry on to the pitch was unseen by many of the tightly packed spectators. Although the venue was a Cricket Ground, the reporter of the day commented on its suitability for Football, and particularly referred to the Pavilion. Despite the many changes over the years, that structure is probably the same as that at the Ground today!

Even by the standards of the day – when hacking, tripping and pushing were all part of the game – the game between these two antagonists was a rough affair, in which the spectators all but took part! On several occasions the large crowd had to be restrained, and kept back behind the ropes that surrounded the pitch. Despite having the wind behind them, Bootle were unable to score in the first half and the teams went in after a goalless period. The advantage then went to Everton, and it was expected that they would now win the match easily, with the elements in their favour. But it was Bootle who came closest to scoring, with an effort that was judged to have gone past, rather than between the posts – goal nets at this time were not used! However, it was Everton that opened the account through Briscoe.

With Everton gradually gaining the upper hand, they added a second goal to their tally. Bootle fought back, and with less than two minutes left on the watch, a whistled stoppage by the Referee, was a signal for the Evertonians to invade the pitch. The players retired to the Dressing Rooms, but by the time that the pitch was cleared of spectators, the Bootle men had partially washed and changed, and refused to play the final seconds of the game! By now the fixtures with Everton were not to be taken lightly!

Matches were still limited to Friendlies and Cup games, since the first League competition was not inaugurated until 1888. Despite Bootle's somewhat regained prowess, it was not until 1888 that another worthy run in the F.A.Cup was made. Old Carthusians, previous semi-finalists, were met in the second series first round – the last sixteen stage in the competition. Although the renowned Old Boys teams from the South had by now lost their dominance in the Competition, the Bootle team lost the match 0-2. The following season the Club reached the re-designated first round proper, (last thirty-two) and were destined to meet the renowned, Preston North End team, the previous season's losing finalists. Great interest in the town was raised by this meeting, and the fans were moved to write a song for the occasion with the chorus:

"There's going to be a match today, and Bootle will be there."

The team was there, but even their vociferous supporters could not help Bootle avoid a 0-3 defeat! Preston went on to win the Cup that year by the same score against Wolverhampton Wanderers.

Next season, the Club reached their furthest ever in the F.A.Cup. The first round proper was contested with Sunderland Albion. The Tyneside Club were an offshoot of the present-day Sunderland Club, had quickly risen in status, and were bidding for overall power in their area. The match in 1889, was lost by Bootle by three goals to one, but a protest was lodged against Sunderland – a not uncommon action which usually centred around the usage of ineligible players – and the match was awarded to the Merseysiders.

The second round produced a 2-1 win over Derby Midland – a leading Club in the newly constituted Midland League – the result taking the Club through to the last eight. In this round Bootle met their match, and were unceremoniously thrashed by Blackburn Rovers, by seven unopposed goals; once again the Club had lost to the Cup Winners – Blackburn went on to register a record Cup Final, score of 6-1 over Sheffield Wednesday.

Friendly matches continued to be played, although the dawning of the age of League competitions was near at hand. The Club's opponents were generally other teams in Lancashire or neighbouring Counties although there were some notable exceptions. In March 1888 a visit to Bootle was made by the Club that originated in London from exiled Scotsmen – London Caledonians. Early the next season, Bootle paid a visit to Cheshire to play Crewe Alexandra, and just after Christmas Kilmarnock made the trip down to Bootle. Everton were still the main 'enemy', and by now they were gradually easing ahead of the Bootle team in the popularity and seniority stakes.

In local Competitions, the Lancashire Cup was played for – with little success – plus the Liverpool and District Cup. By the late 1880's the latter Cup was usually contested for, in the early rounds, by the Reserves, with the first team being played only when felt necessary; the winning of the Trophy was considered a prestigious feat. The run through to the final in 1888, included two games with Southport High Park. This Club were considered a pushover and the Reserve team took part in the game at Hawthorne Road on January the 7th. The Seaside team forced a draw, and it was considered necessary for the first eleven to play in the replay two weeks later, which was also played at Bootle. This hurdle was overcome, and local team, Bootle Wanderers were beaten in the semi–final, the game being played at the Stanley Club Ground. In the end of season Final, the Cup was won when Stanley were beaten at the Stanley Athletic Grounds. One year later, Bootle retained the trophy, with a 5–3 victory over Earlstown, on March the 23rd, although it was the Reserves again, that played in the easy, early ties.

With the introduction of the Football League in the 1888/89 season, many of the Club's games had extra interest, for several matches were against these League Clubs (six of the teams were from Lancashire) who required such matches to augment their fixture list. The season opened with a home game against Accrington – one of the Football League Founder–members – and Bootle's ability was demonstrated with a 3–1 home win. Two days later an even more emphatic win was achieved over the League team Burnley, with a three goal victory. Other early season games with the 'elite', were against Blackburn (1–0), Preston (a 1–4 home defeat) and two defeats versus Bolton Wanderers. By Christmas, the Club had amassed a list of 22 games played – all Friendlies – of which 14 were won, 2 drawn and a very satisfactory total of only 6 defeats. On Boxing Day, a visit was made to Anfield were a scoreless draw was played with Everton, and in March in the return game, six goals were shared – before an enthusiastic 9,000 attendance at Hawthorne Road. Kilmarnock from Scotland visited Bootle again, at the year end, and 3,000 witnessed a good two goal home win; the same day a similar attendance was recorded at Anfield where the Reserves of Bootle and Everton met.

The second half of the season started in an excellent way, with high-scoring home wins over Moffat and St.Helen's, both by 7-1, and within four days of each other, followed by a demolition of Newcastle West End by 12-1. The St.Helen's game was a Liverpool Cup-tie and was 'partially' watched by around 1,000 spectators - thick fog was present throughout the game! The next game in the local Cup was easily won over Police Athletic by six goals before a 3,000 home crowd; around this time, the enemy (Everton) were attracting around 8,000 for their games at Anfield. A late match in the season produced a rare win over their neighbours, when Bootle triumphed 2-1 in the Liverpool Cup. By the season's end, over forty matches had been played between September the 1st and May the 4th, and the Club were able to show a good credit balance in their results.

The forming of the Football League revolutionised the Sport; winning games took on a whole new meaning, the payments to players became paramount for the necessary successes, and consequently, Clubs came to find that - even more - finance would dictate their future. In the Summer of 1889, the Football Alliance was formed. Bootle, anxious to emulate and equal the triumphs of their rivals, Everton, who had strode ahead of them and had been accepted into the Football League, gained entry in to the new Competition. Their past season record was a sufficient recommendation, and they were encouraged with a surge of new Club members - everybody hoped for, and expected success. The Alliance was originated principally by Nottingham Forest and Sheffield Wednesday - two Clubs who had been unsuccessful in their bid to join the Football League. The first season consisted of twelve teams in the league, and therefore for Bootle it was necessary for a number of friendly games to be played, at a serious level, in order to augment their fixture list.

Bootle welcomed the F.A.Cup winners, Preston, to Hawthorne Road for an opening friendly on September the 2nd, and an exciting game finished as a highly encouraging two-all draw before an excellent 7,000 attendance. But the first Alliance match was lost 1-2 at Sheffield Wednesday five days later, when Bootle were represented by:
Jardine, Spencer, Powell, Alsop, Hughes, Campbell, Jones, Hastings, Jamieson, Morris and Woods.

A four goals shared match followed, at Small Heath, and the first home game in the League brought Newton Heath to Bootle. The locals were far superior to their opponents, and ran out easy 4–1 winners. In October, the Club were depleted for one game as no less than eight of their players were called up for the Liverpool and District representative side. Following the 3–1 home win over Sunderland Albion, watched by a 4,000 crowd, Bootle moved up to second in the League after having played eight games, and by Christmas they had maintained this position, just one point behind leaders Sheffield Wednesday.

On Boxing Day a Friendly was played at Hawthorne Road with Everton, and the interest in the game surpassed all others. It was estimated that a staggering 20,000 were present. By now the Ground had undergone a fair degree of development, and the crowds were packed around the pitch and in the open and covered stands. The pitch was very heavy, which did not suit Bootle for they went in two goals down at Half–time. Bootle's Geary retired injured in the second half, and the homesters did well to limit the Everton score to just one more. At the end, both teams received enthusiastic applause. Overall, the season went well for Bootle and they retained the runners–up position in the Alliance, to Sheffield Wednesday, at the finish.

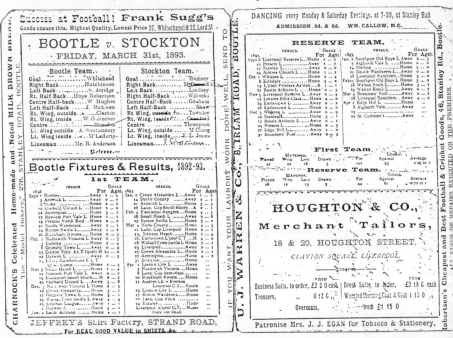

The First (and only) season in the Football League – Many Friendly matches were also played.

Stoke took Long Eaton Rangers' place in the Alliance for the 1890/91 season, but for Bootle it was not a happy time. By the turn of the year the Club lay in the third from bottom position, from one win, six draws and seven defeats, and the match versus Birmingham St.George completed a run of seven successive drawn games. There were certainly no honours for the Club by the season's end for they finished in eleventh place – of twelve – with just 2 wins, 7 draws and 12 defeats, and a goal difference of 40 – 61. In an incredible double turn around, it was even worse for the reigning Champions, Sheffield Wednesday, for they finished up bottom in the table!

By now the Competition had become the unofficial Second Division, and this was recognised by the promotion of Stoke (the Champions) into the Football League. Things were little better by the New Year of 1892, with Bootle languishing in eighth place in the Alliance, whilst the Reserve team were also involved in League Competition – the Liverpool and District. The F.A.Cup produced little, when at Bootle, before a very poor attendance, (no more than for a second team fixture) they lost to Darwen in icy conditions. This second season of poor and generally indifferent results was having its affect on the crowd numbers, and the local Press urged for more support for the local team.

At a Football League meeting in Birmingham on the 23rd of March, it was resolved that the Alliance would form the new Second Division for the next season. This month coincided with troubles for Bootle's great rivals, and resulted in them moving from Anfield, whilst their previous President formed the new Club of 'Liverpool'.

The thought of Football League competition, and perhaps the Club's emulation of Everton's success, appeared to interest the locals, as the last matches generally attracted slightly improved crowd numbers. The final three matches brought Blackburn Rovers and Queen of the South Wanderers, to Bootle for Friendly fixtures (each watched by 2,500 people), and a Liverpool Cup semi–final defeat at Everton, before a 6,000 gate. At the final reckoning, the third season in the Alliance was a little better for Bootle, but even so the record showed an uninspiring 8th place, with eight victories and twelve defeats.

It was always going to be a struggle for Bootle. Their playing ability had appeared to have 'peaked' some years earlier, and the never ending battle with Everton for support from the populace had become more and more biased towards the Anfield Club. The 1891/92 season had ended with a fairly poor playing record for Bootle, plus reduced attendances. Conversely, Everton in the Football League had finished in fifth place, whilst one year later this was improved to third, plus a first ever F.A.Cup Final appearance.

By May 1893, gates at Anfield producing £573, £625 and £736 (32,000) had been recorded, whilst Bootle's best – and this was considered extremely good – totalled a mere £219. Bootle knew they had to emulate their great rivals, and this could only be achieved by the right payments to the right players – finance was going to be the make or break of the Club. In Bootle's case it was the latter!

After a 1–4 defeat in a friendly at Burnley, the first Football League fixture got off to a disastrous start on September the 3rd, with a thumping seven unopposed goal defeat, before 4,000, at Ardwick! The line–up for this, not so auspicious occasion, was:

> *McLaughlin, Hutchinson, Arridge, Nelson, Hughes, Grierson, Montgomery, McLafferty, Law, Finlayson and Gallacher.*

Four goals were then shared in a friendly with First Division Stoke, followed by a somewhat reassuring 2–0 home League victory against Sheffield United. This first ever home game in the Football League attracted a reasonable attendance of around 4,000. Generally, League games were played on alternate weeks, whilst Friendly matches were arranged between times; with regard to the latter an excellent two goal win was recorded over the high flying Preston North End, on September the 19th. Unfortunately, the Club's aspirations were not fulfilled, and as the season wore on the results were not as hoped for. Hence the attendances dropped, not aided by the new 'Liverpool' Club's success. By Christmas, an awful start had been made to the Club's League career; 2 wins, 3 draws and 8 defeats – including a 3–8 reverse at Sheffield United in November. Even the F.A.Cup produced little, for after a ten goal shattering of Gorton Villa, a home local derby with Liverpool Caledonians finished as a surprise 2–3 defeat.

By the New Year, the local press reported that Bootle were doing well! This, perhaps, was not such surprising a statement, for an excellent 5–1 win over Darwen had been obtained on New Year's Day, and the many Friendly fixtures had generally gone in Bootle's favour. League competition was still a novelty, and the full importance of success in this direction had still to be appreciated! In any event, things started to pick up as the second half of the season progressed. In successive League matches at home, first Ardwick were overcome by 5–3, and was followed with a victory over Burton Swifts with a 3–2 scoreline – which should have been more. The League placing was now fourth from bottom, but the next game gave hope financially and further encouragement on the field of play. On the 11th of March, Liverpool F.C. were entertained at home. The visitors, only formed a few months earlier had gained immediate entry into the Lancashire League – which they subsequently won.

This game in the quarter-finals of the Lancashire Cup captured the imagination of the followers of both teams, and a crowd far and away the best for years attended the game at Hawthorne Road. The gate producing £219-1-6d. (an approximate attendance of 10,000), was way above the normal numbers attracted to Bootle's games. The 'icing on the cake', was a 2-1 win to the homesters in a somewhat dirty game. But as so often happens on a big occasion, far better games had been seen at other times. This encouraging support proved to be a flash in the pan as the following Bootle home games were to prove.

On March the 18th, the Club's best ever Football League win in this, their only season, was recorded over Walsall Town Swifts, with a 7-1 scoreline; A match in which Whitehead in goal had shown his worth. One week later, Crewe were also beaten, in a game which finished with only ten men in each team due to injuries. The attendance was between two and three thousand, which could have been considered good, in view of Everton's Cup semi-final at Manchester on the same day.

The season, and Bootle's career was drawing to a close. One of the last matches was played with Preston North End, on April the 8th at Anfield. (now the home Ground of Liverpool) The occasion was the semi-final of the Lancashire Cup, and was attended by a 10,000 crowd. McLaughlin replaced the ineligible Whitehead in goal, and gave a poor display. By half-time Bootle were four goals in arrears, aided by a 'one sided' referee, as the local - unbiased (!) - press, reported. Well into the second period, the score was 0-6, then a transformation took place. In an incredible six minute spell, the team pulled four goals back. Then an uproar greeted a fifth 'goal' that was adjudged by the Official to be offside. Bootle lost the game, but it had been a memorable match.

The last League game for the Club was played on April the 15th, when a 4-1 win was gained over Lincoln City, avenging the earlier 1-5 away reverse. Perhaps sensing the end, and with the bulk of the support now having shifted to either Everton or Liverpool, a miserable attendance of only 1,000 was present. On the 24th of April, the last ever game for the Club was played. Burnley came to Hawthorne Road, and Bootle lost 1-2 in this Friendly before a 1,500 crowd.

At the Club's Annual Dinner in May there was no talk of doom or gloom! It was recognised that more support was needed, and it was expressed that if more notaries such as Councillor Vicars, who was present, would give their backing, then there was every chance that the Club could achieve their goals. No fears were expressed for the future!

But it had been a trying season, for the Club had started the Campaign already in debt from their earlier endeavours to emulate the Everton Club, and although the attendances had slightly improved as a whole over the season, it was not enough. Despite finishing in a respectable 8th place in the Second Division, the Club resigned from the Football League, and by August it was voiced that:

"It is apparent that the Club were doomed and about to sink into oblivion."

On August the 29th 1893, a meeting was held in the Pavilion at Hawthorne Road, where the Company of Bootle F.C. was wound up. This gave other local Clubs the opportunity to rise, where Bootle had failed. Amongst them, Bootle White Star continued playing at the old Marsh Lane Ground, whilst Bootle Athletic took over at Hawthorne Road. However, neither Club – nor any in the future – were ever to reach the heights that the original Bootle F.C. had achieved.

It is interesting conjecture to consider 'what might have been'. Over many years, History has proved that two first class Football Clubs can exist in Liverpool. Yet those two Clubs could so easily have not included Liverpool! Following Everton's Championship winning season of 1890/91, the part owner of Anfield, John Houlding, demanded more rent. Houlding, in addition to owning the adjacent, Sandon Hotel (which was patronised by many of the fans) had the sole concession for refreshments in the Ground, had loaned the Club money (at a high interest rate) – and was the President of Everton Football Club! His non–altruistic attitude towards the Club, was opposed by a large majority of the membership, which culminated in Everton's move to a new Ground at Goodison Park. Houlding then set about creating a new Club, named Liverpool F.C., which quickly became a force in Football, and soon took over from Bootle, the role as the major local opponents to Everton. If this Everton/Liverpool split had never taken place, then it is possible that the name of Bootle F.C. would have lived on to become a Football force, and the title, 'Liverpool' could have remained as just a town! Liverpool in effect were one of the replacements that were necessary in the Second Division, at the end of the 1892/93 season.

Bootle's fate was summed up at the start of the 1893/94 season by the Sports Writer in 'The Liver' Newspaper of the 16th of September:

"Alas! Poor Bootle. The absence of the old North Enders and doings leaves an aching void in the heart of the old time Scribe, whose wont it has been to hold forth year after year concerning them."

THE GROUNDS.

It is quite possible that from the earliest of days, the Club played on Bootle Cricket Field, which was situated off Irlam Road, since this – no doubt unenclosed – area was used by several of the Rugby Clubs around 1880. The first stated 'Ground' of the Club was given in 1881 as Bibbey's Lane, and the same venue was given prior to the commencement of the Club's fixtures for the 1880/81 season. Bibbey's Lane still exists, and runs North off Marsh Lane and is now a residential area. At the time in question, there were open fields. Later in the 1880/81 season, both Bootle Cricket Field, and Marsh Lane, are referred to as home venues. Since the ambitious Club no doubt would want to take entry money at games, it is very likely that due to the open nature of Bibbey's Lane, the other two venues mentioned above were considered more suitable. The Cricket Field was probably enclosed, but the only facility offered was a Pavilion. It is believed that this venue was only rarely used in the early years of the Club. The Fire Station now stands on what was the South–east corner of that Cricket Field. Marsh Lane was used regularly for several years, and although only basic, was developed as a Football Ground, probably enclosed but with very few, if any, facilities, and no accommodation for spectators. The site was a former Convent, is now residential, and lay North to South off Marsh Lane, just to the East of Milton Street.

The final home of the Club was at the (later) Cricket Ground, situated then – as now – to the West and North of the junction of Hawthorne and Bedford Roads. This move was made around 1884 and provided the Club with better accommodation than their status by now required. The Ground was on occasions criticised, despite on the face of it comparing very favourably with the Club's contemporaries, but for the very rare large crowds, of many thousands, and with no banking, then the view of the game must have been very limited for many! Initially, the Ground probably provided only a Pavilion, which although superficially changed over the years is believed to be the same basic building as today; if this is so, then it qualifies as the oldest Football Structure in the World! In the Summer of 1889, improvements were completed, and the Ground could boast of the following spectator accommodation: An open, seated stand behind one goal, a covered seated stand extending approximately one half of the pitch and down the same side two further lengths of open stands. These structures were almost certainly made of timber, and introduced purely for the convenience of the Football Club, as a few years later they had been removed. Wadham Road that now runs parallel with Bedford Road, was built over the side of the Football Ground area that contained the Covered Stand. The remainder of the Cricket Ground appears to be much the same today, as it eventually became before the turn of the Century.

The Hawthorn Road (Cricket Ground) today.
The Pavilion – arguably the oldest football structure in the World! The covered Stand
was located where the houses (top right in top photo.) are now – in Wadham Road.

PROGRAMMES.

Surprisingly, programmes were issued prior to, and during the Club's season
in the Football League. The style was similar throughout the period; Four
pages, with team line-ups and the seasons fixtures and results on the front
page... The Reserve team's fixtures and results, or, (unusually) the
opponents fixtures and results on the back page... and advertisements on the
two inside pages. Should original copies of any programmes still be in
existence then they would, needless to say, be very valuable!

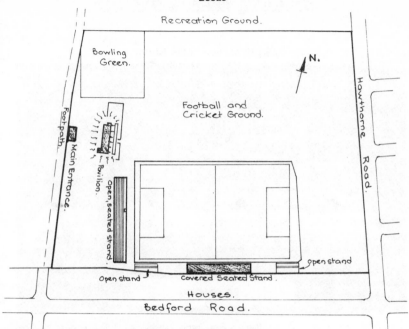

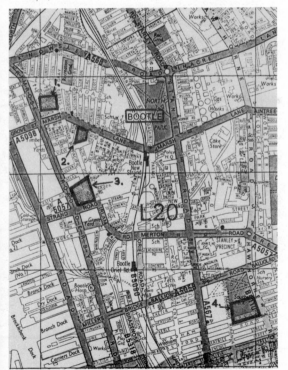

Hawthorn Road Ground in 1892.

The Location of the Grounds.

Bradford (Park Avenue).

1948/49 season Team Group

BRADFORD

STANDING (Left to right): Stephen, Horsman, Farr, Farrell, Layton. SEATED: Glover, Henry, White, Ainsley, Downie, Elliott.

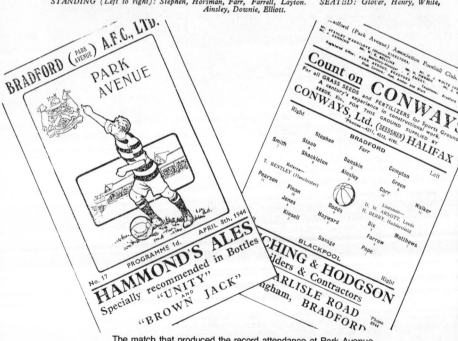

The match that produced the record attendance at Park Avenue
A War-time game!

Bradford (Park Avenue).

Founded: 1907.
Football League. 1908/09 – 1969/70.
****

1907/08.	*Southern League First Div.*
1908/09 – 1913/14.	*Football League Div.2.*
1914/15.	*Football League Div.1.*
1915/16 – 1918/19.	*Midland Section Tournaments.**
1919/20 – 1920/21.	**Football League Div.1.**
1921/22.	**Football League Div.2.**
1922/23 – 1927/28.	**Football League Div.3 North.**
1928/29 – 1938/39.	**Football League Div.2.**
1939/40 – 1945/46.	**Football League North. ****
1946/47 – 1949/50.	**Football League Div.2.**
1950/51 – 1957/58.	**Football League Div.3 North.**
1958/59 – 1960/61.	**Football League Div.4.**
1961/62 – 1962/63.	**Football League Div.3.**
1963/64 – 1969/70.	**Football League Div.4.**
1970/71 – 1973/74.	*Northern Premier League.*

* Competed in regional wartime league of 14 to 16 teams (Principal Tournament), followed by a a six match competition (Subsidary Tournament)
** 1939/40: Football League matches were cancelled after two weeks, and the War-time League was introduced later in the season.

Football League Record:

	Played		W.	D.	L.	F.	A.	Pts.	Posn.
1908/09.	38	13	6	19	51	59	32	16th.	
1909/10.	38	17	4	17	64	59	38	10th.	
1910/11.	38	14	9	15	53	55	37	12th.	
1911/12.	38	13	9	16	44	45	35	11th.	
1912/13.	38	14	8	16	60	60	36	13th.	
1913/14.	38	23	3	12	71	47	49	2nd.	

Promoted to First Division.

1914/15.	38	17	7	14	69	65	41	9th.	
1919/20.	42	15	12	15	60	63	42	11th.	
1920/21.	42	8	8	26	43	76	24	22nd.	

Relegated to Second Division.

1921/22.	42	12	9	21	46	62	33	21st.	

Relegated to Third Division North.

1922/23.	38	19	9	10	67	38	47	2nd.	
1923/24.	42	21	10	11	69	43	52	5th.	
1924/25.	42	19	12	11	84	42	50	5th.	
1925/26.	42	26	8	8	101	43	60	2nd.	
1926/27.	42	24	7	11	101	59	55	3rd.	
1927/28.	42	27	9	6	101	45	63	1st.	

Promoted to Second Division.

1928/29.	42	22	4	16	88	70	48	3rd.	
1929/30.	42	19	12	11	91	70	50	4th.	
1930/31.	42	18	10	14	97	66	46	6th.	
1931/32.	42	21	7	14	72	63	49	6th.	
1932/33.	42	17	8	17	77	71	42	8th.	
1933/34.	42	23	3	16	86	67	49	5th.	
1934/35.	42	11	16	15	55	63	38	15th.	
1935/36.	42	14	9	19	62	84	37	16th.	
1936/37.	42	12	9	21	52	88	33	20th.	
1937/38.	42	17	9	16	69	56	43	7th.	
1938/39.	42	12	11	19	61	82	35	17th.	

(War-time, Football League suspended)

1946/47.	42	14	11	17	65	77	39	16th.
1947/48.	42	16	8	18	68	72	40	14th.
1948/49.	42	13	11	18	65	78	37	17th.
1949/50.	42	10	11	21	51	77	31	22nd.

Relegated to Third Division North.

1950/51.	46	23	8	15	90	72	54	6th.
1951/52.	46	19	12	15	74	64	50	8th.
1952/53.	46	19	12	15	75	61	50	7th.
1953/54.	46	18	14	14	77	68	50	9th.
1954/55.	46	15	11	20	56	70	41	16th.
1955/56.	46	13	7	26	61	122	33	23rd.

Successfully Re-elected.

1956/57.	46	16	3	27	66	93	35	20th.
1957/58.	46	13	11	22	68	95	37	22nd.

Successfully Re-elected. Members of new 4th Division.

1958/59.	46	18	7	21	75	77	43	14th.
1959/60.	46	17	15	14	70	68	49	11th.
1960/61.	46	26	8	12	84	74	60	4th.

Promoted to Third Division.

1961/62.	46	20	7	19	80	78	47	11th.
1962/63.	46	14	12	20	79	97	40	21st.

Relegated to Fourth Division.

1963/64.	46	18	9	19	75	81	45	13th.
1964/65.	46	20	17	9	86	62	57	7th.
1965/66.	46	21	5	20	102	92	47	11th.
1966/67.	46	11	13	22	52	79	35	23rd.

Successfully Re-elected.

1967/68.	46	4	15	27	30	82	23	24th.

Successfully Re-elected.

1968/69.	46	5	10	31	32	106	20	24th.

Successfully Re-elected.

1969/70.	46	6	11	29	41	96	23	24th.

Failed to gain Re-election.

Total Number of Football League Matches Played: 2193. (Including 1939/40 season). This represents the most games played by an 'Ex-League' Club.

Summary of Facts.

Grounds:
1907/08 – 1972/73.	Park Avenue, Bradford, Yorks.
1973/74.	Valley Parade. (Bradford City F.C.)

Nickname: 'The Avenue'.

Colours:
1911:	Red,Amber & Black Stripes, White Shorts.
1911 – 1924:	Green & White Hoops, White Shorts.
1924 – 1932:	Red, Amber and Black Hooped Shirts, Black Shorts.
1932 – 1937:	Red, Amber and Black Striped Shirts, Black Shorts.
1937 – 1956:	White and Red, Amber & Black Hooped Shirts, Black Shorts.
1956 – 1959:	Green, Narrow White Stripes & Trim Shirts, White Shorts.
1959/60:	White, Green 'V' and trim Shirts, Black Shorts.
1960 – 1967:	White, Green and White trim Shirts, White Shorts.
1967/68:	White, Red & Amber Hooped Shirts, White Shorts.
1968/69:	White, Red & Amber Hooped Shirts, Black Shorts.
1969 – 1974:	White, Amber Trim, Red Shorts.

Bradford (Park Avenue)

First League Game:
September 1st 1908. (Home) versus Hull City. (1–0 Win). Attendance approx. 12,000.
(£240 receipts)

Last League Game:
April 20th 1970. (Away) versus Aldershot. (2–4 Defeat). Attendance 4,861.
Last Game:
May 2nd 1974. (Home) v. Great Harwood Town (Northern Premier League) Won 1–0.
Attendance: 698.

Record Attendance:
32,429.   Versus Leeds United. (League) December the 25th 1931.
34,810.   Versus Blackpool. (War Cup) April 18th 1944.
Football League average attendances: 1st season 11,350. Last season 3,137.

Main Achievements.
Football League Division 2 Runners–up: *1913/14.*
Football League Division 1, Best Placing: *1914/15 (9th).*
Football League Div.3 North, Champions: *1927/28.*
Football League Div.4, Promoted: *1960/61.*

International Players:
(England): J.Crayston. L.Scott. A.Geldard. R.Turnbull.(Ireland): S. Burniston. J.Elwood.
A. McCluggage.
(Wales) : J.Parris. Matthews. (Ireland): J. McCandless. (Eire): M. McGrath.

F.A.Cup: (Pre–1926, 2nd round equivalent to modern 4th, etc.) 2nd Round:
1909/10. 1910/11. 1913/14. 1920/21. 1921/22. 1922/23. 1924/25.
3rd Round: 1911/12. 1914/15.
4th Round (Quarter–final): 1912/13. 1919/20.
5th Round: 1928/29. 1929/30. 1930/31. 1931/32. 1935/36. 1937/38.
6th Round (Quarter–final): 1945/46.

West Riding Senior Cup Winners:
1911. 1913. 1924. 1927. 1932. 1936. 1951. 1953. 1963.
West Riding County Cup Winners: 1929. (Reserves)
(Wartime) Midland Section Subsidary Tournament winners:
1916/17, 1918/19.
Top 1st Div. Goalscorer: J. Bauchop. (28) 1914/15 season.
Top 2nd Div. Goalscorer: G.Henson. (27) 1937/38 season.
Top Football League Goalscorer: K.Hector. (44) 1965/66 season.
Most goals in a season: K.McDonald (46 incl. 3 F.A.Cup) 1925/26 season.

Best Win: 8–0, 1925/26 versus Walsall (Home) 3rd.Div.North.
Worst Defeat: 0–7, 1910/11 versus Barnsley (Away) – Div.2., plus 1955/56 versus
Accrington Stanley (Away) 3rd Div.North. Also 2–8, 1930/31 versus Port Vale (Away)
Div.2.

Re–election applied for on 5 occasions.
1967/68: Scored 30 goals in 46 games – (joint) record low for 4th Div.

The Club's initial season saw the first team play in the Southern League, whilst the
reserves competed in the North–Eastern League – opposite ends of the Country and
surely unique in Non–league football.

Youngest ever player in Football League match (Joint record): A.Geldard – 15 years
158 days. (versus Millwall – 16th February 1929)

A football team was playing in the Park Avenue area under the name of *'Bradford'* in the 1890's, and indeed were one of the instigators in the forming of the West Riding F.A. in 1896; however, the start of professional football at Park Avenue commenced in controversy.

Encouraged by the popularity of the football team on the other side of town – Bradford City – founded just four years earlier and operating with success in the Second Division of The Football League, a group of sporting enthusiasts in the Park Avenue area met in April 1907. This band of players had been playing Professional Rugby and the opinion of some within the Club, felt that the time had come for a possible change. Should they continue as they were, revert back to the amateur code or change completely in favour of the round ball game at a professional level? Although the upsurge in football interest was in its prime, there was the nagging doubt that the town would not be able to support two senior Clubs. After much discussion, a vote was taken and by the narrowest of margins the meeting opted in favour of 'as you were'. In view of the closeness of the voting, a recount was decided upon – and this time the numbers favoured a return to Amateur Rugby! Amongst the confusion and indecision, Mr. Harry Briggs, who was the principal financial backer of the Club, decided that his preference was for Football; following the taking of legal advice he announced to the Committee that the meeting had been out of order, and amidst much dissention, his choice was finally adopted in May.

A somewhat audacious suggestion was made that this new, as yet non-established Club, should amalgamate with the highly successful *City* team – a bid that was firmly turned down by the latter!

Around the turn of the Century, an incident happened at the Park Avenue Rugby Club, which suggested that perhaps the Ground was haunted! Mr.Jennings, the Groundsman at the time, happened one night to look out of his bedroom window which overlooked the field. He was surprised to see a light on in the pavilion. Since the pavilion had been visited just one hour earlier, he went to investigate. On looking through the window from where the light shone, he was startled to see a player fully kitted out in the red, amber and black colours of the Club. Somewhat alarmed he summoned a policeman and they both returned to the pavilion within a few minutes to confront the intruder. There was by now no light from the window, and the door to the Pavilion was secured. The door was unlocked and they both entered, only to find to Mr.Jennings surprise that, despite a thorough search of the building, there was nobody there! Mr.Jennings was of a sober disposition, and no rational explanation for the occurrence was ever discovered!

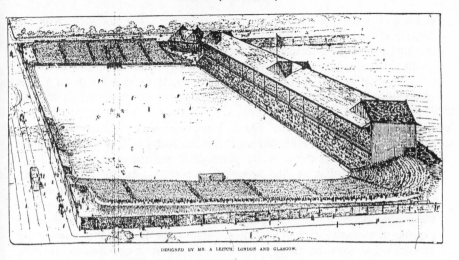

DESIGNED BY MR. A LEITCH, LONDON AND GLASGOW.

The renowned Archibald Leitch's vision of Valley Parade in 1907
(Note the 'Dolls House' in the top right corner)

With their past operating experience as a sporting Club, the ready support both on and off the field, plus a suitable Ground already established adjacent to the County Cricket Ground (where the former Rugby Club had been playing), the Club applied for entry to the Football League Division 2 for the 1907/08 season; the Division that neighbours City were ironically vacating due to their promotion to the top competition.

None other than Archibald Leitch, the Architect of many leading Football Grounds, was commissioned to re-design and improve the Stadium. To the fledgling Club's consternation their application to the 2nd Division was turned down in favour of Fulham F.C., whereupon the Avenue boldly applied to take over the Londoner's place in the Southern League. Despite being the undisputed Senior non-League competition – the geographical situation of the Yorkshire Club resulted in their nearest opponents being Northampton and Norwich – the Prophets of Doom had a field day predicting the immediate financial downfall of the Club. Nonetheless, the newly appointed Manager, Fred Halliday (Ex-Bolton) set about advertising for players.

The first Southern League match was won by 3-1 at Reading in front of a crowd numbering 7,000, although this game was preceded by the first match for the Club, when the Reserves beat Newcastle United's second string in the North-Eastern League at Park Avenue. The Avenue was committed to a large financial outlay with the acquisition of a Professional team coupled with high travelling expenses. Problems were compounded with an indifferent first season, and hence mediocre support, showing a final placing of 13th of twenty teams in the Southern League Division 1. The last match of the season was lost to Southampton by 1–3. So rapid had been the Club's formation that an entry could not be made in time for the F.A.Cup competition !

Less than a year after the Club's formation, they became a Limited Company, and it was fitting and inevitable that Harry Briggs was elected the first Chairman. This decision was particularly merited in view of the large sums of money that he had ploughed into the Club, for without these contributions Bradford (P.A.) would have rapidly disappeared from the scene. During the season the idea was again mooted that the two Bradford Clubs should amalgamate, and therefore form a single, and strong Football League representative for the town. The idea followed a number of meetings, but with the majority of Avenue supporters opposed to the idea, who no doubt considered that their Club's influence would take second place. The talking finally came to a head on May the 27th when a well attended meeting voted 487 for merging and 1031 against.

A bold step was taken at the end of the first season, when the Club resigned from the Southern League prior to their – but on this occasion successful – election application to the Football League. Along with Tottenham Hotspur, the two Clubs replaced Lincoln and Stoke in the Second Division – the latter team opting somewhat surprisingly to play in the Southern League.

The first Football League match was played on Tuesday the 1st of September 1908, at Park Avenue, when Hull City were defeated by a single Fraser goal, before a large and enthusiastic crowd of around 12,000. The team consisted of:

> *Baddeley, Walton, Dixon, O'Rourke, Hartwell, Wolstenholme, Manning, O'Donnell, Wilson, Fraser, Donald.*

The second League game at Park Avenue, four days later, was attended by approximately 15,000 spectators who witnessed another single goal win, this time versus Chesterfield. After four games the Club lay in third position in the League, however this winning start was not to continue. After nine games, their position had dropped to fourth from bottom, and five games later they were bottom but one with only three victories to their credit. Christmas was not a very merry time for the Club as they had by this time sunk to rock bottom of the League table! Results generally improved from then on, although a somewhat disappointing first season resulted with a final 16th placing.

No less than 34 players were used in League matches, with 13 goals from McClarence heading the scorers. No real success was attained in the F.A.Cup as the first round proper was not reached, but the necessity to commence from the preliminary round produced a marathon run with some impressive scores in the qualifying round matches, most of which were played at Park Avenue. The first ever F.A.Cup game was an away tie at South Kirby, but this Club agree to reverse the venue, and the Avenue scored a runaway 8-1 win (Attendance of 4,000). In order to avoid a late season fixture congestion, a Reserve team was sent to Denby Dale in the next round, whilst the first eleven played a League game with Grimsby – this resulted in a £50 fine – even so a 11-0 rout ensued! This was followed by a walkover due to Heckmondwike scratching, and then a six – unopposed – goals win over Mexborough, before a meagre 1,500 attendance. The end came at home to Croydon Common of the Southern League in the final qualifying round and a 1-2 defeat.

The home attendances at matches did not generally match the early turnouts. The Grimsby game attracted only 6,000 in October and the Burnley game started with about 7,000 – although 12,000 were present by half-time. In poor weather Tottenham were entertained with an initial crowd of only 5,000, although the Christmas fixture with Glossop produced a gate of 13,000. In this latter game a penalty was awarded to the Avenue, and for the third successive time was missed! One worthy point of recognition was accorded Bradford, when Park Avenue was used to stage a full International match between England and Ireland; the attendance in excess of 25,000 easily created a new record number for the Ground.

The next few seasons leading up to the First World War produced unspectacular League positions – around mid-table – until the 1913/14 campaign, when an unexpected upsurge in the Club's playing ability resulted in the runners-up position, 4 points behind the Champions Notts.County. The start of 1914 saw Bradford lying in fourth position in the Second Division, behind Hull, Woolwich and Notts.County. On January the 15th a record attendance at Park Avenue of 32,184 turned out for the visit of promotion challenging neighbours, Leeds City. Such was the interest in the match, that several thousand fans were locked out of the ground. The size of the crowd within resulted in the game being held up for three minutes following a barrier surrounding the pitch that collapsed under the pressure. A satisfying 3-1 victory was achieved.

By mid-March, 3rd place in the table had been reached, following the 3-1 win over Hull City at Anlaby Road before a 12,000 attendance. One month later a 20,000 crowd flocked to Park Avenue to see the 2-1 victory over Huddersfield, which took the Club to second place.

The League matches came to an exciting conclusion with a last match home win over Blackpool, and guaranteed second spot. On a fine sunny day, the fans started arriving early and eventually totalled approximately 25,000, to see a comfortable 4–1 winning scoreline.

And so in just a short period of time, the Club had risen to take a place amongst the elite, with two Football Clubs representing the town of Bradford in the First Division – justifying in full the decision taken a few years earlier for the two to maintain their separate identities.

During these initial years some notable successes were accomplished in the F.A.Cup. The second round was first reached in 1910, which followed an eight goal first round proper thrashing of Bishop Auckland. One year later the same round was reached, but was ended with non–Leaguers Darlington's 2–1 home win. In 1912 The Avenue went one step further by becoming one of the last sixteen teams in the Cup; however a single goal, local derby defeat at home to First Division neighbours, and Trophy–holders, City stopped further progress. This match provided a unique statistic for no less than 15 Scots were on the pitch – nine representing The Avenue Club.

However the 1912/13 season produced the most exciting run to that date. Early round victories were gained over Barrow (after a scoreless home draw, followed by the replay which was also played at Bradford), Wolves and the shock result of the third round – a 2–1 defeat of high flying First Division Wednesday (Sheffield). In the latter match, Smith opened the scoring for the home team but right winger Kirkman equalised to produce an all square half–time score; in the 50th minute Howie scored the winner for the Avenue to the joy of the majority of the large crowd. The Club's run came to an end in the next round, the quarter–finals, when despite their luck of all the games having been played at home, they were thrashed 0–5 by eventual winners Aston Villa. The end to the F.A.Cup hopes came in the promotion season at Sheffield United before a huge crowd which provided record receipts of £1,695, and included an estimated 6,000 from Bradford.

The Club's first Manager, Fred Halliday was soon succeeded by George Gillies – the latter's main signing being 19 year old Sam Burniston from Ireland, who became the first International player for the Club. Tom Malley took over the reins in February 1911, and soon made his presence felt with the signing of David Howie – who went on to make 306 appearances for the Avenue – and George Halley who later moved on to Burnley.

During these early seasons some high–scoring results were recorded, notably the 6–0 home wins over Glossop and (final wooden–spoonists) Lincoln, plus an unexpected 0–7 thrashing, at lowly Barnsley; all occurred during the

1910/11 season. But it was three seasons later before The Avenue really made their presence felt. In this, the promotion season of 1913/14, 'doubles' were recorded over six teams, including a 6–1 away win at middle of the table Fulham, and Champions Notts. County were beaten in Nottingham. There were, however, some surprise reverses including two defeats to Woolwich Arsenal, whom The Avenue had beaten into third place (on goal difference) and a 1–5 loss at Leeds City.

The season also produced two record breaking goalscorers for the Club with Jimmy Smith and Tommy Little grabbing 25 and 24 goals respectively; Jack Scott, a 1910 signing from Hamilton, was an ever present in the 38 League games, whilst both Smith and Little were absent only once. Little who arrived from Ilford soon after The Avenue's start in the League became the first Bradford player to be given a Testimonial Match, a game that was played in February 1914 versus Glossop, at which over 13,000 supporters attended.

The Club's first ever First Division season started with high hopes and thoughts of some exciting matches with top opposition. An estimated 25,000 were present at Park Avenue for the first match of the season – a 1–2 defeat to Blackburn – which was a contrast to the next game when a paltry 2,000 attended the game at Notts County. The supporters didn't have long to wait for *'the'* match, when the two Bradfords met at Park Avenue for the first ever competitive game between the two. An (official) crowd numbering 29,802 packed in to the Ground; but there was no happy ending for the newcomers for they lost by the odd goal in five. However, revenge came on April the 28th when The City were defeated by three unopposed goals at Valley Parade, before 30,000 Bradfordians. The season went well, for The Avenue finished in 9th place in the League, remarkably only 5 points behind Champions Everton, in what was a very evenly contested campaign. Bauchop improved on his eleven League goals of one year earlier and set a new record number for the Club, whilst Jack Scott was again an ever present and completed three maximum appearance seasons.

The F.A.Cup run was again halted at Sheffield United by a single goal defeat – but this time before only a moderate 25,000 attendance. Earlier victories were gained over Portsmouth in front of a 12,000 Park Avenue crowd, and a single goal win in the second round versus Notts.County.

With the confrontation in Europe, and many men absent, the attendances at matches had generally taken a dive; by early 1915, around 12,000 fans was the norm. £1,921 less than one year earlier was taken in gate receipts during the season, which resulted in an overall loss on the season of a hefty £1,330. With the First World War well in action, The Football League suspended activities for the duration, however regional competitions were held into which Bradford entered the 'Midland Section Tournament'. The 'Principal Tournament' consisted of between 14 and 16 teams who played each other home and away – as in a normal league fashion. In the late season 'Subsidiary Competition' only six games were played, in which either a mini–league of six teams was formed – from further regionalising – or an order of merit table was formed from the six games that had been played against some of the teams from the Principal Tournament. This football activity was a low keyed competition which carried little glory to its winners, but at least had an entertainment value to those who had not gone to war. However, these absences led to problems on two fronts, for attendances plummeted (6,000 and 5,000 versus Leeds and Nottingham Forest, 4,000 at the Sheffield Wednesday game and only 7,000 for the local match with the City being examples), and there was the necessity to use unestablished local players to make up a team on occasions.

Four years later, in September 1919, the Football League programme got underway again, but for Bradford – as for most Clubs – the start was tinged with sadness for players who had lost their lives during the hostilities. J. Smith who had become a favourite for his goalscoring prowess at Park Avenue had been killed in action, as had Donald Bell. Bell, who made a few pre–war appearances for the Club, became the only Professional footballer to posthumously receive the Victoria Cross medal.

Another respectable mid–table final League position (eleventh), hardly foretold the disasters that were on the horizon! While there were few bad defeats during the 1920/21 season, the only real thrashings being at

Sunderland and Manchester United – both by 1–5 – there were equally few victories, just six at home and two on foreign soil. The two away victories being a single goal win in the local derby with the City, and at West Bromwich. Consequently the Avenue finished bottom of the League, two points below last but one Derby County, and the Club found themselves relegated to the Second Division. There were also troubles on the field other than the results, for at the end of April in the game at home to Manchester City (which was lost 1–2), when the international David McLean was sent off, which led to young spectators throwing stones at the referee; the consequences resulted in the Player's suspension from August the 27th until the end of October, and the non–admittance of boys to the ground until the 1st of October.

There were of course high hopes of an immediate return to the First Division, but this dream became a nightmare when just twelve months later the Avenue were relegated to the Third Division North. This drop represented two ignominious occurrences; the first Club to be relegated to the Northern section – the division having only been formed that season – and the first team to be relegated twice in successive seasons. It was to be many years before two rapid demotions was repeated.

Once again very bad results were rare – apart from a five goal thrashing at Wolverhampton – with most defeats by the odd one or two goals. Only two matches produced away wins, one by a single goal at runners–up Stoke City's ground. But with only ten home successes the Avenue finished in next to bottom place. It was a close run affair however for even twelfth place Derby (who had accompanied the Avenue from the First Division) obtained only six more League points.

But despite the hard luck stories, the Avenue dropped to the Third Division North, whilst Bristol City – two points below the Avenue in the Second Division – moved to the Southern section of the Third. During these two disastrous seasons it was not surprising that many players were used with the aim of fielding a winning combination; 23 during season 1920/21 and no less than 27 one year later. Consistency of maintaining a place in the team was of course difficult, but W.Dickinson was ever present in the first Campaign and missed only seven games in the second. McLean was top scorer in the last First Division sortie with a notable 22 goals, but with his long suspension managed only nine in the 1921/22 season – five less than J.Bauchop the top goalscorer.

Following this depressing period, there was a halt to the downward spiral. Despite a moderate away record, but which saw only 16 goals scored, and five drawn and winning games the Avenue missed out on promotion by four

85

points, finishing runners–up to Nelson. Home matches were the mainstay for the Club in which only one defeat was recorded, and victories included an excellent 6–2 result over the Champions–to–be, plus 5–1 wins versus Accrington and Southport. A new record was set and subsequently became an all–time one, by conceding only 38 goals in League games.

Four encouraging seasons followed, during which the Club finished between 5th and 2nd in the League. McCluggage who played for the Club for three seasons was first chosen to represent Ireland in October 1923, despite recovering from tonsillitis! But,despite these years of relative success, there was a rapid change of Managers; Maley resigning in February 1924, followed by O'Rourke (after a Managerless period) who lasted for just ten months, whilst Howie 'enjoyed' an even shorter time afterwards. Finances, however, were tight and it became necessary to sell McCluggage and Turnbull to Burnley and Leeds United respectively. The 1925/26 season, when the Avenue achieved the runners–up spot again, saw a surprising feat; it was the first of three consecutive campaigns when the team scored 101 goals in League games, mainly due to the scoring prowess of Ken McDonald who in one campaign netted 43 – a Club record that was to remain for some 40 years – and to that date a new Football League best. During these years there were several high scoring games; the 7–1 and 6–1 home drubbings of Ashington and Crewe respectively in the 1924/25 season, plus three further 6–1 home victories and, (what became the highest ever) eight goal win over Walsall the next season.

During the early 1920's, there were few F.A.Cup shocks provided by the Avenue, apart from notable victories over First Division opposition Everton, after two goals shared at Goodison Park in 1922/23 (followed by a 1–4 defeat at fellow Third Division, Plymouth), and Second Division, Middles-brough two years later. Ever aware of the Club's financial situation, it became necessary to sell the local born winger Harold Peel, who com-manded a fee of £1,750 from Arsenal. Peel had appeared for Bradford in 207 League games – in all three Football League Divisions.

The 1927/28 season became an unparalleled successful one. The first record was achieved in November when the team won their 27th consecutive home game – which encompassed parts of two seasons. By December they had reached the top spot in the League, a position that was not relinquished, with perhaps the most satisfying victory coming one month later when their local rivals were thrashed by five unopposed goals. During their occupation of the number one position, it only the other 5–0 home win (over Ashington) that failed to attract a 10,000 plus gate; whilst the local derby attracted a massive 23,598 attendance. The earlier game at Valley Parade attracted a record gate for this fixture, of 38,442.

By the end of the Championship winning season, a new Football League record was established with 15 consecutive undefeated away matches, and their final points tally of 63 became an all time record for the team. McDonald was top marksman with 29 goals (in 33 games) while two players were ever present, namely goalkeeper Clough and Matthews. The home attendances averaged 14,134 a rise of nearly 4,000 over the previous season.

The Club were hardly overawed back in their Second Division company for one year later saw them finish in third position, only one place – but ten points – behind second place and promoted Grimsby Town. By now the crowds were regularly flocking into Park Avenue, and the final tally was a healthy 17,739 average – a figure that became the best ever for the Club. Clough was once again an everpresent, but on this occasion he had no equals. Perhaps one of the Club's most remarkable feats was the losing of only six home matches in seven seasons.

There were many supporters who felt the time had now come for the team to regain its lost First Division status, but it did not materialise, although a final placing of 4th was achieved (this time only 5 points too few for a promotion place). Surprisingly, attendances plummeted to a season's average of only 14,860 per home game. The biggest surprise result was a 5–0 win at Park Avenue over eventual Champions Blackpool. But despite the team's high placing in the League there were some heavy defeats away from Park Avenue – 0–5 to West Bromwich (despite a 5–1 win in the return) and 1–5 at both Oldham and Bury.

The season produced an all–time Football League record for the Avenue with the introduction of Albert Geldard to League football. Geldard was still of schoolboy age when he made his debut for the Club on September the 16th versus Millwall at the record 15 years and 158 days; an amazing coincidence occurred almost exactly 22 years later when the Club's opponents – Wrexham – fielded Kenneth Roberts, the same age to the day as had been Geldard! Despite this early introduction to the big time, Geldard's stay with Bradford was fairly shortlived for he played only thirty-four appearances for the team before being transferred to Everton in 1932 for £4,000; he then went on to become the youngest F.A.Cup winners medal holder at 19 years, and made four appearances for England, two of which at this same age.

Twenty–seven players were used in League games, and there were no 'ever presents', although McLean and Taylor only missed one game each – the former being the top goalscorer with twenty; this was Taylor's ninth season in the Avenue's colours, and there were to be two more before his departure from the Bradford scene.

Although Barnsley were beaten in the F.A.Cup followed by Derby, after sharing two goals at the Baseball Ground, the end came at Sheffield Wednesday in the 5th round with a 1–5 thrashing. The win over Derby occurred when the County were placed third in the First Division table.

The 1930's were not very happy years for The Avenue, and to make ends meet, the Club's top players continued to be sold, including Jack Crayston who moved on to Arsenal, and later played eight times for England. In December 1931, the Avenue's left winger Eddie Parris, played for Wales against Ireland – the first coloured player to appear in the Home Internationals. Although the Club had maintained their Second Division status, their fortunes gradually plummeted to a dismal final third from bottom placing in the 1936/37 season. These poor displays must have come as a shattering blow to Chairman Ernest Waddilove, who one season earlier, on his appointment to this position, had reputedly spent £40,000 on players in an attempt to raise the Avenue to the peak in the football world. The money was poorly spent for the Club's captures made little impact in the team. This campaign produced poor away form with only two wins and five drawn matches to show for their efforts; during their travels, nine games failed to produce an Avenue goal, and included heavy defeats at (Champions) Leicester – by 0–5 – Blackpool (Runners–up) by 0–6, and defeats at both Coventry (0–4) and Aston Villa (1–4).

There was little solace to be found in F.A.Cup games apart from the reaching of the 5th round again in 1931 – when they were surprisingly beaten by Southport – one year later when Watford put paid to their hopes, and in 1936 with a narrow replay defeat at Tottenham, after holding the Spurs to a goalless first game. The first Spurs game drew 24,053 to Park Avenue, but home League attendances in line with performances remained at a poor level, with a 'low' of only 8,984 (average) in the 1934/35 season, although there was a rise to nearly 10,500 two years later. The early thirties however produced widely differing numbers at Park Avenue; for instance, the 1931/32 season showed an average per match of 13,205, but the Christmas day top of the table clash and local derby with Leeds United drew a near all time record attendance of 32,429.

An unusual feat was achieved by Bradford on January the 31st 1931, when Syd Dickenson not only recorded a hat trick in the 4–1 home win over Burnley, but scored two of those goals direct from corners. The next week at Southampton, Bert Davis also scored three goals and both of the Club's wingers had hence scored three goals in successive games. However this season also had a particular 'black spot', a record League (goals against) defeat of 2–8 to Port Vale.

The ex–Cardiff star, Billy Hardy, took on the role of Manager in March 1934, at the same time as George Brigg's appointment as Secretary; Brigg's held this position until the Club's exit from the Football League.

Sensational news was announced in February 1937 to the effect that a London syndicate had offered to buy out the Club ! The intention was to 'transfer' Bradford to the Capital, but such a move never got further than the drawing board.

The final two seasons leading up to the Second World War produced an initial rise to an end of season placing in the League of seventh and then once again a dismal drop, this time to 17th. These last two seasons produced an ever–present in T.Farr who was to return for four post–war campaigns. The F.A.Cup exploits in the 1937/38 season, saw a high scoring 7–4 home victory over Newport County, followed by two matches with Stoke City, but the end came at Sunderland by a single goal. The Newport match on January the 8th was, as could be expected, a thriller. The Avenue went in at half time, 3–1 up, despite being initially one goal in arrears after only 4 minutes. The goals came rapidly in the second half, and after 90 minutes the home team had won through to the next round, aided by four goals from Henson.

Two weeks later, Stoke City were the visitors, and the locals once again turned out enmasse – producing a 31,347 attendance. One down at half–time, Bradford were intent on an equaliser, which came in the 53rd minute. The replay before 30,680 produced a shock win for the Yorkshire team, despite the likes of Frank Soo and Stanley Matthews in the Stoke line–up. Bradford were one up after 16 minutes and increased the lead after 70 minutes (Henson again !). Despite a goal from the Pottery team, the underdogs held on and earned themselves a trip to Sunderland, in a match before a massive crowd of 59,326.

One week later, the indominatable Henson carved his name in the Bradford history book, with a record six goals in the 7–1 home win over Blackburn. At this time the Club lay in a useful 4th in the League, but from then on the promotion challenge faded.

The Club continued playing during the hostilities, in the League North competition. Whilst no honours were achieved during this period, some successful runs were made in the League War Cup. The last eight of the Cup competition was reached in 1942 and 1944, when ties were played on a home and away basis. The quarter finals in 1944 resulted in four goals shared at Blackpool and a 1–2 defeat in the return – before an all–time record attendance of 32,810.

One player throughout these dark years shone out above all others, the renowned Len Shackleton. During most of these seasons he was high on the lists of 'most appearances' for the Club (twice he was top), and he was also a prolific goalscorer – 19, 24, 36, 34, 40 and 12 in successive seasons to 1945/46 – the leading scorer on all but one occasion.

The F.A.Cup competition proper was re–introduced for the 1945/46 season (one year before the Football League reappeared), and for this one season the matches were also played on a home and away basis; for Bradford it led to a record run. In the third round The Avenue scrapped through on a 3–2 aggregate over Port Vale. The fourth round was also won but in sensational style, for despite a first leg defeat of 1–3 to Manchester City, the return leg produced an amazing 8–2 victory! A single goal win followed by a 1–1 draw with Barnsley took the Club through to a sixth round contest with Birmingham. The City were held to a 2–2 home draw in the first leg, but in the away return game Bradford crashed out to six unopposed goals.

The return to Football League competition for the 1946/47 season produced an unprecedented upsurge in football interest throughout the Country. An average home gate of 14,861 was 50% up on the immediate pre–war season, but on the pitch it was a different story with a dismal final 16th place in the League. One year later a slight improvement was made, and the attendances were even higher – a near record average at home games of 17,690. However from the 1948/49 season a downward slide both in performances on the field and in support started, that was never really halted. The drop to the Third Division North was narrowly avoided by four places and just two points, but in May 1950 there was no such escape. Apart from a 0–5 thrashing at Champions Tottenham's ground there were no really bad defeats, indeed home games included a 5–1 win over Hull. But with only 31 points the 'wooden spoon' position had to be accepted, and a drop to the Third Division.

The first match in the Basement Division brought Barrow to Park Avenue, and a 16,623 attendance was treated to a 5–0 win, with the locals convinced that it would be a rapid return to the Second Division. Such a score was not repeated that season (though the same scoreline was recorded as a defeat at Gateshead!), and a disappointing 6th final League position was the end result. The 1951/52 campaign was much the same as the previous, and in finishing in the eighth place in the table at least a reasonably settled team was established when only twenty different players were called upon for Football League games. Suddards – his third season with The Avenue, and Hindle (his second) were ever presents. Apart from five players who only played in nine matches between them, the rest of the squad all managed double figure appearances.

With a rise to a final seventh placing at the end of the 1952/53 season the locals really felt that a turn in the Club's fortunes was now due, whereas from then on things got steadily worse. Ninth, sixteenth and the final humiliation – 23rd of 24 in the League were the end results for the next three years. In line with the declining performances on the pitch, the attendances took a tumble too, with the immediate post war averages gradually dropping to around 50% by 1953/54 and down to 7,323 in this the Club's first ever re–election season. However, the ultimate low came in the home game with Barrow during March 1954, when a paltry 1,881 paid for admission at the turnstiles. The early years of the 1950's produced few high scoring games, that is until the 1955/56 season when Bradford invariably came off worse. An horrendous goal difference of 61 for and a massive 122 goals against was the final tally; such a high final deficit was inevitably produced from some bad defeats – 0–7 at Accrington, 0–6 at Halifax and five goal defeats at Mansfield and York plus the same score at home to Chesterfield.

Just three points were picked up away from home from three draws, whilst the home record was almost respectable with 13 victories, 4 drawn games and only 6 defeats. Re–election became the formality that was expected, but one year later a similar indignity was only just avoided when only one place (and two points) separated Bradford from fourth from bottom Chester. It came as something of a surprise to find that the average home gates were up by over 1,000 despite only a moderate upturn in The Avenue's fortunes. But more amazing was a further rise to 8,744 one year later – the 1957/58 season – when re–election once again would have had to be sought but for the introduction of the new Fourth Division, when the last but one place in the League was the fate of the Club. This latter season required the use of 29 different players in League matches, with the most appearances – just two missed – by Suddards.

This period produced no prolific goal scorers apart from B.Smith in the 1956/57 season who recorded a very creditable 28 of the total 66 scored, in fact two years earlier, the top marksmen (Pickard) could only manage a paltry eight.

There was little joy in the F.A.Cup matches during the first half of the fifties, although Sheffield Wednesday were beaten (before the Avenue lost to Leeds in the fourth round) in 1952. The other seasons saw progression to the third round occur on only three occasions. In view of the poor performances on the field it came as no surprise to see Managers frequently departing! In the years of the decade, Vic Buckingham was followed by Norman Kirkman, the latter winning the position from a short list of two; the other name on the list was Bill Shankly!

It is open to conjecture whether 'Shanks' could have achieved a miracle with The Avenue. Jack Breedon then Bill Corkhill, who was succeeded by Alf Young, completed a set of five different Managers in the space six years.

The lowly final position in 1958 resulted in the Club becoming founder-members of the Fourth Division, when a mid-table placing – but another drop in average attendances – saw the start of the upturn in the team's fortunes. This 14th placing was improved to 11th one year later, and finally a breakthrough with promotion to the Third Division through finishing fourth in the 1960/61 season.

BRADFORD (PARK AVENUE) A. F. C.

Souvenir PROGRAMME

INAUGURATION OF FLOODLIGHTS

BRADFORD (PARK AVENUE)
v.
CZECHOSLOVAKIA
INTERNATIONAL AND WORLD CUP TEAM
TUESDAY, OCTOBER 3rd 1961—7-30 p.m.   PRICE 6d.

Buchanon was the leading scorer with 21 League goals (from a total of 84) an identical achievement of his, two years earlier. The campaign saw a remarkable pair of results when Barrow were in opposition. The lowly Cumbria side were beaten by four goals at Park Avenue but reversed the result at Holker Street – this time to the tune of 5–0! The year saw a revival of interest in the Club, for the average attendances shot up to 9,209 from the previous season's worst ever of just over 6,500. But still no real success came in the F.A.Cup, and they were destined never again to record their pre–war achievements. Walter Galbraith who had joined The Avenue as Manager in November 1958 was the Architect of the team's revival, and his Scottish background produced the situation of including no less than eight players from North of the Border for the April 1960 game versus Northampton; this was not a Club record, since nine such players were included for a League game in 1912. Galbraith's bias was not confined to Bradford, for five years earlier whilst Managing Accrington, all eleven players were Scottish! But even the Scot did not last, and in early 1961, a significant capture was made in the appointment as Player/Manager of the Newcastle wing–half – Jimmy Scoular. Such was his charisma that his first home game saw a 30% rise in the attendance – to 12,718 – over the previous game.

Following their promotion, one moderately good season resulted, when 11th place was reached, but this revival was shortlived for 21st position followed one year later, and relegation was once again the outcome. Bradford never 'escaped' from the Fourth Division, and during their remaining years, seventh place was far and away their best – at the end of the 1964/65 campaign. While the team as a whole had little to enthuse over, one man made his mark in the squad – Kevin Hector.

First appearing on the scene in 1962, he was leading goalscorer for that relegation season with 19. His stay with the Club remained until September 1966, when £34,500 was paid for his transfer to Derby County. Hector's record during these few years was one of the rare bright spots, as he completed four consecutive seasons as top marksman. In the 1965/66 period, despite only finishing 11th in the Fourth Division, Hector became the Football League's top goalscorer with the Club record 44 successes during which he was an ever present. Despite his team mate's worthy title, Bobby Ham found the back of the net on twenty–four occasions (which would have merited the top spot in many previous campaigns), and so between them they scored 68 League goals of the Club's record 102 for the season. The defence however conceded ninety two goals! Prior to his departure, Hector even managed four goals in four games during August and early September 1966. Such feats were insufficient to draw the crowds, and the lowest ever average for a season of 5,365 was announced in May 1966.

Yet another Football League record was established, though debatable to prove conclusively, on April the 25th 1964. Verified by the Referee and both Linesmen, it was adjudged that Jim Fryatt opened the scoring (against Tranmere) in four seconds! As if this were not enough, two other goals were scored in separate matches that season within the first minute of play.

Four Football League seasons remained for Bradford F.C., and they could hardly have been worse; consecutive final placings of 23rd, 24th, 24th and 24th sounded the final death knell for the Club. During this period there were no season 'ever presents', and in their penultimate campaign no less than 31 players were tried, with J.Hardie turning out in the most games – 36 – and Draper, in only 26 League games, leading the goal list with a puny seven. By now the average home attendance had plunged to 3,280, which was little wonder since only five games were won (nil at opponents grounds), 106 goals were conceded, and the team finished 13 points lower than the 23rd placed Grimsby Town. In May the lowest ever attendance for a League match at Park Avenue was recorded of 1,572 for the one goal defeat to the mid–table Port Vale team. In a desperate survival season, the Club, by now deep in financial plight, had a large clear out of players and only 11 of the previous season's large list made appearances during 1969/70.

The departed men included Kenny Hibbitt who was transferred to Wolves for £6,000. With a Player/Manager – Laurie Brown – the Club started this season, their last in the Football League, whilst a Businessman from Manchester – Herbert Metcalfe – took upon himself the financial aspects. Metcalfe soon made his presence felt before even having seen the team in action, by appointing Frank Tomlinson as Manager in October 1969. This drastic step led to the immediate resignation of both Brown and Ray Ambler the Club Chairman. The players were somewhat disillusioned also, for 19 players immediately made transfer requests (most of which were subsequently withdrawn) including Bernard Rafferty who had been with the Club for just one day! Despite his strange actions, Metcalfe nonetheless ploughed thousands of pounds into the Club, followed by up to £700 per week in order to keep the Club alive. His efforts were all to no avail, for again the team finished bottom of the Fourth Division, and with Cambridge United waiting in the wings it needed a supreme optimist to give The Avenue any chance of being re-elected. The final record was little better than a year earlier, just 23 points (seven fewer than one place higher Hartlepool), and yet again the record showed no wins on foreign soil. Whilst the goals against only totalled 96, there were some bad results, including five away games and one at home (to Scunthorpe), in which five goals were scored against them. Only 41 goals were credited to the team, with 18 matches in which none were scored.

26 different players had been used in League games, with John Brodie's 45 appearances and Ray Charnley's 12 goals hitting the two 'highs'. For a consistently unsuccessful team an average attendance of over 4,000 was surprisingly good, the minimum crowd being the 1,864 for the Newport match in March, while Chester attracted the best gate of 5,997. But apart from a reasonable start and an early position of 10th in the League table the Avenue quickly sunk to the lower reaches.

On April the 4th the last home game was played before 2,563 faithfulls and the visitors, Scunthorpe, cruised to a 5-0 victory – the equal worst result of the season! By this time the team were already seven points clear at the foot of the table, with their last four games to be played away. The final game ended as a 2-4 defeat at Aldershot, with the following line-up:

Hardie, Hudson, Brodie, Dolan, Campbell Wright, Tewley, Woolmer, Brannan, Beanlan and Tomlinson.

Danny Campbell had the dubious distinction of scoring the last ever Football League goal for Bradford F.C. As expected the Club were voted out of the Football League; their support totalled 17 votes whilst Cambridge United (whose application was processed with much razamataz) received 31 – even unsuccessful Wigan managed 18!

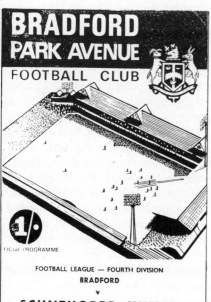

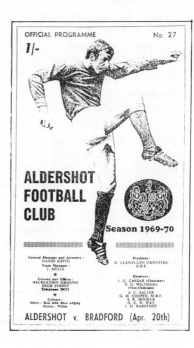

BRADFORD
(PARK AVENUE)
ASSOCIATION FOOTBALL CLUB LTD

Directors:
G. Sutcliffe (Chairman)   M. F. Brown (Vice-Chairman)   T. Horsfall
J. Burkinshaw (Hon. Secretary)
Hon. Medical Officer: J. Howard, MB., B.S.   Manager: Roy Ambler
Registered Office: Valley Parade Ground, Bradford 8.   Telephone: 26565
Development Fund Office: South Parade, Bradford 8.   Telephone: 28000

Northern Premier League

Thursday, May 2nd, 1974

VERSUS

GREAT HARWOOD

KICK-OFF 7-30 p.m.

Final League Match

Souvenir Programme - - 3P

AGENTS REQUIRED FOR DEVELOPMENT FUNDS

If you follow Association Football in Bradford, now is your chance
to help us build a successful team at Valley Parade. There are
two money raising associations issuing Fireside Bingo Tickets with
good prizes and excellent commission.
Why not telephone 28000 or 683208 (Park Avenue Association)
or 26565 (City Pools Office), or call in at Valley Parade?

ANNUAL MEETING

The final meeting of the Bradford P.A. Supporters' Club will be held on
Tuesday, June 25th, at 7.30 p.m. at the Central Library Theatre, Prince's Way,
Bradford. A presentation will be made to Mr. P. Brannan in his benefit year and
also to our Player of the Year, who will be named this weekend.

(Above left) The last Football
League home game.
(Above right) The Last Football
League match and ....

..... (Left) The last ever
Bradford (P.A.) game
which was played
at Valley Parade.

95

The Northern Premier League was increased to include 22 teams, and the Bradford application to join received an overwhelming vote of confidence. The first match in non–League circles produced a 0–2 home defeat to Netherfield on August the 15th, before a highly encouraging attendance of 2,216. But with a three goal defeat following at Wigan, it was obvious that this standard of football was not going to be no easy trip. A poor start was followed by five games without defeat, and the faithful were still present – 1,773 for South Shield's visit and 3,139 for the appearance of the much acclaimed Altrincham team. On October the 24th, the Club's hoped for saviour, Mr.Metcalfe died.

No honours came the club's way in their brief life outside of the big time, and final placings in the Northern Premier produced 14th, 18th and 5th to the end of the 1972/73 campaign. At this point, they were forced to vacate Park Avenue. The rent at their one and only home venue was still a moderate £336 per annum, but the move to Valley Parade, where they shared the ground with their hosts – Bradford City – this outgoing soared to £7,000! The standards on the pitch were insufficient to gain the desperately needed support for they finished in 21st place in a league of 24 teams. By now attendances had dropped to around 500 average, although 1,300 were present for Wigan's 'one–off' Sunday match at Valley Parade. In March, the Club announced that they would not be applying for their lost Football League status, which they had done each season since leaving that company. By early April the position looked desperate, and the disbanding of the Club had become virtually certain.

Ironically the last match was a home fixture to Great Harwood, the same opponents who were the last visitors to Park Avenue. Only 698 spectators bothered to turn up for what was widely known to be The Avenue's final game; with a scoreless draw being on the cards, the team Captain – Mike Fleming – scored a dramatic winner in the last minute. Valiant attempts were made by the (greatly reduced in numbers) Supporters Club, but to no avail, and so another Club, of such recent Football League status, died.

PARK AVENUE.

The Park Avenue Ground which was highly regarded and arguably superior to Valley Parade still remains in part. The Main Stand complete with the pavilion which was often referred to as 'The Doll's House' and the other two covered structures – all of which provided cover for 14,000 spectators – have disappeared, but the terracing at the old covered end, some of the perimeter walls and the remains of several turnstile entrances are still present. The Ground was used for football prior to the Club's formation in 1908 – but for the oval shaped ball game of Rugby.

The Park Avenue Ground in the late 1980's.
(Top) The covered end – now roofless...
...(Bottom) The Canterbury Road end has now disappeared.

Until this time, spectator facilities probably consisted of only a covered seated stand – separating the Cricket from the Rugby pitch – but not for the full length of the field. The opposite narrow side and the area behind one goal were probably flat, but some banking was present behind the Canterbury Avenue end. There was also probably a Pavilion on the Rugby Ground.

The Park Avenue Ground was completely redeveloped during the early years, with the first priority being a covered standing enclosure opposite the seated stand. By the Second World War, high concrete terracing had been built behind each goal, and the Grandstand was probably rebuilt to form the attractive gabled structure together with the unique 'Doll's House' – the only comparable building being that of Fulham's 'Cottage'. The covered standing enclosure was provided in the post–war years.

What is left of the Ground is now a forlorn sight however, with tall weeds growing up through the cracks in the crumbling concrete. For some years the pitch was maintained, and again hosted football matches – albeit at a minor level – but by 1990, a new Cricket School was built at the Canterbury Avenue end, and engulfed half of the former football Ground; how long before the final remains disappear?

A fine aerial view of the Ground – taken whilst a Cricket match was taking place!

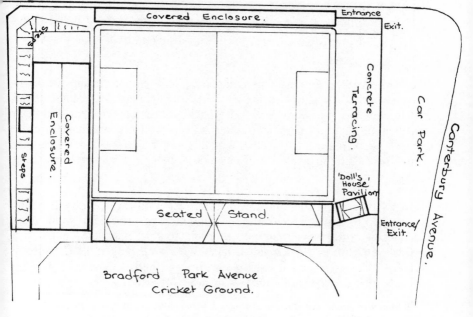

The Ground – as it was ....

.... and its location.

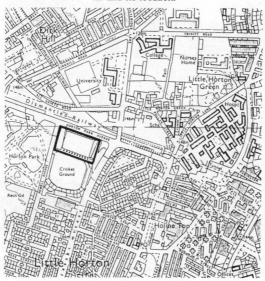

BURTON SWIFTS, WANDERERS & UNITED.

Burton Wanderers 1886/87: (Back) Scattergood, G.Tunnicliffe, Chandler, Nice (President)
Sheffield, Black, Fellows. (Middle) Burton, Parker (Sec.), Soar, Bancroft,
(Front) Murfin, M.Tunnicliffe, Smith.

Burton Swifts c.1890: (Back) Horne (Sec.), Lawrence, Furniss, West (Capt.), Hadley,
Berry, Hindle (Linesman). (Front) Perry, Emery, Worrall, McBeth, May, Sutherland.

BURTON UNITED

1905/06 Season: (Top) Allsopp (Trainer), Grewcock (Sec.), Burton, Shruve,
Starbuck, Kirkland, Davis, Mundy (Finanical Sec.).
(Bottom) Battles, Bradshaw, Hunt, Robinson, Aston, Gutteridge, King.

1906/07 Season: (Top) Allsopp(Trainer), Robinson,Gray, Starbuck,Wood, Kirkland
Nelmes. (Bottom) Bradshaw, Hunt, Stanley, Emmerson, Bradworth, Axcell.

BURTON SWIFTS.
founded: 187?. as Burton Outwood Star.
Changed name to Burton Swifts – 1883.

BURTON WANDERERS.
Founded: 1871.

BURTON UNITED.
Founded: 1901. (Amalgamation of the Swifts and the Wanderers) Disbanded: 1910.

****

Burton Swifts.
187? – 1889/90.	*Friendlies.*
1890/91.	*The Combination.*
1891/92.	*Football Alliance.*
1892/93 – 1900/01.	**Football League Div.2. ***

Burton Wanderers.
1871 – 1888/89.	*Friendlies. †*
1889/90 – 1893/94.	*Midland League. **
1894/95 – 1896/97.	**Football League Div.2.**
1897/98 – 1900/01.	*Midland League.*

† 1888/89 season played in unfinished Combination 'League'.
* Founder–members.

Burton United.
1901/02 – 1906/07.	**Football League Div.2.**
1907/08 – 1909/10.	*Birmingham & District League. ***

** 1909/10 season also played in Southern League Div.2 (only 6 games).

....

Football League Record:

Burton Swifts.
	Played	W.	D.	L.	F.	A.	Pts.	Posn.
1892/93:	*22*	*9*	*2*	*11*	*47*	*47*	*20*	*6th.*
1893/94:	*28*	*14*	*3*	*11*	*79*	*61*	*31*	*6th.*
1894/95:	*30*	*11*	*3*	*16*	*52*	*74*	*25*	*11th.*
1895/96:	*30*	*10*	*4*	*16*	*39*	*69*	*24*	*11th.*
1896/97:	*30*	*9*	*6*	*15*	*46*	*61*	*24*	*14th.*

(Successfully re–elected)

	Played	W.	D.	L.	F.	A.	Pts.	Posn.
1897/98:	*30*	*8*	*5*	*17*	*38*	*69*	*21*	*13th.*
1898/99:	*34*	*10*	*8*	*16*	*51*	*70*	*28*	*13th.*
1899/1900:	*34*	*9*	*6*	*19*	*43*	*84*	*24*	*15th.*
1900/01:	*34*	*8*	*4*	*22*	*34*	*66*	*20*	*18th.*

(Successfully re–elected – but as 'Burton United')

Burton Wanderers.

1894/95:	30	14	7	9	67	39	35	7th.
1895/96:	30	19	4	7	69	40	42	4th.
1896/97:	30	9	2	19	31	67	20	15th.

Failed to gain Re-election.

Burton United.

1901/02:	34	11	8	15	46	54	30	10th.
1902/03:	34	11	7	16	39	59	29	13th.
1903/04:	34	11	7	16	45	61	29	14th.
1904/05:	34	8	4	22	30	84	20	17th.
1905/06:	38	10	6	22	34	67	26	19th.

(Successfully re-elected)

1906/07:	38	8	7	23	34	68	23	20th.

Failed to gain Re-election.

Summary of Facts.

Burton Swifts: *187? – 1901.*
*Grounds: 1891 :   Shobnall Street (Cricket Ground) and Kidger's Field.
                 From 1891: Peel Croft, Burton-Upon Trent, Staffs.*

Nickname: 'Swallows' or 'Brewers'.

*Colours: (Football League)
                 1892 – 1895: Blue Shirts, White Shorts.
                 1895 – 1897: Maroon & Orange Quarters Shirts, Black Shorts.
                 1897 – 1901: Red & White Quarters Shirts, Dark Blue Shorts.*

*First Football League Game: September 3rd, 1892. (Home) versus Crewe Alex.
(Won 7-1)
Last Football League Game: April 27th, 1901. (Away) versus Stockport County
(Lost 0-2)
Record Attendance: (Probable)
Approx. 5,500. versus Burton Wanderers, F.A.Cup. 10th December 1892. (Won 3-2).
Football League average attendances: First season 2,000. Last season 2,500.*

Main Achievements:

*Best League Win: 7-0 versus Middlesbrough Ironopolis (Home) 1893/94.
Also 8-5 versus Walsall Town Swifts (Home) 1893/94.
Worst League Defeat: 0-9 versus Manchester City (Away) 1897/98.*

Total Number of Football League Matches Played: 272.

*F.A.Cup:1st Round (Modern day equivalent 4th round)
1892/93. 1895/96. 1896/97.
3rd Round (equivalent) 1898/99.*

*Staffordshire Senior Cup Winners: 1891/92.
Burton & Dist. Challenge Cup Winners: 1885/86. 1888/89.*

Burton Wanderers: *1871 – 1901.*
Claimed on demise in 1901 to be the fourth oldest Football Club in England.
Ground: Derby Turn, Burton–Upon–Trent, Staffs.
Nickname: 'Wanderers'.
Colours: (Football League): Blue and White Halves Shirts, White Shorts.

*First Football League Game: September 1st, 1894 (Away) versus Rotherham Town.
(Won 3–1)*
Last Football League Game: April 19th, 1897 (Home) versus Loughborough. (Lost 0–1)
*Record Attendance: (Probable) 6,000: versus Notts County, F.A.Cup, 1893 (Lost 0–2),
and versus Leicester Fosse, Bass Charity Vase Final, 1895 (Won 2–1)*
Football League average attendances: First season 2,600. Last season 2,700.

Main Achievements:
*Best League Wins: 9–0 v. Newcastle. 8–0 v. Manchester City. 7–0 v. Walsall Town
Swifts. (All home games, 1894/95 season)*
Worst League defeat: 0–6 v. Loughborough 1896/97 (Away).
Total Number of Football League Matches Played: 90.

F.A.Cup: 2nd Round: (Pre–League) 1893/94. (Modern day equivalent 5th Round)
1st Round: 1894/95. 1895/96. 1896/97. (Equivalant 4th Round)

Midland League Champs.: 1894/95. (Joint record, nil defeats)
Staffordshire Senior Cup Winners: 1894/95.
Burton & Dist. Challenge Cup Winners: 1883/84. 1884/85. 1886/87. 1887/88.

Burton United: *1901 – 1910.*

Ground: Peel Coft, Burton–Upon Trent, Staffs.
Nickname: 'Crofters'.
Colours: (Football League):1901 – 1902: Light Blue & White Quarters, Dark Blue Shorts.
                    1902 – 1903: Maroon Shirts, Black Shorts.
                    1903 – 1905: Green Shirts & Red Collars, White Shorts.
                    1905 – 1907: Brown & Blue Quarters, White Shorts.
First Football League Game: September 7th 1901 (Away) versus Barnsley. (Lost 2–3).
Last Football League Game: April 27th 1907 (Home) versus West Bromwich.(Won 2–0).
*Record Attendance (Probable): Approx. 4,000. Versus Blackpool, Football League.
14th of September 1901. (Drew 1–1)*
And versus Wellingborough, F.A.Cup, 29th November 1903. (Won 5–1)
Football League average attendances: First season 2,800. Last season 3,600.

Main Achievements:
Best League Win: 7–0 v. Stockport County 1903/04. (Home)
Worst League Defeat: 0–8 v. Woolwich Arsenal 1903/04. (Away)

Total Number of Football League Matches Played: 212.

F.A.Cup:1st Round: 1905/06. 1906/07. (Modern day Equivalent 3rd Round)
3rd Round (equivalent) 1902/03, 1903/04.
*Probably unique to any Football League Club (of more than two seasons duration);
recorded best and worst League scores in same season (1903/04).*

It is something of an honour for a town with a population of around 40,000 (Burton's total in 1880 was 39,972) to have had a team playing in the Football League – yet incredibly for three years this Staffordshire brewing centre went one better and had two representatives in the competition!

With the Burton and District Football Association claiming the title of the oldest District Association – they were formed in 1871 – it comes as no surprise to find a number of active Clubs in the area during this period. Of particular note were the *'Burton's'*: Strollers, Rangers, Wanderers and Outwood Star. The former two could not last the pace and within a few years became defunct, whilst the Wanderers (formed around 1871) and the Swifts – the renamed Outwood Star – emerged as the two Senior Clubs and a battle for supremacy ensued in the area.

Throughout the life of the Wanderers, the Club played at the Derby Turn Ground. Whilst no traces of this venue remains, the approximate location can be surmised from the title, since the junction of the earlier two main roads in Burton was literally the *'Derby Turn'*, i.e. the point at which the carts and horses would terminate their journeys between Derby and Burton. Initially Derby Turn was the premier Ground in the town, for although probably limited in its facilities for spectators, Athletics Meetings were regularly held their, and Club Meetings took place in the 'large room' in a building adjacent or within the Headquarters. With a superior home venue, the Wanderers tended to have the edge on their main local rivals, for the Swifts – in their formative years – had to depend on a shared or very basic Ground that probably lacked facilities of any kind. The Swifts first home was located at the local Cricket Ground before a move was made to nearby Kidger's Field where they remained until this was built over to become the present day Gordon Street.

It was to be several years before either Club were to become known outside their own locality, and newspaper references of either outfit were few and far between, until the early 1880's. It can be assumed that these early days produced little more than Friendlies between other Burton teams in somewhat rudimentary conditions. During the 1876/77 season the Wanderers match versus St.Pauls was declared a draw when in the 82nd minute the ball burst! The same day, another match between the two Clubs' reserve teams was terminated in a similar fashion. Presumably the finances of each Club did not stretch further than the ownership of one football per Club – the loss of two on the same day no doubt represented a heavy financial loss!

The first honour of note fell to the Wanderers with their winning of the Burton and District Challenge Cup in the 1883/84 season, the previous two winning Clubs being the Strollers and the Rangers – two names that soon disappeared off the scene. This success was repeated one year later when the Wanderers beat their newly renamed rivals, Burton Swifts, in the final. The match was played at Derby Turn before an enthusiastic crowd of 1,500, a record attendance at any football match in the town to that time.

The start of the 1885/86 season saw a change in the Wanderers formation when the Club technically became a professional outfit. Local man, Measham Tunnicliffe – a centre half – was paid for his services. This move naturally gave the Club an edge on their keenest rivals, the Swifts, but the latter caused a minor sensation in local Football circles when they beat their Professional rivals in the Challenge Cup Final. The enterprise for the adoption of professionalism which was credited to the Wanderers Secretary John Parker, did not go unheeded for in 1886 the Swifts also left the Amateur ranks. By the end of that season the lasting dominance of these two Clubs in Burton became obvious when the two met yet again in the final of the local Challenge Cup. By now the Swifts were on a par with their previously superior opponents, but on this occasion the honours fell to the Wanderers.

The match was played at the Alma Club Ground – another somewhat prominent team that were winners themselves two years later only to disband in 1893 before later reforming, albeit in only a minor capacity. On a windy day a sizeable crowd were entertained to a fast moving game that saw honours even with one goal each at half–time, a 2–2 draw at full time, and the winner coming seven minutes before the end of extra time. One year later the Wanderers retained the trophy, but strangely despite both their, and the Swifts ascendency in the football world, it was only won once again – by the Swifts. Possibly in later years their new elevation precluded them from considering the Competition worthy of a serious challenge!

One player who did appear in a later final however was to become a world renowned figure in the football world. The inside left of the victorious Tutbury Hawthorn team in 1893 was the legendary Steve Bloomer. The aftermath of this match however was wrought with controversy, for it was alleged that the 19 year old, who had moved to Burton whilst still a child, was ineligible. It was claimed that he had already, at the time of the final, signed professional forms for Derby County. The casting vote of the Chairman of the Association decided that the matter was not proved either way and that Gresley Rovers – the other finalists – should also receive medals! Would football history have changed if either of the 'Burtons' rather than the Derby Club had captured Bloomer's signature ?

By 1890 the introduction of football league competitions were a welcome innovation to both Clubs after years of prestigious – but little more – friendly games and local cup competitions.

Both Clubs had their influential supporters but it was the Swifts who attracted substantial financial help. The *notables* for the Wanderers included Sammy Wellings the Landlord of the 'Derby Turn' Public House, and Mr.C.Grewcock who continued as an Official after the amalgamation of the two Clubs in 1901 and right up to the end of the United.

...ton Swifts Football Club.

WINNERS OF BURTON CUP, 1885-6.
WINNERS OF BURTON CUP, 1888-9.
WINNERS OF DUDLEY CUP, 1888-9.
...NERS UP FOR GAINSBORO' CUP, 1888-9.

Swifts Rangers (Reserve Team)—
...NNERS OF BURTON JUNIOR CUP, 1887-8.

*President—*ALDERMAN WRIGHT.

Vice-Presidents—
...Burton ; W. H. Worthington, Esq.; F. Hol-Esq.; F. Thompson, Esq.; J. Thompson, S. Evershed, E.q., M.P.; S. H. Evershed, P. Evershed, Esq.; J.T.C. Eadie, Esq. ...amble, Esq.; F. W. Porter, Esq.; J. N. ...e, Esq.; J. Stirk, Esq.; T. Sykes, Esq.; A.T. ...t, Esq.; P. Robinson, Esq.; W. Newton, Esq.; G. Meakin, Esq.

Committee—
MR. W. MATTHEWS (Chairman).
J. J. BUXTON. | MR. WALTERS.
M. CLAY. | ,, C. GREWCOCK.
W. GOODWIN. | ,, J. FERNYHOUGH.
J. ROBINSON. | ,, W. COX.

Hon. Secretary—
MR. W. BARSON, 44, Newton Road.

*Hon. Treasurer—*MR. J. RUSHTON.

Captain—   *Deputy Captain—*
...R. G. KINSEY. | MR. W. HUBBARD.

...ners—Messrs. H. HORN & J. KEIGHTLEY.

Ground—   *Colours—*
...NALL STREET. | CHOCOLATE AND BLUE.

STATEMENT OF ACCOUNTS FOR YEAR ENDING APRIL 30th, 1889.

	£ s. d.
To Balance in Treasurer's hands, April 30th, 1888	7 1 3
,, Subscriptions for 1888-9	24 15 6
Outstanding*	1 12 6
	16 13 0
,, Gates and Guarantees	
,, Hire of Ground :—	
Alma F.C.	0 5 0
Wanderers F. C.	0 10 0
Staffordshire Football Assn.	1 0 3
Burton Junior Football Assn.	1 0 0
	2 15 3
,, Fares refunded by Railway Co. :—	
Midland Ry.	0 1 2
L. & N.W. Ry.	1 1 2½
	1 2 4½
,, Half-time Refreshments, April 27th.	
Amount allowed by Burton F. A.	0 2 6
,, Profit on Annual Dinner	0 0 6

* These are now realised.

£199 3 1

LIABILITIES.

	£ s. d.
By Sundry Accounts outstanding	10 13 2
,, Balance of Assets	10 8 11

£21 2 1

W. BARSON, HON. SECRETARY.
J. RUSHTON, HON. TREASURER.

	£ s. d.
By Ground Expenses :—	
Rent to April 30th, 1889	8 0 0
Repairs, Marking, &c.	1 13 2
	9 13 2
,, Match Expenses :—	
Travelling	44 0 7
Umpires and Referees	6 3 1
Visiting Clubs	50 8 1
Refreshments for Players	18 7 11
Loss of Work (Professionals)	9 12 0
Gate Men	0 9 0
	129 0 8
,, Training Expenses	4 14 6½
,, Postage, Telegrams, P. O., &c.	5 9 5
,, New Boots and Repairs and New Shirts	5 11 9
,, Subscriptions to Football Associations :—	
English Association	1 0 6
Birmingham ,,	0 15 6
Staffordshire ,,	0 10 0
Burton ,,	0 10 6
Gainsboro' ,,	0 5 6
Wednesbury ,,	0 5 0
Walsall ,,	0 5 0
Dudley ,,	0 5 0
	3 17 0
,, Official Expenses, Association Meetings, &c.	3 10 11
,, Printing and Stationery :—	
Tresise's Account, Jan. 1, '89.	11 7 11
Jan. 1, '89.	11 7 11
Mc.Corquodale's Account.	0 19 0
Williamson's ,,	0 4 9
Osborn's ,,	0 6 0
Billamy's ,,	0 8 0
	23 14 2
,, Oil, Whiting, Towels, Xmas Boxes, Errands, &c.	0 19 10½
,, Subscriptions outstanding*	1 12 6
,, Balance in Treasurer's hands, April 30th, 1889	10 19 1

* These are now realised.

£199 3 1

ASSETS.

	£ s. d.
To Club Property	8 10 6
,, Balance in Treasurer's hands	10 19 1
,, Subscriptions outstanding	1 12 6

£21 2 1

Examined and found correct { J. FERNYHOUGH, T. B. CHARLES.

Extracts from a Burton Swifts Handbook

The Swifts best *'captures'* were those of James and J.T.C.Eadie. The Eadie family became the loyalist of followers of the 'Maroon and Gold' team, a devotion which was carried on by their sons up to the final disbanding of Burton United. The financial support of the Eadie's provided a valuable edge for the Swifts over the Wanderers, the most valuable of which was their purchase of Peel Croft in 1890 for use by the Swifts.

The Ground, prior to the Swifts occupation, had been used by the Burton Rugby Club, and to which use it returned some twenty years later. Over £5,000 was spent on the Ground which included perimeter enclosure fencing plus a combined Pavilion/Grandstand, and was generally regarded as one of the best equipped Grounds in the Midlands. This development must have helped, in no small way, for the Club to gain a league entry of a high standard – that of 'The Combination' for the 1890/91 season.
On September the 2nd, 1891 the Ground was formally opened with a friendly match versus Derby County in front of 3,500 spectators.

The Wanderers, however had already upstaged their rivals with their entry into the Midland League one year earlier. The Midland League, in this the first season, was the oldest professional football league (outside of the Football League itself) and contained eleven Clubs.

Included with the Wanderers were the teams of Lincoln City (eventual Champions), Derby Midland (who later combined with Derby County), Rotherham Town and Gainsborough Trinity all of whom were to become eventual members of the Football League.

On the 7th of September 1889, Burton Wanderers had the distinction of staging – one of the two – first Midland League matches, and hence jointly, the first ever Non–league, league game (ignoring the uncompleted 'Combination' competition one year earlier) The team consisted of:

Brentnall, Chandler, Collins, Lowe, Tunnicliffe, Haywood, Heath, Dooley, Wheatcroft, Richards and Bancroft.

They were matched against Rotherham Town at Derby Turn.

A 'large attendance' greeted the teams as they appeared on the field – Wanderers starting the match with only ten players – and in bright summer weather Rotherham kicked off. After only five minutes the Town were one goal up through McCormack who then doubled his tally just two minutes later. All seemed to be lost for the homesters when a third was added, but Richards reduced the arrears to provide a 1–3 half–time score. The second half started quietly, but then the Wanderers began to command the game, and two goals were scored in quick succession to the delight of the home supporters. By the close of the game there was only one team in it, and the Wanderers managed to score just once more to run out eventual 4–3 winners in what was a very satisfying opening match. One week later, with the same team, the Burton Club won 3–2 at Derby Midland, and after five games the third position in the league was attained with seven points. By the season's end, the final league placing was 4th, with eleven wins, three draws and six defeats.

Whilst the Wanderers continued in the Midland League, the Swifts entry into The Combination for the 1890/91 season signalled probably the real start of the latter's gradual rise to become Burton's premier Club. The Wanderers second league season produced a slight drop to 6th place (of ten teams) whilst the Swifts (who had within their company eventual Football League Clubs in Chester, Northwich Victoria and Wrexham) despite no honours, applied for and were accepted into The Football Alliance for the next campaign.

This shortlived competition quickly established itself as the premier league outside that of the Football League and almost immediately was regarded as the unofficial Second Division of the latter.

Surprise was expressed when Burton Swifts applied for membership in 1891, and some locals unkindly referred to them as a 'fourth rate Club'! However, despite such elite company they completed a very satisfactory campaign, and all members were accepted into the Football League at the end of this, the last of three seasons of the Football Alliance. The final league record showed twelve wins, two draws and eight defeats (goal difference of 54–52). They finished in 6th place and were hardly overshadowed by such illustrious opponents as Sheffield Wednesday, Nottingham Forest (Champions) Newton Heath (later Manchester United) and Grimsby Town. The final game in the Alliance produced a 5–1 (half–time 2–0) home win over Bootle on April the 16th. The Club's total income for the year of £1143–9–0, produced a profit of just two shillings and sixpence halfpenny (approx.13p)!

The final 'icing on the cake' was their defeat of Aston Villa in the final of the Staffordshire Cup played at Molineux; the holders Villa were so confident of retaining the trophy that they didn't even bother to bring it to the match! To commemorate the rise up the football 'ladder', J.T.C. Eadie – the President – was presented with a Cup from the Swifts for his outstanding efforts.

The Swifts entry into the Second Division of the Football League for the 1892/93 season signalled their final acceptance in Burton as the town's top team. Although somewhat overshadowed by their neighbours, the Wanderers were none–the–less making headway in the Midland League with their eventual fifth place in 1892. To Burton Wanderers went the dubious honour of playing against Staveley in the latter's last ever game on the 5th of December 1891 (an 8–0 win to the Wanderers) following the game, this Club were expelled from the League. Support for the Wanderers was generally good, especially for prestige matches. In the relatively minor 'Burton Charity Cup', Derby County were beaten by two unopposed goals at Derby Turn before a crowd of over 3,000 providing, £66 gate receipts; entry to the Ground at this time being 3d. and 6d.

Burton Swifts assembled for their first season in the Football League an experienced team that included in its ranks the likes of Donald Sutherland (Ex–Grimsby Town Captain), Arthur Worrall (Wolves) and the near identical brothers W. and E.May – both from Nottingham Forest. Apart from these signings the Club relied basically on the players that had played in the Football Alliance plus some new and promising youngsters. On the 3rd of September 1892, the Swifts opened their season – and also the first ever for the Football League Second Division – with a home game against Crewe Alexandra; these opponents were for some time, the only amateur team in the League. The result after 90 minutes exceeded the Club's officials and supporters expectations with a 7–1 victory.

The team that day consisted of:

Hadley, Furniss, Berry, Lawrence, West, Sutherland, Perry
Emery, Worrall, Marriott and May.

Seven days later a narrow victory was inflicted at Barley Bank on Darwen with the odd goal in five, before a 5,000 crowd, and the Swifts confirmed their second from top early League placing when they inflicted a 2–1 home defeat over Bootle two weeks later. Of their twelve home games, just three were lost during the season, the first coming on Christmas Eve when Darwen gained revenge by 2–0. There was however little success on their travels, for the only other victory was achieved at Crewe on October the 1st.

At the completion of the season, the Swifts could consider their final placing of 6th as reasonable and hardly that of a 'fourth rate team'! Despite the eleven defeats and only nine victories the goal difference was even with 47 scored and conceded. Meanwhile the Club's best ever run in the F.A.Cup was achieved which started with a victory over fellow–Leaguers Burslem Port Vale. The final qualifying game produced a draw which set the town 'alight' – Swifts versus Wanderers at Peel Croft. The gates were opened at 1.00 p.m. and a massive crowd of approximately 5,500 (the all time high for the Swifts, and to that time a record for a football match in Burton) assembled, including many enthusiasts from outlying villages. Both Clubs' supporters were in evidence, many with their team's favours on their hats. An exciting game gave the Swifts the edge with three goals of the five, after sharing four at half–time. The run ended in the 1st round proper (the last 32 teams) with an embarrassing 2–9 defeat to eventual Football League runners–up Preston North End.

Whilst the Wanderers did not achieve glory in the premier Cup Competition – the first match at Ironbridge – they were determined to emulate their, by now, more successful local rivals. The team in Blue and White did seriously consider changing their home Ground to another that had been offered them. But after serious consideration, a decision was taken not to move, and work was put in hand – and completed – during the Autumn of 1892 for the provision of a new Grandstand. Derby Turn remained the Wanderers home venue until their amalgamation with the Swifts some eight years later. The first game of the 1892/93 season at Derby Junction was abandoned after 70 minutes due to bad light, the delayed start having been caused by the late arrival – of the Home team! The match was ordered to be replayed at Derby some months later, but with the Wanderers taking only half of the gate takings and their travelling expenses.

In the Midland League, things were improving and the final record of 15 wins, 4 draws and only 5 defeats gave the Club the runners–up slot.

The 1893/94 season was the same for the two Clubs as a year earlier, the Swifts in the Football League (Division 2) and the Wanderers striving to attract extra support in the Midland League. With competition so keen in the town, the Swifts opened the campaign with the most experienced and most expensive squad ever, including by now, Sam Jones the Welsh International goalkeeper and Walter Perry from West Bromwich Albion. The season started in awful fashion with a crushing 1–6 defeat at the home of the eventual runners–up Small Heath on the 9th of September. This poor start was more or less compensated, when two days later, the Swifts ran out 4–1 winners at Ardwick, and on the 20th of September they completed an emphatic double over the same team with a clear five goal victory.

Good home wins became frequent during the season with 6–2 successes over both Northwich and the Royal Arsenal, 6–1 versus Crewe, a seven goal unopposed demolition of Middlesbrough Ironopolis (the North–East Club's first and only Football League season, and the Swifts record League victory), and an incredible 8–5 victory in February when Walsall were the visitors. However the home record was not as good as a year earlier (4 defeats), but with five wins on their travels, the final placing in the League was the same – 6th. However, since the League had increased from 12 to 15 teams it was overall an improved position. The F.A.Cup produced little with elimination at the 1st round stage.

Down the road at Derby Turn, things were improving still further. The Midland League membership had decreased by two, and so only 11 teams were in competition, but by the season's end the remarkable final record of the Wanderers was; 17 victories, 3 draws and no defeats. (an undefeated record only once equalled – although with more games played). 82 goals were scored whilst just 12 were conceded. The Club finished only 3 points above Leicester Fosse, as two were deducted for playing an ineligible player.

As if this record was not enough for the Club's increasing number of followers, the Wanderers reached the 2nd round proper in the F.A.Cup, their furthest progress ever. Early victories were achieved over Leek by nine clear goals, Old Hill Wanderers by five, a seven–two victory over Hednesford and a last qualifying win over Brierley Hill with the odd goal in three. In the first round Stockport County were defeated by a single goal. The next game decreed that the Club would entertain high flying Second Division Notts.County. Despite the Football League Club's inducements to reverse the venue, the Wanderers remained faithful to Burton and were rewarded with their probable all time record attendance.

Six thousand fans packed in to the Derby Turn Ground: *"The attendance reached gigantic proportions at what was the largest number of spectators ever seen in Burton at a Football Match."*

Accommodation at the Ground had been increased with the provision of temporary extra stands, but the crowds were unable to lift the team sufficiently to avoid a two goal defeat; but since the County were the eventual winners of the Cup, the Non-league team were hardly disgraced.

The last game in the Midland League was a fitting eight goal victory at home to Kettering, at which... " *A large assemblage of spectators were present to pay homage to the old Club... never in the whole twenty-three years of the Club's existence have there been such rejoicings.* " The success story for the Wanderers extended to other Cup competitions where they appeared in an unprecedented three semi-finals, but perhaps most surprising of all, the Club had only called upon 14 different players for all of the first team matches. As support had increased, the spartan facilities were improved at the ground at the season's end, and also included new posts and ropes to all sides of the playing pitch. A membership drive was instigated by the Club, when it was hoped for a total of 300; in the first three days 45 new names were 'signed on'. After such a successful campaign, a Special General Meeting was held at the Derby Turn Inn on May the 11th. With only one vote against the proposal, the Club decided to apply for election to the Football League With Ardwick and Middlesbrough Ironopolis dropping out, and an extension to sixteen Clubs, the Wanderers just scraped in on the voting to become members of the Football League Second Division, for the 1894/95 season.

The 1894/95 pre-season trial matches of the Swifts produced large attendances, in this a period when the town could boast two teams with membership of the Football League – never had such interest in the sport been so apparent. On September the 1st, whilst the Swifts were defeating Crewe by four unopposed goals before an encouraging 3,000 attendance at Peel Croft, the Wanderers were experiencing their first game in the same League. Despite an excellent 3-1 win at Rotherham, before a 'large crowd', the game was somewhat disappointing entertainment value. The Wanderers team for this historic match consisted of:
> *Brentnall, Cunningham, Draper, Hayward, Ward, Draycott, Garfield, Brown, Ade and Arthur Capes plus Moore.*

Two days later, the new Club of Manchester City (who had in effect replaced the defunct Ardwick) were visited, and a very creditable 1-1 draw was played before 3,000 spectators. On Boxing Day the Burton team had a lot more to celebrate when they inflicted on the same team, the City's all time record (joint) defeat, a crushing 8-0 (half time 3-0) Wanderers victory, before 2,000 fans.

The eagerly awaited first home game came on September the 8th when Newton Heath were in opposition. The Ground had taken on a new look, complete with improvements to the new Grandstand on the reserved side – part of which was for members only – and included a Press Stand in the centre. The kick–off was delayed until 4 o'clock due to the special Manchester Supporters train arriving late! The final result – with a third match unchanged team – was a satisfying single goal win to the homesters before a 2,500 crowd.

The Wanderers 5 points from 6 was matched by the Swifts who also achieved two wins and a draw from their first three games, all at home. The Burton newcomers excellent start continued with a 2-1 win at Leicester, but they finally met their match when they appeared at Darwen and lost by two goals one week later, with Ade Capes a virtual passenger throughout the game due to his illness on the outward journey. Additional entertainment was provided before the match and at half–time from the 'Pickup Bank' prize Brass Band. The same day saw the Swifts lose by the odd goal in five at The John 'O Gaunt's Ground, to Lincoln, but this defeat was revenged four months later with an emphatic 6-1 return victory.

After such an encouraging start, the Wanderers hopes took a tumble in the weeks leading up to Christmas with defeats becoming the norm, but a recovery after the turn of the year balanced the – match – balance. On the 27th of October, the match that all of Burton was waiting for was staged – Wanderers versus Swifts.

Special trains from outlying villages brought the fans into the Brewery town, and well before the kick–off many had assembled within the Derby Turn Ground. At the start of the game, a total of over 3,000 supporters were present, and as the teams took to the field the majority of the cheers were for the Swifts. However a local derby that could only attract such a low attendance on present day standards was at the root of the two Burton Clubs fairly short life within the Football League. The town was just not big enough to attract sufficient support for even one high–flying team, never alone two! The final result finished in the favour of the Swifts, repeating the results of their recent encounters with the Wanderers – three Friendlies and a Birmingham Senior Cup–tie match one year earlier, plus the F.A.Cup encounter in 1892 – all of which went against the Wanderers. Another top crowd–puller for the Wanderers was the visit of Bury, Champions–elect, when well over 3,000 spectators saw the visitors continue their winning ways. The most amazing result of the season occurred on April the 15th, when Newcastle were humiliated with their all time record defeat to the tune of nine goals to nil; a unique feat for a Club in their first Football League season to inflict subsequent all–time record League defeats over **two** opposition teams! The final place in the League for the newcomers was a somewhat disappointing seventh.

The Swifts fared even worse, for apart from the Lincoln home victory, there were few other notable wins, but some heavy defeats including five goal thrashings at Peel Croft (by Leicester), and at Darwen. A final 11th place in the 16 Club League table gave cause for concern.

The F.A.Cup produced easy early round wins for both Clubs, before they were destined to meet each other in the 3rd qualifying round at Derby Turn. 3,500 supporters were present, many of them lining the ropes well before the start, and at last the Wanderers achieved a win over their neighbours – by 5-2. The end in this competition for the Wanderers came with Blackburn's narrow victory in the first round proper.

The 1895/96 campaign produced a surprise for the Wanderers, for after several years of living in the shadows of their other opponents in Burton, they excelled themselves and came within three points of possible promotion. The season got off to a late start with a 3-0 home victory over Darwen before a 2,500 attendance (quite good by Burton standards) plus away wins at Crewe on the 14th of September and Leicester two weeks later. Between times a 2-1 home victory over Burslem Port Vale, produced an early second from top place in the League. All conquering Liverpool (eventual Champions) halted the Wanderers progress with an emphatic 4-1 Anfield win, but apart from a heavy defeat at the Royal Arsenal in October no other League matches were lost until a three goal setback at Darwen on January the 4th. By this time the Club found themselves in unfamiliar surroundings – second from top in the table!

For the Swifts, things were not so good. Early season topsy turvy form saw them both lose and win by comfortable margins on their travels, while their eight matches at Peel Croft produced five wins and three defeats, which resulted in a mid-table placing by the New Year.

The F.A.Cup Competition included both Clubs at the first round proper stage, but for both of them, defeats. The Swifts succumbed lamely before a 3,000 crowd at Raikes Hall Gardens, Blackpool (by 1-4), but the Wanderers nearly produced a minor shock with two goals shared at First Division Sheffield United. The replay at Derby Turn encouraged a near record crowd, but the 5,000 went home disappointed with their team's single goal defeat.

The second half of the season saw the Wanderers promotion chances fade away due to unexpected losses on their travels, and a final fourth place was insufficient for them to contest the play-offs for the First Division. Nonetheless just 3 points behind Liverpool and runners-up Manchester City hardly represented a failed season! A bizarre incident occurred on March the 21st when Rotherham visited Derby Turn.

The visitors turned up with only 10 men, but more importantly the Referee was also missing; Mr.Buxton of Burton Wanderers officiated!

Things went badly for the Swifts. Following two heavy losses at Darwen (0–3) and Notts.County (0–5) in February, there were wholesale changes made to the forward line for the visit of table topping Liverpool on February the 29th. The team changes did not have the desired effect, for in front of a disappointing crowd of only 3,000, the locals – three goals down at half–time – ended up on the wrong end of a seven goal defeat. The season trailed off in poor fashion, and included Liverpool's return 6–1 win at home before 4,000 fans, to put the Swifts in final eleventh place in the League. One of the season's top crowds to watch a Swifts game occurred at Kettering, when 8,000 were present for the Kettering Charity Cup Semi–final with Aston Villa.

The brief courtship with the table–toppers did not enhance the coffers at the Wanderers, and the Swifts also found it hard going on the financial front. At the start of the 1896/97 season players from both Clubs were transferred to provide desperately required finance. From the Wanderers, both of the Capes brothers plus Draycott and Garfield – all of whom had played in the Club's first ever Football League match – together with goalkeeper Watts, and Handford left. Meanwhile the Swifts lost their goalkeeper, Jones, along with Crone, Campbell, Arnott and Willocks. These were desperate measures for the two Clubs, but necessary as neither had been able to meet their expenses over the last two years. " One day, perhaps, they will see fit to amalgamate ", was publicly expressed, and also seriously considered some two years earlier; this was to be the final outcome – but five years later.

Apprehension rather than optimism greeted the start of the campaign, and this fear for the Clubs' endeavours became a reality. Both teams lost their opening games, Wanderers at Walsall – where the Press accommodation consisted of a 'sodden plank alongside the middle of the pitch' – and the Swifts when they were hosts to Newton Heath. Apart from an uncharacter-istic 5–1 home victory at Derby Turn over the strong Grimsby side on September the 12th, it was downhill all the way for the Wanderers, and by early November they were stuck at second from bottom in the table. Things were little better for their close foes, for by this time the Swifts found themselves only four places higher. The situation by the New Year showed little change – just one place – higher for the Wanderers and lower for the Swifts! Home results for the former in the second half of the season were generally good, apart from the 2–6 reverse dished out by promotion chasing Small Heath in mid–February, but away from home the record was dismal; apart from a success at Lincoln on Boxing Day, just one more point was obtained.

Poor Attendances, and hence money, continued as the main problem for both Clubs. The Swifts games at the Arsenal and Newcastle, with attendances of 7,000 and over 5,000 respectively, could rarely be even half matched at games in Burton. On Easter Saturday, the Wanderers started with only ten players at Loughborough, but were down to nine when the injured Lowe left the pitch after twenty minutes. Later, Brettle *"... was rushed at by a Loughborough forward and kicked in a dangerous part..."* This left the Burton team with only eight players, balanced in part by the sending off of the assailant! The match ended 0–6 against the Wanderers, the Club's record Football League defeat. Two days later at Derby Turn, the attendance was well up – but only due to the number of travelling fans! This 1–3 defeat to Loughborough was to be the last ever Football League match for the Wanderers. The last match (as a League team) for the Club was a local (home) cup–tie played against Derby County, with a line–up of:

Brentnall, Lowe, Archer, Wheldon, Handley, Devey, Brown, Flanegan, Dyke, Arkesden and Lumsden;
The Derby line–up included Steve Bloomer.

The only matches to attract anything like good crowds were inevitably the two local derbys with each other, the match at Derby Turn attracting nearly 5,000, which contrasted sharply with the 1,500 (including many away supporters) when Leicester Fosse were the visitors! Across town, the Swifts playing record was as bad! They did have the encouragement of a few surprise home victories – 5–0 over Manchester City plus 4–0 results versus both Lincoln and Gainsborough – but like their neighbours, it was an uphill struggle for them away from home.

With the Derby Turn Club finishing in 15th (second from bottom) place, and the Swifts just one position higher, the *'Beeropolis'* (as Burton was popularly called – 'opolis' being a popular town name suffix by the Press of this time) had the embarrassment of both its teams having to apply for re–election; probably the first and only time that this has happened to a town with two representatives in the Football League.

The Swifts were given another chance, but not so the Wanderers. With all the Football League aspirants represented at the Football League election meeting – except Millwall Athletic and Long Eaton Rangers – the Wanderers received nine votes, the second highest of the seven unlucky hopefuls. Despite their loss of status, the Wanderers still featured in some matches – two in particular – that on the face of it did not warrant their inclusion. Early in the 1897/98 season they appeared as the opponents to Leicester Fosse at Filbert Street in a Benefit Match for a Fosse player, which finished as a 1–5 defeat before an attendance of 4,000. Shortly afterwards they were invited as opponents to a newly formed Club by the name of 'New Brighton Tower'.

This honour turned out to be something of a nightmare as they slumped to a five goal defeat. Competitively the Wanderers now played in the Midland League, their first game being at Chesterfield where a single goal defeat ensued. 1,500 spectators were present at Corbridge for the second league game, when four goals were shared with Burslem Port Vale – the Potteries Club despite only finishing in 5th place in the table, moved up to the Football League at the end of the season. A scoreless draw was played out with Kettering in the first home game. All things considered it was a far from successful re–start in Non–league circles. The Club's fortunes did not change, and the final league placing was a dismal second from bottom (of twelve) with 5 victories, 3 draws and 11 defeats. It was in the F.A.Cup competition where some progress was made. Playing through from the early qualifying rounds – the first time for three years – the vanquished included; Wrockwardine Wood (a leagueless Club) with a 5–3 scoreline, followed by Stourbridge (more of the latter below) but finally beaten 1–2, by Burslem Port Vale in the final qualifying round.

The F.A.Cup was something of an embarrassment to the Swifts. They too had to meet Stourbridge, and at Peel Croft after a terrible display fell by two goals. Between the posts for the visitors was Hadley the ex–Burton Swifts custodian. This defeat was a bitter pill to swallow, and there were many changes in the Swifts team line–up for the next game. The Football League season was little better than a year earlier, with a final placing of thirteenth. A reasonable home match record was balanced with a grim list of defeats on the Club's travels which included a 0–9 hammering by Manchester City and a 2–7 reverse at Grimsby.

The Century was drawing to a close as was the existence of the two Clubs as separate organisations. Plagued with money problems they none–the–less struggled on for three more years. The 1898/99 season provided a near identical record in the Football League for the Swifts – more points from more games – but the same final position. For the Wanderers the position was somewhat brighter, enough to stave off amalgamation at least for a while, with a final position in the Midland League of sixth in a table of 14 teams. The Midland League at this time was composed of several reserve teams of Football League teams, plus a number of prominent Non–leaguers. The most dramatic turn around was for wooden–spoonists Mexborough, who had been league Champions one year earlier. One year later and the situation was even worse for the Swifts. Once again the home record was reasonable – apart from a five goal defeat to eventual Champions Sheffield Wednesday on October the 7th. But two six goal defeats (at Sheffield and Grimsby), two of five without reply and a 1–8 thrashing at newcomers Middlesbrough put paid to any respectable final record – fourth from bottom being the outcome. The Wanderers meanwhile sunk to 10th of twelve in their competition.

The first season in the Twentieth Century proved to be the last straw for both Clubs. For the Wanderers, despite their reduced costs in running a Midland League team, finance had become critical, whilst over at Peel Croft money and playing credibility became the joint enemies.

The sons of the Eadie family had ensured that the Club kept its head above water, but a dreadful playing season placed the Swifts in a final bottom position. Their campaign started in disastrous fashion with a four goal defeat at home to Chesterfield – a result that surprisingly and subsequently turned out to be the team's worst of the season. Two days later defeat came at Burnley, and on the 15th of September the first win arrived with a single goal victory at home to Woolwich Arsenal, followed a few days later with an encouraging 5–1 success at Walsall. But there was no real recovery on the way, and the team soon slipped to the lowest rung in the League ladder. The Swifts last ever game produced a two goal defeat at Green Lane, Stockport before a miserable attendance of a few hundred, while the Wanderers said goodbye – ironically at borrowed Peel Croft – with a 1–2 defeat to Newark. An unusual friendly was played at Peel Croft in October 1899, when a *'capital attendance'* watched a friendly between the Swifts and the Kaffirs (Blacks) from the Orange Free State (South Africa), with the homesters running out winners with the odd goal in seventeen!

An agreement by the Swifts and the Wanderers to amalgamate – on two occasions the idea had been previously raised – at the Station Hotel on May the 15th probably saved Burton from losing its one representative in the Football League. This new initiative provided a vote of confidence for Burton *'ex–Swifts'*, at the Football League election meeting, for they – along with newcomers Bristol City – received equal top votes. Injected with new enthusiasm, the Masonic Hall was crowded to overflowing, with hundreds shut out, when a meeting on July the 3rd was held to agree the final details of the merger. The past failures both on the field and in financial terms – on some occasions the Wanderers home gates provided less than £3, to pay a weekly £8 wages bill – were now hopefully in the past. A name for the new team was decided upon. *'Burton County'*, an apt title since 1901 coincided with the first year that the town had become a County Borough, was rejected in favour of the more obvious choice of 'Burton United' – the latter proposed by Mr.T.Bidder. A Committee was to be formed, consisting of four members from each of the former Clubs plus four neutral gentlemen. This body was to inevitably include the redoubtable Mr.Grewcock.

With a gradually rising population – in ten years the numbers had increased by some 10% from 45,000 – Burton United could hopefully depend not only on improvements on the pitch, but also home match attendances; ideals that were never to be fulfilled!

BURTON WANDERERS F.C.

Allsopps' to the Rescue.

ROSY PROSPECTS.

The prospects of the Burton Wanderers are brightening rapidly. The rumours which were widely circulated during the summer months that the old club would not be able to face another season, were ruthlessly dispelled by the report presented by the chairman at the annual meeting last week. It was then shown that a temporary run of bad gates, owing to the lack of proper shelter and accommodation for the visitors was not to be allowed—thanks to generous outside support—to kill the club. The existing state of affairs has received the serious consideration of Messrs. Allsopp and Sons, and as an outcome a conference was held this morning between representatives of the firm and the chairman of the club at the brewery offices. The outcome will be very gratifying to the well-wishers of this now nearly thirty year old club.

Mr. C. J. Stewart, the newly-elected managing director of the firm, presided, and speedily presented himself in the light of a staunch and generous supporter of sports in general and football in particular. Amongst others present were Mr. R. Hutton, Mr. J. Hartshorne, Mr. McGilph, and Mr. W. D. Manton.

The exact position of the club's affairs was placed before the meeting by its representative, and was attentively listened to and carefully considered by Mr. Stewart. After some discussion the genial chairman expressed himself in sympathy with the aims and objects of the club, and promised to do all in his power to help the Wanderers to recover their prestige. He generously agreed to a rearrangement of the playing ground so as to avoid damaging the cricket pitch. He gave the necessary instructions for a grand stand and pavilion to be erected for the comfort and convenience of the patrons, and expressed his wish that the work should be put in hand without a moment's delay. This, so far as the plans have already been matured, will extend almost the whole length of the field of play. Substantial financial support was also very kindly promised. Amongst other business transacted, by far the most important and gratifying to the club supporters will be the announcement that Mr. R. Hutton and Mr. W. D. Manton have consented to become members of the Wanderers Committee; and, in accordance with the powers conferred upon the committee at the annual meeting, have been duly elected.

It will thus be seen that the future prospects of the club are such as will gladden the heart of all supporters of local football.

It would be needless to add that in the name of the club, Mr. Woolrych thanked the representatives of the firm in general, and Mr. Stewart in particular, for so generously coming to their assistance in a time of great need. He expressed the hope that when the club had regained its old name and position in the football world, its supporters would look back with pride and pleasure upon that day, which he felt confident would be marked as the turning point in the club's career.

The remedy, I think, for our present difficulties lies in another direction. We are not alone in our troubles in Burton. It is the same cry all over the country, and the time is fast approaching when some radical changes will have to be effected, such, for instance, as a county qualification, the same as at cricket, and a consequent reduction in the absurd and ridiculous wages paid to and for players. Neither the Swifts nor the Wanderers can keep up a winning career by selling their best men, and people in Burton, as elsewhere, won't go in sufficiently large numbers to pay expenses, to see a team lose more matches than they win. I am wandering a little from my point, hence I will bring my remarks to a close by expressing the hope that whatever decision is come to, will be for the best. Common honesty compels me to say that I shall feel with regret the day

THE BURTON FOOTBALL AMALGAMATION.

Yesterday morning Mr. A. J. Woolrych, the chairman of the Burton Wanderers Football Club, who have recently agreed to an amalgamation with the Burton Swifts, received a letter from Mr. A. Kingscott, the hon. secretary of the Midland League, informing him that the Management Committee had agreed to an alteration of their name from "Burton Wanderers" to "Burton United Reserve." The Swifts management have applied to the League authorities for a similar concession. The club at a meeting last night decided to have athletic sports on Peel Croft on Saturday, August 10.

The amalgamation saga:
On the 25th of March 1899 (Top right), Mr. Woolrych gave his opinion.
On the 16th of August 1900, the Wanderers were determined to go it alone.
But less than one year later (10th of July 1901), the amalgamation was confirmed.

Several new players were signed on for the 1901/02 season including: Peers (Nottingham Forest), Mann (Aston Villa), Jones (Wales and Leicester), Joyce (Portsmouth), Arkesden (Derby) and Rae the Irish International; the total cost of transfers plus summer wages amounted to approximately £500. With a new trainer – George Kinsey the former International and Swifts player, plus several improvements to the Ground and the Grandstand, the new United looked optimistically towards the first games in September. The Club's practise match in August attracted over 2,000 spectators, the best for many years and indeed more than many recent League games. With their sights fixed firmly on the First Division they kicked off on the 7th of September – and lost 2–3 at Barnsley! The team consisted of:

Gray, Peers, Kirkland, Waterson, Mann, Garlick, Arkesden, Lewis, Joyce, Martin and Clarke.

A 1–1 home draw followed one week later, and was attended by around 4,000 fans (an attendance that subsequently became a probable joint record for the Club). But with a four goal reverse at the Fosse on September the 21st, things were looking far from rosy. Apart from the 3–2 win over Stockport on the 28th of September, it was not until the last day of November that another success was achieved, a welcome 4–1 win at Gainsborough – and this period had included a six goal home thrashing by the strong Lincoln side. A surprise single goal victory was achieved over Woolwich Arsenal before Christmas in front of a 6,000 crowd in London, but there was still little to enthuse over. In the New Year there was something of an improvement, at least at home, but by the season's end a somewhat disappointing final place of 10th in the League was the outcome. By the end of 1901 attendances had dropped to the more familiar 1,500 or so! With no good run in the F.A.Cup – which was terminated in a replay at Northampton – the euphoria that had greeted the new team a year earlier had already waned, and the Committee were faced with a deficit on the season in excess of £700.

A very respectable start was made to the 1902/03 campaign, with 2 wins, 2 draws and 1 defeat in September. However things then started going wrong, and by the turn of the year, the United found themselves languishing in twelfth position in the League table. Once again it was the away matches that were principally letting the team down, although in the game at Bristol City on December the 27th, they could consider the 1–3 reverse almost respectable, since the homesters had had no fewer than four goals disallowed!

The team had included reserve goalkeeper Waterson (for first choice Gray), whom it was reported had to take a large share of the blame in the United's defeat. The end of season run–in produced some bad displays, and the final 13th place in the League reflected yet another poor campaign.

Once again money was a problem; attendances had always been low, and hence there was hardly room for them to drop appreciably! However, it was always hoped that a combined team would attract combined support. This expectation was proved wrong, and the 2,000 who attended the Glossop match in September, was by now an average representative attendance, and no more than the former Swifts Club attracted.

By now the full title of the Club was, *'Burton United Football and Athletic Club'*, since Athletics meetings were being regularly held at Peel Croft to slightly ease the financial strain. The F.A.Cup slightly relieved the financial pressures with a run to the final qualifying round. Northampton (2–0) and then Kettering (3–1) were beaten, the latter match at Peel Croft attended by 2,000 but included some 350 visitors. The next round also attracted the travelling fans, for the Wellingborough team were supported in an exceptional attendance of around 4,000 (a joint – approximate – record attendance), which the homesters won by 5–1. On December the 13th a money spinning tie was played with Manchester United, when the Burton Officials succumbed to the temptation and agreed to play in Lancashire. 10,000 Mancurians were present to see two goals shared on a quagmire of a pitch, followed a few days later at the same venue with a 1–3 defeat.

The close season revealed some desperate measures in an attempt to pull the Club round. Five players were not re–signed and the impoverished United were unable to pay summer wages to those that remained. Replacements to those that had departed were found, but all were free transfers. Travel was of course a meaningful expenditure, and with the reserves having covered 1,497 miles in the Midland League – despite the Club's fairly central location – the 'stiffs' were withdrawn from this competition and entered for the somewhat minor Burton League. The first team had travelled 2,639 miles on their journeys.

The Committee set out to clear the Club's debts – most of which were owed to themselves and the continually supportive Eadie family – although at £200 less than a year earlier the economic measures were taking effect. An indifferent start hardly got the crowds flocking in, and a record eight goal thrashing before 14,000 enthusiasts at promotion heading Woolwich Arsenal did nothing to help the cause; the United had in fact played well in this game, and were only two goals in arrears after 45 minutes. Three weeks later on October the 10th, a seven goal thrashing was dished out, at home, to Stockport.

The United's best win and worst defeat in the Football League had hence both occurred within a three week period! After eight games and a fifth from bottom League position, it was obvious that another struggle was to be played out.

Playing through from the qualifying rounds, the F.A.Cup sortie produced some relief. Hinckley were easily disposed of (5-1) at the Leicester Fosse Ground, followed by a 4-0 home victory over Kettering – the fourth F.A.Cup meeting with this Club in five years. Whitwick were easily overcome followed by three games with the Fosse. On November the 28th, the best attendance at Peel Park for many months (aided by around 500 from Leicester) saw two goals shared, and after another drawn match, their fellow struggling neighbours were finally defeated at Derby. A marathon Cup run ended in the final qualifying round at Corbridge, when on a quagmire of a pitch, the United were beaten by Burslem Port Vale, by three goals; the United's share of the gate amounted to £18! Back to the Football League matches, the grim struggle continued, and a final place in the League of 14th was the outcome.

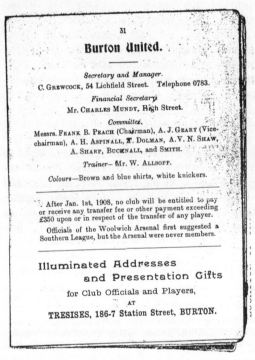

31

Burton United.

Secretary and Manager.
C. GREWCOCK, 54 Lichfield Street. Telephone 0783.

Financial Secretary
Mr. CHARLES MUNDY, High Street.

Committee.
Messrs. FRANK B. PEACH (Chairman), A. J. GEARY (Vice-chairman), A. H. ASPINALL, T. DOLMAN, A.V. N. SHAW, A. SHARP, BUCKNALL, and SMITH.

Trainer— Mr. W. ALLSOPP.

Colours—Brown and blue shirts, white knickers.

After Jan. 1st, 1908, no club will be entitled to pay or receive any transfer fee or other payment exceeding £350 upon or in respect of the transfer of any player.

Officials of the Woolwich Arsenal first suggested a Southern League, but the Arsenal were never members.

Illuminated Addresses and Presentation Gifts
for Club Officials and Players,
AT
TRESISES, 186-7 Station Street, BURTON.

An extract from the 1906/07 season
Burton-on-Trent Football Guide.

The next three seasons, the last in the League for Burton United, produced a gradually worsening situation. Further economies reduced the Club's capacity to employ quality players, which in turn led to poor results and hence little support at matches. Even in the earlier more successful days of the Burton Clubs, good attendances never materialised, and crowds of over 3,000 were rare occurrences. The continued financial support of the Eadies Family – sons of the earlier men who had done so much to establish the Swifts as a Football League team – allowed the United to maintain their status.

The 1904/05 season, with Mr.C.Grewcock now in the position of Secretary/Manager ended with the Club's lowest League position to that date – 17th – and only an increase to twenty teams in the Second Division prevented the necessity of the United having to seek re-election.

Once again it had been a very poor away record, and narrow defeats, that had let the team down apart from an end of season, six nil defeat to the mediocre West Bromwich team; the home matches produced 16 of the team's 20 points.

Inevitably finance was at the root of the Club's troubles. How the Officials of the Swifts must have envied the 16,000 crowd for the Manchester United versus Burton game. The biggest crowd of the season attracted for the visit of Liverpool, only provided the required numbers for an average gate! Some finance was raised when the Mayor supported a *'Penny Fund'* in which all moneys raised went to the Club. The Liverpool game had a different problem, for the home player, Evans, was sent off for kicking an opponent. The Club were also in trouble with the Authorities when the Referee in the Leicester home game became so unpopular that he was bombarded with snowballs at the end of the match!

Just two of the playing staff could be persuaded to remain (without even the inducement of summer wages) and a team as best as could be raised in the circumstances was formed. Twelve months later the situation had not improved and a second from bottom League placing required the need to seek re-election. *"The most disastrous season in their history... fate as far as Senior Football goes, hangs in the balance."*

The League Clubs kept faith with the Burton team, and the scales tipped in Burton's favour with 32 votes to ensure their continued survival with the elite. Ironically in these days of free scoring teams, there had only been one really bad result, the 0-6 away defeat to runners-up Manchester United in the last match of the campaign. For the first time in several years an appearance was made in the first round proper of the F.A.Cup, after a three goal win over Accrington Stanley, but was followed by a single goal defeat at Southern league Club, Millwall. Even so re-arranged numbering of the various rounds that had started in this, the 1905/06 season, would only have been equivalent to the last qualifying round of earlier years! Although the 1906/07 season was to be the last ever in the Football League for Burton United, and the Club's worst ever record in matches, it was also the period when after years of money worries the Club at last appeared to have 'turned the corner' on the financial front! After the first five games – one win two draws and two defeats – signalled a poor, but not disastrous start to the season. But from then on things rapidly deteriorated. All matches were lost up to the New Year, apart from two home victories against fellow strugglers Clapton Orient in November, and versus high-flying Bradford City on December the 15th. The last ever 'away' Football League match was played at Valley Parade where the United completed a surprising double (a single goal win on April the 20th) against a team that had at times looked like promotion contenders.

The first two games of 1907 produced a glimmer of hope with a home win and a rare point in an away match. On February the 23rd, a slaughter at table topping Chelsea was confidently predicted, but the one goal defeat was almost a morale booster. One week later the match at Peel Croft versus Wolverhampton Wanderers was full of drama. In front of an unusually good attendance of around 4,000 (£110 receipts) both teams lost their goalkeepers through injuries; two penalties were later awarded to the United, one of which was missed, and with the final score of 4–1 to the homesters, this League result became the highest of the day!

Good Friday, the 29th of March, was to go down as perhaps the most disastrous in Burton football history. A home match in the afternoon had resulted in a single goal defeat to neighbours Leicester Fosse. But at around 9.00 p.m., a fire occurred in the Grandstand of such magnitude that the crowd that gathered to see the firemen in action was greater than at some of the United's football matches! The incident which preceded the tragedy at Bradford City some eighty years later had many similarities. The cause was put down to a carelessly dropped cigarette earlier in the day, which had smouldered before catching alight the debris below the wooden structure. A report of the day stated that... *"It was fortunate that the fire had not occurred during the game... the possibility of a stampede from the stand is terrible to contemplate... the rapid spread of flames too would have made an escape extremely difficult."*

This accident was a morale deflator to a team that was struggling on the field of play, but a mini–revival in the last undefeated four games (three of which were away) was insufficient to prevent the Club from finishing bottom in the Second Division. During the previous months, a nineteen game period passed without a United goal being scored, yet conversely nine games had been lost by only a single goal.

On April the 27th, Burton United took the field (at Peel Croft) for their last ever Football League match. The team consisted of:
> *Starbuck, Warren, Kirkland, Stanley, Nelmes, Price, Bradshaw, Wileman, Hunt, Wilkins and Vann.*

For Hadyn Price, the Welsh International, it was his debut for the team! After an even first half, the United gradually took command and were unlucky not to record a more emphatic win than the 2–0 final result. During this last season, twenty–five players had been called upon in Football League matches, with Stanley an ever–present and Bradshaw the top goal scorer with just six. Once again an appearance was made in the first round proper of the F.A.Cup. After a scoreless home draw, the replay was also drawn scoreless before a 5,000 crowd, but abandoned after 10 minutes of extra time. At the third attempt, the United bowed out, by two goals, to New Brompton – both replays having been staged at Fulham F.C.

The poor season was heavily blamed on poor management by the Committee. At the turn of the year when the Club were in their best financial position since their formation six years earlier, there was the chance – and the money available – to increase and improve the playing staff; the Manager, Mr.Grewcock, was not however given a free hand and the opportunity passed by. In a final desperate bid to lift the Club, several players were transferred to Peel Croft just before the season's end, and these were no doubt the reason for the late revival.

On May the 31st a large crowd gathered outside the local Newspaper Offices awaiting the result of the Football League re–election poll. With promised support from other Midland Clubs and that of Chelsea, it was with dismay that the supporters were relayed the message that with only a paltry seven votes (Oldham Athletic the best supported of the non–elected teams had received 17 votes), Burton United had been banished from the Football League. The Club's expected support had not been forthcoming, at a time when the United could realistically hope for a revival in their fortunes both on and off the field. The final indignity was dealt out when the Club's recent playing captures were allowed to depart to other Clubs on free transfers, due to the Football League rules at that time that did not allow fees for players leaving non re–elected Football Clubs; the United suffered an estimated £1500 to £2000 loss in this respect!

A successful application for 1907/08 membership of the Birmingham League was made when 14 out of a possible 15 votes were obtained. The Burton football public, fairly small though it was, had enjoyed (or endured!) fifteen years of Football League football. The United were now faced with new opposition in the rapidly spreading Non–league, league world.

In view of the past poor performances, the public trial match attracted an encouraging crowd of around 1,000, and the first match in the Birmingham league gave rise to optimism for the future, with a 6–1 home win over Kidderminster. The next game at Worcester brought the Club back to earth when a 0–4 reverse was experienced!

Six months after the devastating fire – that had all but completely destroyed the Grandstand – the new structure was formally opened on September the 21st. Once again the James and J.T.C. Eadie family had come to the rescue of their local team, and at a cost of £500 had built and presented to the Club a fine new seated stand. The Grandstand, built of pitchpine, was able to seat between 600 and 700, with a central Press Box area and contained (underneath) Dressing Rooms and four Bars. This gesture by the Eadie's was a godsend, for the Insurance claim on the old stand had only produced £200 – once again the family had ensured the continued survival of the Town team.

On the playing front, a moderate start turned sour, and the players were criticised when the first five away games were all lost, resulting in an alarming fourth from bottom position in the league by the end of November. By the end of the year things had improved slightly with the Club laying in 11th place of 18 teams, but with four games played at this time in the space of four days only one game was won! No success was achieved in the F.A.Cup for progress was terminated at Stockton with a 1–2 defeat which none–the–less was considered to be the best game of the season, and before a 5,000 crowd. Yet again finance became the main problem, and receipts at home matches gradually declined; the Stoke match produced £31, Wrexham – £28, and Shrewsbury just £12, were prime examples – all this with a weekly wages bill of some £27! The only two exceptions in this decline were the Easter matches which produced more healthy figures of £69 and £80 against Worcester City and (regular Champions) Aston Villa Reserves respectively – such figures were never even nearly reached again. By the end of the season, despite a final mid–table position in the league, the serious question was raised on how long could Burton United F.C. struggle on.

The Club did, however, manage to struggle on – for two more seasons – but the heart had gone from the United, as its monetary lifeblood dwindled further. After two poor seasons in the Birmingham League, the third, and last attempt for a revival was made for the 1909/10 campaign. By the turn of the year things had reached an all time low. Thirteen league matches had been played, of which just one had ended in victory plus a single draw. " Never have they been in such sore straits as present " was the local press comment. A re–structured Southern League saw the team also enter the second division section A, but only six matches were played.

Administration had been pruned further to counterbalance even less revenue coming in from home matches, despite a reduction in admission prices in attempt at attracting more fans. Another 'low' on the field was reached when the United were humiliated by an eight goal defeat at Stoke in January, but this surprisingly signalled something of a change in fortunes and several good victories were then achieved. These successes included a single goal win at Birmingham, the City's Reserves first home defeat. But these rare wins had all come to late, and the United were already destined for the 'wooden spoon' position in the league when the last game of the season, and for the Club, was played on April the 23rd. Kidderminster were the visitors – the same opponents as the United's first on their Non–league football return. Before an almost non–existent crowd Burton United won by 3–0, and they could have had more!

In spite of the failings of the First Team, the Club's Reserves had one of their best ever season's, winning four Cups during the campaign. Several

Clubs had assured the United of their support at the league's election meeting, but when certain facts came to light, such backing became very unlikely. Most of the Club's Committee lived out of town and were not fully in touch with the day to day running affairs. Seventy pounds ground rental had not even been paid to the owners of Peel Croft for the previous season, and it was only the goodwill of those owners that they had not pressed for payment. In their dire financial situation, the United had relied on the good nature of other Birmingham league Clubs who had made loans to them to cover their travelling costs, but no attempt had been made to repay the lenders. And so it could not have come as any real surprise to the Committee when the league firmly rejected their application for re-election.

Despite the seemingly hopeless plight of Burton United, little encouragement came from the Club's Officials. It was then revealed that entry into the coming season's F.A.Cup had been overlooked, and confirmed in many peoples eyes that the affairs of the Club had become slipshod in the extreme. No criticism was levelled at Manager and stalwart Mr.Grewcock, but by now it was accepted that it was almost inevitable that the organisation would disband. It was then revealed to the Press that an application had been made and accepted for the Club to join the re-organised Southern League Division 2, but with few competing teams this would provide too few competitive games. A meeting was called at the 'eleventh hour' in the Queen's Hotel on August the 29th, in an effort to keep alive senior football in the town, at which sixty present and past Officials and supporters were present. A proposition had been put to the local brewing 'giants' Bass that they should help the town's football Club financially. Bass had in the past been willing to give moral support, and now in the Club's hour of need they promised to donate £20 for every £80 raised by the United. A public appeal was subsequently made, but little was forthcoming. The Chairman, Mr.Dolman also proposed a radical move which caused consternation among the rest of the Committee and supporters; he claimed that another football club had offered a substantial sum of money to take over the United's fixtures in the Southern League, a transaction that he assured those present, did not break the F.A.'s rules.

If this offer had been made, and many questioned its validity, it was argued that whilst this may have paid the Club's debts, all that would be left would be a Football Club with no fixtures! With the proposition that the Club should be taken over and reformed, a Sub-committee was elected with a view to raising in excess of £300. £131 was required to pay back the Club Officials' unsecured loans, and the remainder for the payment of outstanding bills. Such enthusiasm had however come too late, and the first Southern League fixture date arrived – a home game versus Stoke on September the 5th – but passed by without a ball being kicked.

Another meeting at the Queen's Hotel on September the 6th resulted in the new Committee issuing a statement to the effect that it was impossible for Burton United to play matches during the 1910/11 season. A new Club would be formed immediately with the intention of commencing matches at the start of the 1911/12 season. During the interim period the Committee would endeavour to raise funds for the new Club. A new Club was never formed, neither did Burton United or any successor of the Club ever appear again.

PEEL CROFT.

The former Ground of both Burton Swifts and later Burton United, was and is still a neat and well enclosed venue. After the demise of the United, Burton Rugby club took over the Ground, and after three–quarters of a century it has not changed a great deal. The main entrance, off Lichfield Street, led straight through to the Grandstand. To the right of the entrance stands a large building that appears to be almost within the enclosure itself, and is very much as it was in the late 19th century. The entrance hut, probably with turnstiles is no longer present. Another entrance off Lichfield Street probably existed at the other side of the ground. The slightly raised banking behind the Lichfield Street goal was and still is composed of soil. Behind the other goal a narrow, covered enclosure was present in the Football League days, which also ran a short way down the side opposite the seated stand. Almost at the other end of this side another small structure was present, possibly another covered enclosure, or more likely a Tea Bar. Along the side of the pitch, between the two structures, there was a narrow terrace – the current stepped banking was installed after the Second World War. The present covered enclosure opposite the Grandstand is also a relatively recent addition. The present Grandstand is that built by the Eadie family for the United Club in 1906 – although no doubt superficially changed. A plaque commemorating the town's fallen during the Great War confirms its age...

Although there was no direct successor to Burton United F.C., two different Clubs have kept senior football alive in the town. Burton Town first appeared in local Junior football around the turn of the Century, and on the demise of the United donned the crown as the town team. The 'Town', developed their own well enclosed ground – 'The Crescent', which was located just off Victoria Crescent (long since built over with factories), and no further than a long goal kick from the old Derby Turn venue of the Burton Wanderers. The Ground was completely enclosed and could boast of a small seated stand and two larger standing enclosures. The Club achieved senior status with their entry into the Birmingham League which lasted from the 1924/25 to 1932/33 seasons – becoming runners–up in 1926/27 and Champions one year later. They then moved 'up' to the Mid–land League, without gaining any major honours. In 1939 they disbanded. In the shadows of the former Clubs, the present Burton team – Albion – was formed in 1950, although an unrelated Club of the same name competed locally as early as the 1880's. They have made their way up the Non–league ladder via the Birmingham and Midland Leagues (and currently the Southern League), much like their predecessors in Burton that had worn the title of 'The Town Team.'

Peel Croft as it is today: The Grandstand that was built in 1907, still stands and is in very good condition. The 'terrace', opposite, although re-laid, probably similar during the Club's League days. (Photos: Dave Twydell 1987)

Peel Croft c. 1900 ..... Plus the location of the Ground and of Derby Turn.

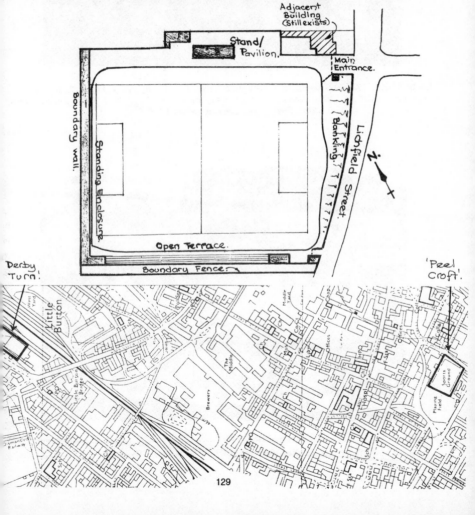

Gateshead/South Shields.

South Shields 1928/29 Season: (Back) Percy (Assist.Trainer), Hope, Sinclair, Turnbull, Shevlin, Taylor, Creighton, Grenyer, Lyllycrop (Trainer). (Middle) Matthewson, Loftus, Kennedy, Maycock, Douglas (Sec/Man.), Parker, Stevenson, Reilly, G.Scott. (Front) Davies, Littlewood, Neilson, J.Scott, Dunn.

Gateshead 1951/52 Season:
(Back) J.Callender, Wyles, Gray, Woodburn, Robinson, T.Callender (Front) Ingham, Buchan, Wilbert, Winters, Campbell.

Gateshead/South Shields.

South Shields Adelaide Athletic.
1905 – South Shields Adelaide.
Reconstituted 1909.
1910 – South Shields.
Became defunct 1930.
1930 – Gateshead. Became defunct 1973.

Football League:
South Shields   –   1919/20 to 1929/30.
Gateshead   –   1930/31 to 1959/60.

****

South Shields Adelaide:
1899/00 – 1903/04.   Shield and District League.
1904/05 –   Tyneside Junior League
1905/06 – 1906/07.   Tyneside League.
1907/08 –   Northern Alliance
1908/09 – 1909/10.   North Eastern League.

South Shields:
1910/11 – 1914/15.   North Eastern League.
1915/16 – 1916/17.   Tyneside Combination.
1917/18 –   Ceased Activities.
1918/19 –   Northern Victory League.
1919/20 – 1927/28. **Football League Div.2.**
1928/29 – 1929/30. **Football League Div.3 North.**

Gateshead:
1930/31 – 1938/39. **Football League Div.3 North.**
1939/40 –   Friendlies. *
1940/41 –   Northumberland & Durham War Lge.
1941/42 – 1944/45.   Football League North.
1945/46 –   Football Lge. Div.3 North East.
1946/47 – 1957/58. **Football League Div.3 North.**
1958/59 – 1959/60. **Football League Div.4.**
1960/61 – 1961/62.   Northern Counties League.
1962/63 – 1967/68.   North Regional League. **
1968/69 – 1969/70.   North Premier League.
1970/71 –   Wearside League.
1971/72 – 1972/73.   Midland League.

* Three Football League games were played before the competition was abandoned.
The rest of the season consisted of occasional representative matches and the Football
League Cup.
** A League, initially for Northern Football League Reserve teams, Gateshead being the
First Non-league first team entered therein.

<<<<<<<<<<<<<>>>>>>>>>>>>>

Football League Record:

	Played	W.	D.	L.	F.	A.	Pts.	Posn.

South Shields:

	Played	W.	D.	L.	F.	A.	Pts.	Posn.
1919/20.	42	15	12	15	58	48	42	9th.
1920/21.	42	17	10	15	61	46	44	8th.
1921/22.	42	17	12	13	43	38	46	6th.
1922/23.	42	15	10	17	35	44	40	13th.
1923/24.	42	17	10	15	49	50	44	9th.
1924/25.	42	12	17	13	42	38	41	9th.
1925/26.	42	18	8	16	74	65	44	9th.
1926/27.	42	11	11	20	71	96	33	19th.
1927/28.	42	7	9	26	56	111	23	22nd.

Relegated to Division 3 North.

	Played	W.	D.	L.	F.	A.	Pts.	Posn.
1928/29.	42	18	8	16	83	74	44	10th.
1929/30.	42	18	10	14	77	74	46	7th.

Club disbanded, to be replaced by:

Gateshead:

	Played	W.	D.	L.	F.	A.	Pts.	Posn.
1930/31.	42	16	13	13	71	73	45	9th.
1931/32.	40*	25	7	8	94	48	57	2nd.
1932/33.	42	19	9	14	78	67	47	7th.
1933/34.	42	12	9	21	76	110	33	19th.
1934/35.	42	13	8	21	58	96	34	19th.
1935/36.	42	13	14	15	56	76	40	14th.
1936/37.	42	11	10	21	63	98	32	21st.

Successfully re-elected

	Played	W.	D.	L.	F.	A.	Pts.	Posn.
1937/38.	42	20	11	11	84	59	51	5th
1938/39.	42	14	14	14	74	67	42	10th
1946/47.	42	16	6	20	62	72	38	14th
1947/48.	42	19	11	12	75	57	49	4th
1948/49.	42	16	13	13	69	58	45	5th
1949/50.	42	23	7	12	87	54	53	2nd
1950/51.	46	21	8	17	84	62	50	8th
1951/52.	46	21	11	14	66	49	53	5th
1952/53.	46	17	15	14	76	60	49	8th
1953/54.	46	21	13	12	74	55	55	4th
1954/55.	46	20	12	14	65	69	52	7th
1955/56.	46	17	11	18	77	84	45	13th
1956/57.	46	17	10	19	72	90	44	17th
1957/58.	46	15	15	16	68	76	45	14th.

Founder-members of 4th Division

	Played	W.	D.	L.	F.	A.	Pts.	Posn.
1958/59.	46	16	8	22	56	85	40	20th
1959/60.	46	12	9	25	58	86	33	22nd.

Failed to gain Re-election.

* Wigan Borough resigned during season, their record was expunged.

SOUTH SHIELDS.

Summary of Facts.
Grounds:
1899 – 1905: Mortimer Road, South Shields, Co.Durham
1905 – 1908: Stanhope Road
1908 – 1930: Horsley Hill Road.

Nickname:
The Laides.
Colours (Football League):
1919 – 1922. Green and Red Quartered Shirts, White Shorts
1922 – 1930. Royal Blue Shirts, White Shorts.

First League Game: 30th August 1919. Versus Fulham (Away).
Lost 0–1. Attendance 20,000.
Last League Game: 3rd May 1930. Versus Accrington Stanley (Home).
Drew 2–2. Attendance 1,500.
Record Attendance: 24,348. (Receipts £1886)
18th February 1927 versus Swansea Town (F.A.Cup). Drew 2–2.
Football League average attendances: First season 14,975. Last season 3,300.

Main Achievements:
North-Eastern League: Champions 1913/14. 1914/15. Runners-up 1912/13.
Tyneside League Champs.: 1905/06. 1906/07.
Tyneside Combination (Wartime): Champions 1915/16 (1st & 2nd Competitions).
Durham Challenge Cup Winners: 1910/11. 1913/14.

F.A.Cup: (Until 1924/25, 1st round equivalent to 3rd round, etc.)
(As Non-league Club)
1st Round: 1912/13. 1913/14. 1914/15.
(As Football League Club)
5th Round: 1925/26. 1926/27
3rd Round: 1922/23.
2nd Round: 1920/21.
1st Round: 1919/20. 1921/22. 1923/24. 1924/25.
3rd Round: 1927/28.

Number of Football League Matches Played: 462.

Best League Win: 1928/29, 10–1 v. Rotherham United. (Home)
Worst League Defeat: 1927/28, 0–6 v. Chelsea. 1928/29, 1–7 v. Stockport County.
Also 1929/30, 3–8 v. Darlington. (All Away)

International Player: W.Cresswell. (England)

Football League Players: W.Cresswell (1921) and A.Maitland (1922)

Most Football League Appearances and Goals:
J.W.Smith – 260 and 82 Goals. (1919 –1928).

GATESHEAD.

Summary of Facts.
Grounds: 1930 – 1972.   Redheugh Park, Low Team, Gateshead.
1972 – 1973.   Gateshead Youth Stadium.

Nickname: The Laides.
Colours (Football League):
1930 – 1936. Claret with Light Blue Sleeves, White Shorts
1936 – 1959. White Shirts, Black Shorts
1959 – 1960. White Shirts & Black 'V', Black Shorts.

First League Game: 30th August 1930 versus Doncaster Rovers (Home). Won 2–1.
Attendance 15,545.
Last League Game: 30th April 1960. Versus Carlisle (Away). Lost 0–4.

Record Attendance:
20,752. 25th of September 1937. Versus Lincoln City.(League). Drew 1–1.
Football League avaerage attendances: First season 5,938. Last season 3,412.

Main Achievements:

Football League Div.3 North. Runners–up 1931/32. 1949/50.

F.A.Cup:6th Round (Quarter Finals): 1952/53.
4th Round: 1948/49. 1951/52.
3rd Round: 1930/31. 1932/33. 1933/34. 1945/46. 1946/47. 1950/51. 1954/55.
(As Non–league Club)
2nd Round: 1961/62. 1962/63. 1963/64. 1965/66.
1st Round: 1960/61.

Tyne–Wear–Tees Cup Winners: 1944/45.

Division 3 North Cup Semi–finalists: 1945/46.

Number of Football League Matches Played: 1007.
(Includes 3 matches 1939/40 season).

Best League Win: 7–0. 1947/48, v. Hartlepools and 1950/51 v. Accrington Stanley.
(Both Home)
Worst League Defeat: 1–12. 1933/34 v. Barrow. (Away)

The Brothers, Jack and Tom Callender recorded the most and second highest number
of League appearances for the Club:
J. Callender – 470 (1946–1958)   T. Callender – 439 (1946– 1957).
Most Football League Goals:
R.J. Ingham – 109. (431 appearances) 1947 –1958.

The research into the historical side of football, in respect of the Gateshead and South Shields area is a veritable minefield. With five completely separate *'Gateshead's'* and four different *'South Shields"*, not to mention lesser Clubs of similar names, it is necessary to disseminate between the Clubs. This History is principally concerned with the two Clubs applicable to the Football League, but appended is a brief resume and 'Chronological Bar Chart' to prevent confusion when 'Gateshead' and 'South Shields' Football Clubs are mentioned!

Westhoe (a Southern suburb of South Shields) is acknowledged as having the first properly organised Football Club in the area, having been formed in 1875 by H.C.Green (President) and R.C.Bell (Secretary). However, as early as the 14th Century the local Courts had prohibited *"The game of Football"* – the principal reason probably being that it interfered with the practise of Archery!

By 1500, South Shields had become an important Seaport, and Shipping, in it's various forms – not surprisingly – became the main Industry in the area. By the late 18th Century the already heavily populated area was to increase even more; from 56,875 in 1881 to 78,391 ten years later and 106,598 by 1901. The Town, located as it is in the far North–East of the Country, with many 'immigrants' from Scotland, helped to produce a natural thriving centre for the new phenomena – *'Football'*. However the Seaport town was not without competition, for there were several already successful Clubs within easy travelling distances in Sunderland and Newcastle – factors which have, and still, stifle any progressive Clubs who wish to identify themselves within the area of the Tyne.

Whilst South Shields Athletic were still the local dominant force in the Sport, South Shields Adelaide Athletic were created in 1899. The new Club was the brainchild of Jack Inskip who joined the local junior Club of Adelaide Albion in 1897, but after two years decided, together with a number of friends, that there was room for another Football outfit. The team members, little more than schoolboys, joined the Shield and District League for the 1899/1900 season and the five seasons spent in this company produced many minor Cup honours. The enthusiasm of Inskip, by now the Secretary/Treasurer and Captain, encouraged a higher grade of football. An entry was made into the Tyneside Junior League for the 1904/05 season, and during the ensuing months four more Cups were added to the Club's awards.

By now the members had outgrown the local Junior Leagues – in age and ability – and a move was made to a much higher sphere, that of the Tyneside League in 1905. By now the Adelaide (they dropped the 'Athletic' at this time) had risen to become the district's principal Football Club with the demise of South Shields Athletic some three years earlier. The first season provided a limited competition with the league only consisting of eight teams, but with the quality of the Reserve teams of North Shields and Hebburn Argyle, it was a big step up the 'ladder'. By the season's end all the Club's expectations were more than fulfilled when they became the League Champions. One year later this success was repeated, by which time the competition encompassed 11 teams.

The Club by now had once again reached the peak within its limitations, and so a further upward move was made to the part professional Northern Alliance. This competition was nearly on a par with the most senior of Non-leagues, and until only a few years earlier had within it's membership the Reserves of Newcastle United and Sunderland. Even so, by 1907, with such opposition as Ashington, Blyth Spartans and Willington Athletic, the league was still one to be reckoned with. At this time the Club made a move that a few years earlier when they were little more than a schoolboy team, would have seemed inconceivable – they turned professional. However the facilities at Stanhope Road were all but non-existent, and the acquisition of an enclosed ground with spectator facilities was of paramount importance.

Their achievements of earlier years were not repeated, although a final placing of third in the League was hardly a failure. But the ambitions of the Club, headed by Inskip, led to an application and acceptance into the North-Eastern League – the most senior Non-league in this region of England.

The start of the 1908/09 season coincided with a new home venue. An undeveloped Ground in Horsley Hill Road had been used as a home venue for the local Rugby Union Club, but was now available for rental, and offered a good prospect for development. The ground was owned by the Club's main force, Inskip, a point in the Club's favour, but a fact that could also have gone against the Club just a few months later, when the Laides where to become embroiled in controversy.

The first game of the season, on September the 5th, was played at home against Huddersfield Town – the latter's first game as a professional outfit – and a good start was made to the season with a two goal victory. Despite the wet and miserable weather an excellent attendance of 3,000 (that had nearly doubled by half-time) was present. The first three games were won and the Laides did not suffer defeat until the 21st of November, in the F.A.Cup at Workington. Earlier Cup games had resulted in home wins over Wallsend before a near 5,000 gate, Mickley (a reversed venue game) and another 4,000 plus attendance, when Morpeth were crushed by 6–0.

Despite losing at Gateshead Town in a preliminary round of the Durham Senior Cup, the Laides protest regarding their opponents playing an ineligible player was upheld, and the following round produced a victory over Dipton. In the first round proper of the County Cup, a similar incident to the Gateshead match – but reversed against the Laides – occurred which was to have the most drastic repercussions on the young Club. Between times a local derby was played at North Shields before *"an enormous"* crowd of 8,000 which produced match receipts of £120. The Durham Cup incident centred around a protest made by Darlington St.Augustines following the Laides 5–2 victory in the game at Horsley Hill in December 1908. The dispute related to the attempted concealed playing of Hales – an unregistered player – instead of Irvin who had been included in the team sheet. The facts that eventually emerged, and the drastic action that was subsequently taken, went far beyond this indiscretion, when such indiscretions were quite prevalent amongst various Clubs at this time. In any event an investigation by the Durham F.A. – in almost total secrecy – resulted in the Club being referred to the highest football Authority, The Football Association. By now, the Club were enjoying unparalleled support in the area, and with none of the supporters knowing what was happening, a meeting was publicly announced for the 26th of January.

The interest shown to attend this meeting was way beyond the Durham F.A.'s expectations, and in a room designed for around 50 persons, a crowd of six to seven hundred clamoured to gain entry. It had been assumed that this was to be a Public Meeting – and in view of several earlier private, and somewhat secret, meetings between the Club's Officials and the Durham F.A., plus the lack of concealment for this one – a reasonable assumption. In the final event, and using the vast numbers of those present who clearly could not all gain access as a valid excuse, the meeting – from the public's point of view – was abandoned, and another secret session was held over for two hours. At the end of this period, the previously barred Press were informed that the Durham F.A. were ordering the complete reformation of the Football Club!

Another meeting was announced for February the 13th, and on this occasion some tangible facts emerged! It would appear that the Football Club had not in fact been a properly constituted Club, for there were no rules, and no members – in the strict definition of the word. The Club was being run by five self–elected *'members'*, i.e. a self proposed Committee. Further revelations showed that The *'Committee'* were illegally paying themselves wages – the Chairman and Vice–Chairman at 50p and the Secretary 75p etc. per week! Club meetings had been held at the Licensed Premises of the Chairman, Mr.Stoker, with the refreshments being paid for out of Club funds!

There were no records of moneys taken at the Ground's four turnstiles, the Ground was being sub–let, and no records were kept! There were no proper record books recording the income or outgoings of the Club! The statement issued was careful to point out that *"The matter was very serious and open to fraud"* (It appears that no actual accusations were made and the matter was not referred to a Court of Law). However the final outcome was that a new Club was in effect properly constituted and a properly elected Committee was formed. The previous 'Committee' was praised by the new, for the high level in the Football World that South Shields Adelaide had undoubtably reached – legally or otherwise! Just one of the old *'Committee'* remained, that of Jack Inskip – the owner of the Horsley Hill Ground!

The first game of the 'new' Club was played on the 30th of January, and an unbelievable attendance of 8,000 – a record gate – and takings of £100 for the match versus Newcastle Reserves was present. The match ended in a two goal defeat. These numbers prompted the Press statement that: *"There is room and support for a Second Division team."* But the 'new' Club's troubles were still not over, as the gate money which as agreed should have been handed directly over to the Durham F.A. in the interim – whilst the Club was in the process of reforming – was not so done; in fact an unsigned cheque was sent instead. However despite the local F.A.'s threat to suspend the Club and the Ground, when looked at reasonably it was acknowledged that, on this occasion, it was a genuine misunderstanding.

There were still worries for the Club, as it was rumoured that the Ground would be lost at the end of the season, but the owner – Jack Inskip – gave an assurance that this would not be so, despite the earlier upheavals in which he had occupied the central spot! As the season drew to a close, the Laides, with their avowed intention of progress, surprisingly signed on several new players. Because of the earlier disruptions and cup matches, the Club were forced to play many games at the season's end, but victories continued, as did the support which was averaging between 4,000 and 5,000 at home games. With a final placing in the League of runners–up it was even mooted that they should immediately apply for election into the Football League! There were 28 players signed on for the 1909/10 season, including Ford and Hall from Newcastle, Burns (ex–Sheffield Wednesday) and Howe (Hull City), and the outlook was bright. Although a surprise early exit was made from the F.A.Cup, in a replay at Willington Athletic, by Christmas the Laides held the 5th place in the League.

With average gates of 4,000, the locals objected to a rise in admission charges, but the Club claimed that the entertainment that they were providing justified the decision.

Four local Cup finals were reached, but none were won! The Durham Senior Cup final was played at Bishop Auckland, and an astounding attendance of around 10,000 (hundreds were shut out) witnessed a 2-3 defeat to Hartlepools. By the season's end, although the final placing was not as high as twelve months earlier, it had been none the less another good campaign. Some high scoring victories included the 7-1 victory at Workington and a 8-1 home win over Darlington. Despite their successes and good support, a financial loss was made on the season, although with the engagement of many professional players the Club were operating somewhat beyond their means.

A name change, when the *'Adelaide'* was dropped to become plain *'South Shields'* was made in 1910, and the first game under this banner was lost by the only goal, on September the 3rd, to North Shields before a crowd of well over 5,000. Another reverse was suffered to their near neighbours in the F.A.Cup. Although second place in the League was held at Christmas, the end of the season saw no league honours come their way, but for the first time the Durham Senior cup was captured.

During 1912, £175 was paid to Sunderland for the transfer of Arthur Bridgett, who came as Secretary/Player/Manager! It was not until May 1913 that a repeat of the earlier runners-up spot was achieved again, and this signalled a first - but unsuccessful application for Football League membership. A record attendance was set at Horsley Hill in the 1912/13 season when 12,880 were present for a F.A.Cup replay with Darlington. By now the Club had rapidly become one of the League's 'top dogs', and this was proved in the next two seasons when the Championship came their way on both occasions. At the start of 1915, the Laides were seven points and one place below the leaders Newcastle Reserves - but having played four games less. As the season progressed some outstanding victories were recorded, including; 9-2 over North Shields, 6-1 at Gateshead Town (a year earlier it had been 11-4!), 6-0 at home to Sunderland Rovers, 8-1 versus Wallsend and 12-0 over Jarrow. In one period of six league games, a phenomenal 46 goals were scored, and Thornley (who had recorded 44 successes by January the 9th) ended the season with 70 goals to his credit! The last match produced an 8-1 home victory over Carlisle, despite the 1-1 half-time scoreline, and the final record showed: 31 wins, 4 draws and 3 defeats, with a staggering goal difference of 160 to 35!

The F.A.Cup produced a new record attendance, when on January the 9th, a crowd of 14,594 (receipts of £496) were disappointed to see their favourites lose by 1-2, in the first round, to Fulham. It was the First World War starting that spoilt the party, for this era proved to be the happiest time for the Club, and a blight on the scene was the rapid fall in normal attendances. By now the Country had been at War for some time, and many of the supporters were in Europe. As the season wore on, and despite the Fulham game, the crowds dropped from the normal 5,000 to a late season 2,000 and finally 1,000 in the last game. Fortunately the finances were stable, mainly due to their F.A.Cup exploits and the share of a 10,000 gate, when – as holders – they visited Sunderland in a County Cup tie. The way was clear for a hoped for successful application and entry into the Football League, but the War was to prevent this for four years.

The opportunities for War–time Football activity was somewhat limited, and certainly frowned upon in many quarters. The 1915/16 season saw the Laides competing in a local competition devised for the special circumstances, entitled the *Tyneside Combination*, in which the Laides were the masters and became Champions for both 1st and 2nd competitions – the year being effectively split into two 'seasons' due to the limited number of competing teams. For two seasons the Club ceased activities, then this period was followed by an interim competition, the Northern Victory League. Whilst there were only nine competing Clubs, the Laides finished in 3rd place, with such opponents as Newcastle, Sunderland and Middlesbrough.

With the War over football clubs everywhere were ready for a brand new start, not least of all South Shields. With the Football League being extended to 44 Clubs, and the Laides excellent post–war performances, it came as no surprise when they were elected to fill one of the vacant places in the Second Division. During the War years their situation had enabled them to borrow many League players, now it was left to them to build a new team to suit their new status. Under Chairman William Stephenson and the other eleven Directors, plus Manager Jack Tinn – the latter to achieve fame nearly twenty years later as the Portsmouth leader – signings were made including: Chatt from Aston Villa, Mitchell the ex–Sheffield United and Luton player and Burkinshaw from Sheffield Wednesday. Local favourites included Warney Cresswell and George Keenleyside who were to prove themselves worthy of the Football League. A total of 27 Players were signed for the season.

The Horsley Hill Road Ground became the property of the Club, and extensive alterations and improvements were undertaken. Over a period of two years, a new Stand was built at the Sea end, and a total of 15,000 spectators could be accommodated under cover with an overall claimed capacity of 40,000.

The first match in the Football League was played at home with Fulham in opposition, on August the 30th.

The team that day consisted of;
Hoffman, Cresswell, Maitland, Stothard, Frith, Trayner, Higginbotham, Roe, Burkinshaw, Woods and Keenleyside.

The Laides got off to an excellent start with a two goal win, before an estimated new record attendance of 20,000. Two days later Birmingham were entertained and also beaten, this time by the only goal scored a few minutes before the final whistle, in a fast and entertaining match. The return with Fulham on September the 6th was not so successful for the visitors lost by a single goal, before around 20,000 Londoners, in a game dominated by two strong defences. After a bright start, things turned for the worse and four defeats followed; 0–4 at Birmingham by two goals, at Tottenham (before a 30,000 crowd), a three goal reverse at home, plus another four goal loss at Clapton Orient. The Club slipped down the table, and a 2–0 win in the return with Clapton was a welcome result, played before 15,000 fans.

There was a temporary 'hiccup' in the League programme whilst the affairs of Leeds City were sorted out by the Football League, resulting in this Club being thrown out of the competition for making illegal payments to players! Their last match was played at Wolverhampton on the 4th of October, and the 'Peacocks' were replaced with Port Vale who took over their fixtures. The Potteries team's first League game was played at Horsley Hill where the newcomers made an inauspicious start with a two goal reverse. After an even and goalless first half the second period came to life when Smith scored from the penalty spot, then missed after another penalty award. Smith made amends with a second goal before Hill of Port Vale also missed from the 'spot'! The attendance of 18,000 was 3,000 more than attended the next home game, for a scoreless match with Bury. After such excellent attendances, the novelty began to wane and there was a further drop to 12,000 for Nottingham Forest's visit in mid–November – but the fans were treated to a 5–2 home win.

By the New Year, the Laides held a respectable 12th position in the League, which was improved to 9th by the season's end. The leading goalscorer for the season was Jack Smith, and notable home victories included 6–0 versus Blackpool, 7–1 against Hull City and the 6–2 victory over Rotherham, whilst the two four goal away defeats were the worst reverses. The F.A.Cup campaign was cut short in the first round when the Club bowed out at Liverpool following a 1–1 home draw.

The 1920/21 season got off to an excellent start. Birmingham were first beaten at home by three unopposed goals on August the 28th, followed by a 2–1 victory at Leeds (Not the 'City' but the new 'United' – their first home Football League match), and a draw in the return at Birmingham.

The winning ways continued, and the first defeat was not recorded until October the 2nd at Rotherham, by which time they had accumulated five wins and two draws. This encouraging start did not continue, and inconsistent performances led to a disappointing, but none the less respectable, final 8th place in the League. The big Clubs were taking note of several of the players who were shining with the Laides, and Cresswell came to the fore when he was selected to play for Wales near the season's end. Despite playing attractive football and maintaining respectability in the League, the lure of Newcastle (just over the Tyne) and Sunderland (a short way down the coast) was beginning to take effect on attendances! The visits of Sheffield Wednesday and Leicester could only entice crowds of 12,000, whilst the visit of high–flying Cardiff encouraged an extra 4,000 to Horsley Hill.

A three goal home win over Portsmouth in the 1st round of the F.A.Cup, before a disappointingly low crowd of 15,510, was followed in the next round by an embarrassing 0–4 defeat on Tyneside to the mediocre Luton Town of the newly formed Third Division. A new record attendance of 21,003 was set for this match, on February the 5th, with match receipts of £1776.

A moderate start was made to the 1921/22 season, and initially the attendances held at a reasonable level – 15,000 for Hull's appearance and 14,000 when West Ham were beaten by a single goal on October the 1st. But as winter approached, and a poor run put the team in only a mid–table placing, further crowd desertions meant lower attendances, such as just 10,000 for the Bury match. Fortunately a good second half of the season led to a final position of 6th in the League. But for a somewhat indifferent home record (3 defeats and 7 draws), a serious promotion challenge would have been possible, for the team were only 10 points behind Champions Nottingham Forest. The Laides fell at the 1st round stage in the F.A.Cup at Third Division South Club, Southampton. With the financial situation in a far from healthy state, the Club were forced to part with Cresswell, to neighbours Sunderland, for the enormous (at that time) sum of £5,500.

A definite turn for the worse occurred next season, when although a similar home record was obtained, there were few victories on their travels – despite only one heavy five goal defeat at Barnsley – and seven places lower in the table resulted. The F.A.Cup results produced the best run to that date. Halifax Town were easily beaten in the 1st round proper, followed by an excellent performance at First Division Blackburn after a scoreless draw. But yet again defeat came at the hands of a Third Division team, this time to Queens Park Rangers at Park Royal by three goals. Of most concern were the attendances which were steadily dropping, and following a near £5,000 loss on the season, another home grown player was sold – Maitland to Middlesbrough.

Yet again the season started well enough in August 1923, with consecutive home wins over Blackpool, Barnsley, and Fulham, plus an away win and a draw in the return matches in Lancashire and London. But a good enough home record (just two defeats) was spoiled by a poor record on the Laides travels – including a 1–6 defeat at Derby County and 0–5 at Sheffield Wednesday – even so a slightly improved final placing in the League of 9th was accomplished. The same position in the table was obtained twelve months later, but with three points less. However, apart from a five goal thrashing again at Blackpool, and a 1–3 reverse at home to the same team on September the 1st, no games were lost by more than the odd goal. While the two seasons were satisfactory, this was not good enough for the public, and attendances continued to fall. Finances were not improved by the F.A.Cup, for on both occasions matches were lost at the first round proper stage.

In Football League matches, it was very much the same one year later, this time with a final placing of tenth, but at least in this period there had been some highlights. Notable wins occurred at Preston on Boxing Day, by four unopposed goals, and five goals were scored at home on four occasions, although Blackpool proved to be the Laides 'bogey' team by accomplishing the double over the Tynesiders yet again! It was the F.A.Cup that produced the main excitement.

An easy home victory over Non–leaguers Chilton Colliery was followed in the second round with a surprise win at Horsley Hill Road over First Division Birmingham City. The fifth round (there had been a revised numbering system) decreed a game at Bolton Wanderers, and although a 0–3 defeat was the result, the game was closer than the scoreline suggested; Bolton went on to become the winners that year.

In order to meet their commitments, £5,000 extra income was generated from the transfer of promising players. But if the Club had struggled to make ends meet, even with a moderately successful side, then the 1926/27 season proved to be not far short of disaster, and it was only the revenue generated from another good Cup run that kept them in business! In the League it proved to be the worst campaign to date with a final placing of 19th, just two positions and seven points from relegation. But the actual results produced a number of extremes. The first home game was won by five unopposed goals over Notts.County and the highest League match score of 7–1 was achieved on November the 20th when Barnsley were the visitors.

But in contrast the results on the team's travels were terrible – defeats in six games by four or more goals, including a 2–8 demolition at Darlington (who were relegated) and 1–6 losses at – ironically –Barnsley, and perhaps inevitably at Blackpool!   By the turn of the year, after the home win over Hull City – attended by the season's best attendance to that date of 10,000 – the Club were 14th in the League table.   Then the League results took a back seat as the spotlight fell on the F.A.Cup, and the Public showed that they could support the team given the right situation.

In the third round, Third Division Plymouth, were beaten 3–1, after a 1–1 half–time scoreline before a moderate crowd of 9,811.   The fourth round required a trip to Sheffield to meet the First Division Wednesday side, and following a surprise one goal lead at the break, the Laides held out to force a draw, before an attendance of 33,471.

The midweek replay was attended by a healthy 23,470 who paid £1,847, and saw their favourites triumph by the only goal of the game.   On the face of it, the fifth round tie should have been an easier tie for fellow Second Division Swansea Town were the visitors.   With their eyes on a sixth round appearance the locals poured into the Ground in unprecedented numbers. Many fans were waiting to take their places when the gates opened fully two hours before kick–off, and one hour later there was already an estimated 15,000 crowd inside.   The final official attendance was 24,348 (receipts of £1886), an all time record, and the teams came out to a rousing reception. Such was the size of the crowd that a barrier collapsed on the popular side, but fortunately the only injuries were minor.   The homesters were surprisingly soon down by two goals, but to the delight of the majority, pulled the score back to 2–2 by half–time.   South Shields dominated the second half but to no avail, and with no further goals a replay was necessary in Wales.   The Club had failed their big chance, and lost before another 24,000 attendance, by 1–2.

Typically the locals deserted the team when it came to ordinary Second Division matches; the late season home games with Fulham and Portsmouth attracted gates of only 5,000 and 4,000 respectively.   Despite the extra revenue from the Cup matches, the overall situation was still bleak with total receipts at the Gate down by £8,000 on the previous year.   Players had to be sold, which in turn incensed the dwindling number of supporters, and things looked grim!

The 1927/28 season was one long period of failure and depression for the Club and it's loyal fans.   Only 7,000 attended the first home game in August, a demoralising 1–5 defeat to Leeds.   Defeat followed defeat, and the first win was not achieved until October the 8th.

By late September attendances had plunged further – 5,000 for Preston's visit – and after seven games the bottom position in the League was reached, from which the Club never looked like vacating. Notts.County's 3–2 win at South Shields in late October produced the lowest Football League attendance to that time of less than 3,000. Whilst home games were generally close contests, the opposite applied to the away matches.

By the season's end eleven games had been lost by three or more goals, including the 0–6, 2–7 (twice) and 3–6 hammerings at Chelsea, Nottingham Forest, Preston and Swansea respectively. By the New Year with six fewer points than bottom but one Blackpool, a miracle was required – but not forthcoming – and so the Club were relegated to the Third Division North of the Football League. No less than 111 goals had been conceded in League games, and the team had finished ten points below Fulham, the other relegated team. The F.A.Cup run got no further than a good attendance at Middlesbrough, where the Laides lost by 0–3. It was now obviously going to be an uphill struggle for the Directors to ensure that the Club would survive.

Any hopes of a quick return to the Second Division soon looked unlikely as only a moderate start was made to the 1928/29 season. The first match, at Darlington, was drawn, followed by an encouraging four goal victory over Southport. An equal share of the spoils in the next few matches was to prove the norm for the remainder of the season, and the final League placing was a not so encouraging tenth. The 5–0 win at Hartlepools was balanced with the same score defeat at Lincoln, but on March the 16th the Laides recorded their best ever League victory when double figures were recorded over Rotherham (10–1).

Moderate results were not enough for the local fans however, even more so now that two Divisions separated the Laides from Newcastle and Sunderland, and the attendances continued to fall. By now the Club were in dire straits, with a £14,000 overdraft, and the idea was first mooted regarding a move of the Club to hopefully a better supported base.

The 1929/30 season was to prove the last for the Club at Horsley Hill Road and under the South Shields name – yet ironically it was quite a successful period with an end of season placing of seventh. With home gates barely covering 50% of expenditure, and as an 'away' team their share often exceeding their percentages at 'home', things had to happen. By the end of January rumours abounded of a proposed move to a Newcastle suburb. Initially the Directors were loathe to confirm or deny this, but within a few weeks they had to admit to the plan of selling the South Shields Ground – for housing – and moving the team to an area more responsive to a Football

League Club. The Newcastle Council expressed a cautious welcome towards a move to within their boundaries, while the Newcastle United Football Club were less keen; a Club that could regularly attract attendances for their Reserves in excess of that of some Second Division teams would hardly welcome the possibility of local competition!

The reality of the move was the final straw for the South Shields public, for at the Rotherham game on February the 1st – a 5–0 win – there were less than 1,200 spectators present. Within weeks it was announced that the move may be to Gateshead, just South of and on the opposite side of the Tyne, to Newcastle. This news impressed the public to the extent that there was less than 1,000 who attended the mid–February match with Wigan Borough! By mid–March it was announced that the move to Gateshead was definite, and the Town Clerk confirmed that a new Football pitch would be laid out in a suburb of this highly populated town. In view of the subsequent fortunes of the hapless Gateshead Football Club, it was perhaps an ironic prophesy, that the area of Gateshead chosen should be that known as – *'Low Team'*! The site of the future Redheugh Park was the locally named 'Clay hole'.

Goal!! The last League match for South Shields – and the last goal?

Meanwhile alternative plans were being considered for the Horsley Hill Road Ground, one suggestion being that the Ground would not be demolished but leased out intact or sold to the South Shields Corporation. The fast moving negotiations regarding Gateshead again did not impress the football public as the attendances at home games continued at between 1,000 and 1,500. A moderate annual rental at the Gateshead venue of £1,000 was confirmed, and it was hoped that the new local fans would take up some of the £6,000 share capital in the Club that was available.

On May the 3rd around 500 people turned up, but this number increased to around 1,500 after the kick–off, to witness the final game under the name of 'South Shields'. Accrington Stanley were the visitors and they set the ball rolling, but it was the Laides who scored first through Laycock after 13 minutes. By half–time the score was 2–1, following a lucky equaliser and a second home goal through Kennedy. The final result was a 2–2 draw, but the few that were present had little to enthuse over, in what was generally regarded as the worst match of the season! The last Laides lineup consisted of: *Carr, Sinclair, Turnbull, Neilson, Littlewood, Reilly, Mustard, Maycock, Kennedy, T.Charlton and Talbot.*

The last F.A.Cup match played by the Club resulted in a 2–4 home defeat before just a few hundred faithfulls in appalling weather, when Wrexham – a fellow financially struggling Club – were the visitors.

The first unofficial game by *'Gateshead'* was played on April the 30th (the formal name change, was finally approved by the Football Association on July the 9th) when 4,000 saw a Charity match played against an Eslington Park X1, and played at Eslington Park. This bold move had been given, of course, much thought, and the Directors obviously considered it a wise financial decision. Gateshead as a whole welcomed the chance of a Football League team in their midst, there was plenty of potential support, and no doubt the local Corporation relished the prestige that could accrue. However, it can now be viewed objectively many years later – was there ever any hope for the 'new' team? The South Shields Club support was poor, due to the locals preferring to travel a few miles down to Sunderland, or a similar distance to Newcastle. But Gateshead's situation was very similar, possibly even worse, with Newcastle on their doorstep and also Sunderland scarcely any further away than from South Shields. Down the ages, Tyneside fans had thrived on successful teams but would not tolerate failure; therefore promotion to, at least, the Second Division was paramount for Gateshead. South Shields had tried and failed, were there any circumstances more favourable towards Gateshead? On hindsight and in the final reality – No!

Redheugh Park was officially opened by Mr.Sutcliffe – the Football League Vice–President – and on August the 30th the first match of the season saw Doncaster Rovers as visitors. The pre–season practise game had attracted an amazing 10,000 spectators to the ground, and 15,545 fans went home delighted with the new Club's 2–1 League win over Doncaster. The Gateshead team that day consisted of:
Crowther, Sinclair, Turnbull, Neilson, Davies, Reilly, Charlton, Barkas, Maycock, Kennedy and Taylor;
Seven of the players who had played in the last match at Horsley Hill.

Gateshead's first Football League match

After a scoreless first half, the honour went to Maycock – who had also scored the last South Shields goal – to open the account for the new team, whilst Barkas scored the winner a few minutes from time. Two days later a three goal reverse resulted at Halifax, followed by an even worse defeat by 0–4 at Hull before a 6,000 crowd. New Brighton were the second visitors to Redheugh, the result being an encouraging 4–0 win. Five days later Gateshead were at home again, but only 6,000 spectators were attracted to the ground – the euphoria and novelty had already begun to wear off! A single goal defeat by Lincoln did not help matters.

A spate of draws, but only one home win, took the team up to a reasonable mid-table placing by mid-October; included in this sequence was a drawn local derby with Darlington before a 10,000 gate. On October the 25th, another home match with relatively local opposition – Carlisle United – also attracted a five figure attendance, but included an estimated 3,000 Cumbrians in the crowd, the residue of 7,000 locals was less than the Directors had hoped for. Entrance to the paddock in front of the 'spacious grandstand' was reduced to 1/6d. (7.5p), but even so an alarmingly low attendance of only 4,000 was present for the next home match, versus Southport, who witnessed a 2–3 defeat.

By Christmas the Club held an eleventh position in the League, which was improved upon by two places at the season's end. Although the home results were generally good, the away record left a lot to be desired, not least of all a last game reverse at Champions Chesterfield's Ground by 1–8! Whilst the overall record was by no means a disaster, it was hardly a success, and the alarm bells were already sounding with regard to finance.

In the F.A.Cup, the new Club's first match resulted in an eight equally shared goals thriller at Tranmere, followed by a replay victory. Folkestone were required to make the long journey to Tyneside in the next round and were narrowly overcome by 3–2 before a 6,000 attendance. However the encouragement of a large home crowd in the third round could not prevent a 2–6 defeat to Sheffield Wednesday.

Although this opening season produced nothing exceptional, the 1931/32 campaign must have exceeded the expectations of all but the most optimistic supporters of the new Club. A perfect start was made with an opening day victory at New Brighton by 3–2, followed by two home wins over Barrow and York – games in which no goals were conceded and ten were scored. A fourth consecutive victory – at Hull – on September the 12th, put the Club in the driving seat at the head of the table. Although a home reverse followed when Champions–elect Lincoln came to Redheugh (one of only two home defeats that season), the Club's consistently good form made them one of the favourites for promotion. In all there were five 4–0 home victories, and whilst the only high scoring away match was at Crewe (a 5–3 win), the season ended on a high note. By the narrowest of margins, Gateshead failed to secure the one promotion position, for although equal on points with Lincoln and with a goal difference of 94–48, Lincoln's 100–47 produced a slightly better goal average.

This exceptional performance proved to be a 'flash-in-the-pan' rather than a sign of better things to come, for the points tally of 57 was never later exceeded, and the 1932/33 season was a bitter disappointment.

Whilst a final placing of seventh was in itself quite good, the Supporters and Directors had hoped for so much better. Much of the Club's decline could be attributed to the loss of promising players for financial stability, such as one of the favourite's, McNaughton to Hull City. Although the third round of the F.A.Cup was reached, and a healthy gate produced with the visit of First Division Manchester City, even this turned sour. A very creditable 1-1 draw was obtained at Redheugh Park, and although the proceeds from the replay gate was more than welcome, the 1-9 thrashing was not!

The 1933/34 season was to be the start of a very bleak period for the Club. Fired with such enthusiasm only three years earlier, and having nearly achieved promotion in only their second campaign, the Club were now to come close to extinction. A disastrous year followed, and by the turn of the year a moderate mid-table placing was held, but by the season's end the Club had sunk to 19th place in the League. Although fourth from bottom and nine points above tail-enders Rochdale, the defence had proved to be the real problem. Goalscoring was not at fault, a total in the League of 76 was only two short of a year earlier, but the 'goals against' column was abysmal. In 42 games no fewer than 110 goals were conceded – seven more than tail-enders Rochdale! There were two surprisingly emphatic victories, by 4-0 and 6-0 at home to Halifax and New Brighton respectively, but some of the defeats were awful – 0-4 at home to Stockport, and some heavy away losses, not least of all an incredible thrashing by 1-12 at mediocre Barrow in the last match of the season.

The closing matches became a nightmare, six successive defeats were suffered, and financially it could hardly have been worse! Tranmere's visit on January the 20th attracted just 2,000 spectators, two weeks later the visit of Mansfield produced 1,500. York's appearance in mid-April saw a drop to around 1,000, and the last home game on April the 28th produced a crowd of barely 800. The situation was such that Gateshead's attendances were now less than those of the former South Shields during their final days. Although the third round of the F.A.Cup was reached, an embarrassing 1-4 loss at Non-league Workington prevented any further progress. The Cumbria Club attracted a 13,000 crowd including an estimated 500 from Tyneside. After these first four seasons, things had already become desperate; low gates, financial problems and supporters dissatisfaction with the selling of the best players – it had all been seen before, up the road at South Shields! Serious doubts were expressed regarding the Club's continued existence.

From the early days, one man in particular had involved himself with the Club, Bill Tulip. In 1930 the Club were £24,000 in debt, and as the hard times continued he was to become the mainstay of Gateshead F.C., with much of his own money being ploughed into the Club to keep it going. Whilst not being everybody's most favourite man, this extrovert – he always wore an orchid in his buttonhole at matches – was regarded as faultlessly fair, and carried his passion for the Club right up to his resignation as Secretary/Manager at aged 77, and maintained interest until he passed away nine years later, in 1961. Even the family name was synonymous with Gatehead F.C. until their final days. As well as being the Club's first President, Bill Tulip at one time held the joint post of Chairman, Secretary and Manager – and in all his twenty plus years he received no money for any of the payable posts! By the summer of 1934, the charisma and cash of Tulip was required again, for the Club announced a loss on the past season of £1,110.

Although all manner of schemes had been tried to win the fans, it was a hopeless battle – success and nothing else would suffice. Any hopes of a recovery on the pitch were soon dashed, with an opening home defeat of the 1934/35 season, by 2–4 to Chester before an encouraging attendance of over 6,000, but a three goal victory four days later at Redheugh gave cause for renewed hope. Despite an excellent 5–2 home victory over Crewe on September the 22nd, support had by now dipped to 5,000, and although at this time the Club were placed in mid–table, an eventual uplift in the Club's fortunes was not to be. With financial restraints necessary and unable to employ the desired number of players, a Reserve match in late November – a 1–5 defeat at Walker Celtic – was played with only ten Gateshead players!

Rumours at this time were rife that the legendary Chelsea star Hughie Gallacher was to sign for the Club, supreme optimism perhaps, but the move remarkably came to pass four years later.
By late October the home crowds had again dropped to around 2,000, and in November a near all time low of around 500 – admittedly in pouring rain – paid their pennies at Redheugh. The post–Christmas position saw a slump to 17th in the League and with worse to come. The season finished as it had started, a home defeat, this time by 1–4 to middle of the table Chesterfield – leaving Gateshead in 19th position again. There was not even any recompense from the F.A.Cup, with an early exit in the first round. The defeat was to neighbours Darlington, a match attended by a reasonably high crowd of 6,000.

Solvency was only sustained by the transfer of promising forwards Meek and Wesley and the situation could not have conceivably got any worse. But something of an improvement was made twelve months later when a position five places higher in the League was reached. If only the Club could have produced better away form it would have been much higher, for at home they remained unbeaten. Three particular away defeats were best forgotten; a five goal hammering at Rochdale – who finished in 20th place – the same score at Lincoln, and 1–6 at middle of the table Accrington. Yet again there was no success in the F.A.Cup.

This near middle of the table position was but a brief respite, for the 1936/37 season was to become the worst to date. The first victory did not come until the last day of October, a two goal win at Rochdale (one of only two successes on foreign soil), and the first celebratory victory at home was nearly a month later. A last match disaster at Tranmere to the tune of 1–6 sealed the team's fate and on goal average they finished one place and two points above wooden–spoonists Darlington. With only their first ever re–election application, they convinced the League that better days were ahead – which they were. Although the balance sheet showed an inevitable loss, this time of £550, there was the promise to the faithful fans that improvements to the Ground would be carried out. With the introduction and the necessary upheaval to the playing arena caused by the introduction of Greyhound Racing a few months later, this sentiment was questionable.

However there was no doubt that with greatly reduced upkeep costs, that at least on the financial side the situation should be greatly improved. At this time an ironic twist of fate became manifest. A new South Shields Club had been formed, and played at the old Horsley Hill Stadium – which by now had also been adapted for Greyhound Racing. While Gateshead could not expect more than three to four thousand fans at their run–of–the–mill home matches, the Non–leaguers were rapidly approaching and even exceeding these figures!

The Tynesiders attitude towards the local poor relations of the Football League was amply illustrated by the local football press, who despite giving plenty of coverage to the 'Big Boys' (and even the Non–leaguers), they virtually ignored poor Gateshead!

With now less pressure on the money side of the Club, things began to work well on the pitch. With the way clear to expenditure in respect of players, which included Davidson's arrival from Newcastle, Bob Keen was promoted to Trainer, and late in the season Thompson was signed from Manchester United. A new optimism was in the air, and the Club got off to a satisfactory start with four goals shared at Port Vale; this was followed by a two goal home win over Crewe, before a remarkable attendance of 9,000 and then a 3–1 success at Barrow. By the 25th of September, the Club were undefeated and riding high in the League, and the mid–October visit of Tranmere attracted no fewer than 12,000 to Redheugh.

Proof that the axiom of the locals supporting a successful Club was even more evident, when an all time record League match crowd of 20,752 were at Redheugh Park for the top of the table clash with Lincoln City – final runners–up in the table a few months earlier – to see a 1–1 draw. Steady good form led to a promotion challenging position throughout the months to come, with only one bad aberration – a 1–5 Christmas defeat at York. This was offset by two excellent victories over the hapless Barrow and Southport, by 6–0 and 5–0 respectively. A final placing of fifth was a vast improvement from a year earlier, and even the Press realised that the Club existed! Once again fame and fortune did not come the team's way in the F.A.Cup with their exit at the first round stage.

The 1938/39 season opened with news that was to gladden the hearts of the Gateshead fans; the transfer of the legendary Hughie Gallacher from Grimsby Town. Although at the twilight of his career, the charisma generated by his appearance was inevitable, and in September he found the back of the net on no fewer than five occasions in the 7–1 demolition of Tranmere Rovers. With the arrival of Gallacher, the locals were already talking of promotion as a mere formality, and as interest rose the attendances remained high.

However, after all the years of struggle, and when the Club deserved a little luck, Dame Fortune turned the other way. The absence of Gallacher through injury between October and December, saw the team's performances plummet, the position in the League drop, and the crowds at Redheugh dwindle. By the New Year promotion was a virtual impossibility, however, the return of the fans' Hero resulted in eighteen wins in the last twenty games, and a final 10th position in the table.

Just three games were played in the 1939/40 season before the War in Europe forced a halt on the proceedings. Unlike their local fellow League Clubs, Gateshead joined the Northumberland and Durham War League for the 1940/41 season, and in competition with former Non–league Clubs it came as no great surprise to see them finish as Champions. This success coupled with the chance of better gates provided the incentive to move to the League North. Wartime football took on an unnatural look, with many players 'guesting' for other Clubs; Gateshead were no exception, and included on their books six 'foreign' members, not least Billy Scott from First Division Brentford. For Gateshead the war years were to provide (crowd–wise) perhaps the best sustained period in the Club's existence. With many matches in opposition to the North–East giants, less travelling, and coupled with frequent changed and sometimes well known faces, it was a rare period of enthusiasm from the public and solvency for the Club.

Peacetime brought with it a return to normal football, starting with the 1946/47 season. The loss of the guest 'stars', was not so dramatic for Gateshead, as in the pre-war days they had begun to assemble a worthy team, and the signings made during the conflict had further enhanced their chances. Notable players were; Bill Cassidy who had signed on for the Club in 1935 (and remained until 1953), and the Callender Brothers – Jack who joined in 1942 plus Tom three years later. Over the years and into the mid-1950's the Brothers amassed between them over 900 Football League appearances for the Club, the only player to approach this number in the Club's history, being Ingham who commenced in the 1947/48 season and totalled 431 showings.

The end of the War also marked the end of competitive equality for the Club with the likes of Sunderland and Newcastle. Once again three Divisions separated the combatants, and the attendances once again emphasised the point!

The first Football League match for seven years was enacted at Redheugh Park on the 31st of August, hardly an auspicious start for a 1–2 reverse was suffered at the hands of Crewe. The hopes of the Club took a further jolt four days later when another home defeat was suffered, to Hartlepools, by the only goal of the match. As the season progressed, things improved to a degree, and apart from a five goal thrashing at home to Barrow, an unremarkable – but disappointing – term ended with the final position in the League of 14th. The third round of the F.A.Cup was reached – as was achieved a year earlier – the farewell coming with a 0–3 reverse at Manchester City.

One year later there was a vast improvement, and fourth place was achieved, although eleven points behind Champions Lincoln. With an improvement on the five home defeats, the position would have been a lot better. Three out of the four points at stake were obtained over third placed Wrexham, and excellent home victories versus Hartlepools (7-0) and Rochdale (5-0), were balanced by some poor showings against other unimpressive teams. The latter half of the season had seen a gradual rise up the League from a turn of the year mid-table position. No progress was made in the F.A.Cup, but in this department, excitement was to come in the next few years!

The 1948/49 season produced a consolidation of the Club's high placing, a one place drop and four points less, but it was almost a runaway Championship win for Hull City who finished a clear twenty points ahead of Gateshead. The real excitement was reserved for the F.A.Cup, when the fourth round was reached, and the Club entertained West Bromwich Albion.

It is likely that an all–time record attendance would have resulted from the tie, but with the recent Bolton Wanderers tragedy in mind, the F.A. had reduced the capacity of the Ground. 17,500 spectators packed into Redheugh, and although the final result was a disappointment, it was only after extra time (such periods this season being played in all first tie matches) that the Club finally succumbed to a score of 1–3.

If the 1949/50 season did not produce the excitement of a good F.A.Cup run (progress only to the second round was achieved), then this was more than compensated for by the equal best ever placing in the Third Division North. The latter years of the 1940's were without doubt the most successful – a fourth round F.A.Cup appearance and placings in the League of; 4th, 5th and now runners–up. Finishing only two points behind Doncaster Rovers, it could have been promotion had it not been for only a moderate away record of 10 wins, 2 draws, but nine defeats. Four notable home victories had been achieved; 5–0 over Accrington Stanley, 4–0 versus Chester (with a three goal win in the return), 7–1 over lowly Halifax – although the away game was lost 2–5 – and 5–1 when fellow high flyers Tranmere were the visitors. Three out of the four points were taken from Doncaster.

The next three years – despite the encouraging earlier signs – were to prove disappointing to the Gateshead supporters as far as promotion was concerned; successive positions of 8th, 5th and 8th again were the end of season placings. Initially the finances of the Club were not in the usual desperate state, and in fact the 1950/51 season actually produced a moderate profit of nearly £600. One year later the Club were back in to the all to familiar money crisis situation – lack of real success had resulted in the inevitable desertions from Redheugh – and a loss of over £800. In March 1952, the claimed lowest ever (official) attendance at a Football League match – in normal conditions – was recorded with a paltry 484 when Accrington Stanley were the visitors. Yet again the fickle public were demonstrating their apathy towards the Club, even when the team were not even struggling on the pitch!

However the period did bring in some much needed revenue following three good Cup runs. Although beaten at Sheffield United in 1951 at the third round stage, a single goal was hardly a disgrace. One year later, and the Club's record of an appearance in the 4th round was equalled. Three games were necessary before Stockport County were disposed of, followed by a 2nd round game at Redheugh with Non–league Guildford City. Despite being embarrassingly outplayed by their Surrey opponents, the locals triumphed by two goals. The third round again required three games before the decider, this time over another Third Division Club – Ipswich. The fourth round draw was awaited with excitement, and the fans hopes were realised when it was decreed that West Bromwich Albion would again travel up North. For financial reasons the tie was switched to Newcastle's, St. James Park. Despite the fanatical encouragement of 40,000 'supporters' (nearly one hundred times the number for the Accrington all time low crowd). A shock was not to be and the Club were defeated by two unopposed goals. The unparalleled eight F.A.Cup ties had produced nearly £7,000 in gate money – over one third the total received in all games – without which the financial prospects would have been very gloomy indeed!

The 1952/53 F.A.Cup campaign was to eclipse all others. Unspectacular victories over Crewe (at home) and at Bradford City led to a third consecutive appearance in the third round. Over 15,000 fans were present for the visit of struggling First Division Club, Liverpool – but few saw much of the game! With thick fog clouding the issue, the homesters ran out shock winners from a headed Winters goal.

The players in training prior to the Liverpool Cup-tie.

The fourth round tie required a journey, this time to Second Division side Hull City. Against a gale force wind, the visitors went into a surprise two goal lead before Hull reduced the arrears before half-time. To the delight of the many Gateshead fans in the 37,000 crowd their team held out and progressed on to another Cup match, the fifth round. Whilst bemoaning their luck – a long journey to Second Division promotion contenders Plymouth – the final result was ample reward. Before a crowd of 29,736, Winters' head was again all that was required to secure another notable victory.

To the joy of many thousands (!) of Gateshead supporters, the draw for the sixth round, was to bring the mighty Bolton Wanderers to Tyneside. No doubt if it had been possible, the game would have again been played at the more lucrative nearby venue of St.James Park, but with Newcastle due to play a First Division fixture at home, the Cup game was declared an all-ticket Redheugh Park affair.

17,692 fans packed into the ground – 3,000 less than the earlier record in 1937 – although over twice as many people wanted tickets – to hopefully witness an unprecedented appearance of a Third Division team in the Semi-finals of the F.A.Cup. The minnows were not to be outdone by their illustrious opponents, who were able to parade five Internationals, including the legendary Nat Lofthouse. Gateshead, however, played a quality of football far above their League standing.

The Gateshead full back clears, but Bolton scored the winner soon afterwards

The match proved to be a typical, exciting Cup tie, but was to finish as a bitter disappointment to the majority of those present. With the score at 0–0, Gateshead vigorously claimed a penalty following a 'handball' incident (the perpetrator – Bell – subsequently admitted the offence), but the Referee waved play on. To the dismay of the locals, the ball was cleared upfield, and Lofthouse scored for the visitors! The end of the run had come in such unfortunate circumstances, but had proved to be the pinnacle of excitement for the 'true' supporters of Gateshead F.C.

The F.A.Cup exploits realised over £10,000 – nearly equalling that of all the Football League matches together – but with a profit of only £260 on the season, it was clear that the Club was still balanced on a precarious tightrope. One year later saw something of a change in fortunes.

Whilst there were no wins in the F.A.Cup, a serious promotion challenge was mounted, which put the Club in a final 4th position – but a clear 14 points behind runaway Champions, Port Vale. Results had gone more or less to form, apart from a shock five goal defeat at Wooden–spoonists Chester, and three points from four from the final Champions, Port Vale; the latter having been defeated on only three occasions in the League. More encouraging were the finances, for despite virtually non–existent F.A.Cup receipts, the Gate income had increased on League games by nearly 10%, season ticket sales were up by 50%, and a welcome overall seasonal profit of £115 was realised. Gateshead were one of the early 'Floodlights Supporters', with an opening match in 1953 against Middlesbrough, but it was another three years before such games were allowed to be played in the Football League.

The 1954/55 season signalled the start of a slow downward slide that was never halted. The early season showings put the Tynesiders at the top for an all to brief period, before a succession of defeats resulted in a final League position of seventh. The campaign was also to be the last in which a third round Cup appearance was made. Chester were first brushed aside with a six goal defeat, followed by victory at Barnsley – following the six goals shared at Redheugh before a way above average 13,000 attendance. The third round tie was to prove as popular as the earlier visit of Bolton. Tottenham Hotspur of the First Division were the visitors, and an increased capacity crowd, to 18,840 (the second all–time high), saw the locals go down lamely by two unopposed goals.

The final five Football League years were full of doom and gloom, as the League record hit a regular 'low' (13th, 17th and 14th up to the end of the 1957/58 season), and attendances decreased by a greater percentage than was experienced elsewhere throughout the Football World.

The best crowd of the 1955/56 season was a meagre 6,235 for Carlisle's visit, whilst the average was only 3,135 – only the active Supporters Club donations kept the loss on the season down to manageable levels. Eventually, disharmony in the Boardroom led to the resignations of five Directors who could not live with Chairman Bill Tulip's (now eighty years old) intransigent ideas – although he was soon to hand over control to his son. A January 1957 match watched by only 1,322 summed up the public's feelings towards the Club, and at the season's end a loss of nearly £4,000 was recorded; but one year later that sum had risen by a further two thousand pounds.

The 1958/59 season gave the Club an unenviable honour, that of being Founder–members of the new Fourth Division; one point had deprived them of a place in the new nonregionalised Third – but the last two games ending in defeat had sealed their fate. Hopes of promotion were soon dashed, and defeats of 1–8 at Aldershot and 0–8 to Port Vale put the team at the bottom of the League in October. New players were regularly signed on in an attempt to halt the team's slide, but continuous wrangles from within the Club led to more bad feelings and finally resignations. By May 1959 the Club could only achieve a final, lowly 20th place, in a League that in theory was of a reduced standard than before. Attendances were now at a desperate low average of approximately 4,000.

Any hopes of a revival in the Club's fortunes for the 1959/60 season were dashed during October and November when nine defeats out of ten games left them struggling. To add to this was an immediate exit from the F.A.Cup at home to Halifax. By the turn of the year the Club were placed third from bottom in the Fourth Division, just two points more than Hartlepools and Oldham. An incredible number of sixty players were on the books – nearly half of whom were professional; four of these were later to resign. Now desperate for money and an improvement on the field, both Manager Ron Batty and Trainer/Coach Tommy Rigg were also asked to leave. By mid–April the Club's fate was known, re–election into the League would be required. Yet such was the Directors optimism, that Charlie Ferguson was appointed on a three year contract as new manager, from his former Chief Scout post at Sunderland.

As the season drew to a close two rare victories were achieved – one over Champions Walsall. But the last two games summed up the season. On April the 23rd, fellow strugglers Oldham walked off with two points from Redheugh from a two goal win that could have been more. The final match was played at Carlisle, on the 30th of April, when the Cumbrians strolled through the match, running out as 4–0 winners – all goals resulting from demoralised defensive blunders.

The season had terminated, in which no away wins had been achieved and the Club left in a third from bottom position, five points above wooden-spoonists Hartlepools.

The last – home and away – matches for Gateshead in the Football League.

Having had to apply for re-election only once before in their thirty year Football League membership, the Directors had already set about planning a revival for the Club – assuming quite logically that their League membership would be intact. Fifty local Business Directors and Managers had been persuaded to back the Club by agreeing to purchase all available season tickets for the next season. However, the Football League meeting on Saturday the 28th May was to stun the Club and their loyal band of supporters. With an average attendance through the season of only 3,412, this represented the lowest of all 92 Clubs, but with Southport making a third consecutive re-election bid – bottom in 1959 and one place higher in the last season of the North Division – this record was seen as a cushion for Gateshead. Likewise one place lower, Oldham, were also re-applying – for the second year running – whilst Hartlepools trailed five points behind the Tynesiders. Meanwhile, Peterborough's bid for League status – their 21st attempt – could hardly be denied, in view of them sweeping all before them so consistently in the Midland League.

It was only fair that one Club should be rejected, and on balance Gateshead reasonably considered that they presented the best case for support. In what was arguably the most unjust voting ever, Gateshead polled just 18 votes, whilst the next lowest was Southport with 29! It has since been argued that the Football League were unhappy with Clubs who shared facilities with Greyhound Racing – as Gateshead did – but the more convincing argument for rejection was the reluctance of most other Clubs to travel to this North–East outpost of England, which was inevitably coupled with a guaranteed poor return from gate receipts!

A forlorn attempt was made for entry into the Scottish League – Berwick Rangers who are based in England were members – but when this failed the Club settled for the Northern Counties League. With a first match attendance of only 1,368 for the three goal win over Stockton on August the 20th, it was obvious that along with the Football League, the local population had all but deserted the Club. Three days later, a somewhat ironic fixture was played at South Shields, the Club from which Gateshead had evolved; the changeover some thirty years previously had been brought about due to poor support at Shields – whereas the attendance for this game was close to 4,000! In 1961, Bill Tulip died, and although by now his connections with the Club had been severed, his love for Gateshead F.C. had not waned.

No honours came the Club's way, nor the next season, and on the disbanding of the Northern Counties League, Gateshead became the first Non–league Club to gain membership of the North Regional League for the 1962/63 season. At this time a new Team Coach was appointed, Laurie McMenemy, who was destined for football management fame in later years. Alongside the newcomer – as Assistant Trainer – stood Tom Callender the Club's former long term player.

In May 1964, a League Championship Honour came at last, but this distinction was somewhat dimmed as Gateshead's opponents were all Reserve teams of Football League Clubs. The ambitious Directors of the Club were determined to regain the team's Football League status that, in their view, had been so unjustly wrenched from them, and as an alternative, membership of the Scottish League was again sought. The English Football Association refused to support them in this quest, and the Club were left with the tiny flicker of hope that a re–organisation of the Football League may allow an influx of Non–league teams. The Club's ambitions whilst praiseworthy, were also somewhat unrealistic. As ever, they were in debt, and with Redheugh Park crumbling into disrepair, the cessation of Greyhound Racing – and consequent loss of revenue –in 1966 plus support at the gate as ever low (attendances very rarely met expenditure), it is difficult to imagine how all these adversities could be overcome with a re-entry into the Football League. A public meeting was held in 1968 to discuss the Club's future, but this received little response.

The first few years in Non-league football produced five appearances in the F.A.Cup first round proper, and even progression to the next round on four occasions. The only results of note were the two victories over Football League opposition; 3-2 at Tranmere in 1961, and a giant-killing 4-1 win at Darlington two years later.

The 1968/69 season saw the formation of the Northern Premier League, a combination designed to compete on equal terms with the accepted most senior Non-league competition, the Southern League. At the conclusion of the second season, disaster struck yet again when by finishing in the second from bottom position, the Club were forced to apply for re-election. Once again they found themselves virtually friendless, when they were voted out and their place was taken by Bradford – the latest casualty from the Football League. Gateshead had little option but to enter their first team into the less senior, and more local competition, to that of the Wearside League, where their Reserves had been performing!

It was imperative for the Club to seek an upward move if there was any chance to progress once again to the Football League, and one year later, they were accepted into the – somewhat geographically unsuitable – Midland League. This 1971/72 season also coincided with a fire at Redheugh Park which hastened the Club's transfer to the nearby International Athletics Stadium, a proposed move that had already been seriously discussed. But financially the new venue was no better, as support dropped even further.

The end of the Club's days were rapidly approaching, and their second season – 1972/73 – in the Midland was to be the last ever for the Club. At the start of 1973, the situation had become desperate, not only on the financial front but also on the pitch, with the team languishing in second from bottom in the League. In play an outstanding recovery came about from the end of January, which produced a gradual rise up the table. The top Club – Frickley – were beaten in Yorkshire and in a run of only one defeat in fifteen matches a healthy 8th place was achieved by the end of March. The third of that month produced an astonishing result, and the Club's record score in any League – despite this being their last season! Hapless Loughborough United, also on their last legs, were beaten by 13-0, and this was followed seven days later with a 5-1 victory over Retford. Better support had accompanied this revival, but it had all come to late, for by now the Club were hopelessly in debt.

The last two games played by the Club, both at home, produced a reversal of their improved form, for both were lost; 3–4 to Worksop, and on April the 28th, a 0–2 defeat to Alfreton. A desperate appeal was made for financial assistance, £7,000 minimum being needed in order to meet their commitments for the next season. The plea, as usual, fell on deaf ears, and after a few weeks the sum had not even reached £1,000. Probably the greatest snub of all was the Club's begging letters to Newcastle and Sunderland. Newcastle claimed that they had their own financial difficulties, whilst Sunderland did not even reply to the letter!

On the 13th of August the Directors met, and the next day the Secretary wrote to the Midland League and informed them that all the Gateshead fixtures should be cancelled. On August the 23rd it was announced that the Club would fight on, but it was not to be, and 'this' Gateshead rapidly slipped into liquidation and oblivion.

HORSLEY HILL ROAD AND REDHEUGH PARK GROUNDS.

1932: The Horsley Hill Road Ground. South Shields F.C. were by now no more, but the Ground remained and work was underway to turn it into a Greyhound Stadium.

When football commenced in an orderly fashion in South Shields way back in 1875, the first Club – Westoe – in common with other clubs of the time shared the facilities of the local Cricket Club for their matches. Later South Shields teams had the opportunity to play their games at the Athletic Ground, off Mowbray Road, a few hundred metres North off Horsley Hill Road. This Ground was enclosed and could boast of open stands running half the length – and each side – of the arena, together with a small enclosed area.

It was not until South Shields rose up the Football ladder and started to develop Horsley Hill Road in 1908, that a proper Football Ground was available in the shipping town. By 1915, the old Athletic Ground had been replaced by housing, and the Football Ground was little more than an enclosed pitch with an entrance in the South–west corner plus a pavilion at the East end. Large scale development work commenced, and a half pitch length open stand on the North side, plus a 50 metre long covered stand and paddock opposite, were erected. By the time that the Football League was entered a well enclosed Ground had been formed. Terraces appeared on all four sides, covering to the East end and the North side were added, and the Seated Stand was extended. By now the old Pavilion had been demolished and a large Administration block plus Dressing Rooms, etc. had arisen in the South–east corner. Several entrances were available, but only at the Horsley Hill Road side. When the Football Club moved out in 1930, the Stadium was not demolished as originally intended, but instead was converted into a Greyhound Stadium in 1932. This remained until the 1960's and became the site of a bowling alley before it's final development into a housing estate. From 1936 until 1949 the Ground was used by 'another' South Shields Football Club!

Redheugh Park 1971 – By now the end of Gateshead was near.

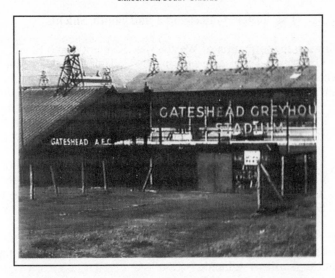

The Redheugh Park Ground (not to be confused with 'Redheugh Park' that still exists), was formerly a clay pit, and was changed into a Football Arena by the local Council at the Club's creation in 1930. Despite the situation, the Ground did not appear to suffer unreasonably from drainage problems. Redheugh was situated in a poor, badly run-down area of Gateshead, and the Football Ground provided the opportunity for the menfolk to brighten their life with the entertainment provided there – but an opportunity that was generally taken by too few.

Within a few years of it's inception the Ground offered terracing all round, with a two-thirds pitch length seated stand along the West side and covered standing extensions each side, that continued round to the North end.

With the introduction of Greyhound Racing in 1936, the playing arena was sufficiently large, to not seriously affect the football pitch width – as has restricted a number of other Football Grounds. The introduction of a large Totaliser board at the West end, coupled with a reduction in the terracing behind that goal, limited the capacity in that area. By the Autumn of 1971, after the move, but before the actual demise of 'this' Gateshead F.C., the Ground had become a derelict site; weed infested and with crumbling terracing and dilapidated structures. A year or so later the Ground was demolished. Until 1990, it was still possible to define the outlines of this once Football enclosure, but only by the grass covered humps that were once the four raised sides of the Ground. However for the Garden Festival that was held in Gateshead that year, the site was commandeered as a car park, and the 'humps' removed.

The 'other' Gateshead's and South Shields'.

(1): Following the formation of Westoe (just South of South Shields proper) in 1875, Gateshead Town emerged in 1887. This Club were not without their successes. They played at Old Ford Ground, which provided a 13,000 record attendance, and they were for a time a professional Club, principally playing in the Northern Alliance and North–East Counties League. They became a Limited Company in 1911, but following several poor years did not re–form after the first World War.

(A): The 'first' South Shields F.C. were formed around 1897, and played all or most of their time in the Northern Alliance. Their home venue was the Athletics Ground in Mowbray Road, but they folded in 1902, at the time that *'the'* South Shields were nearly ready to rise in stature.

(2): In 1919, a *'new'* Gateshead Town was created from the formerly named Close Works. Their existence lasted until 1924, during which time they played in the Northern Alliance.

(C): 1936, saw the formation of another South Shields F.C. They emulated their former namesakes and played at the Horsley Hill (now Greyhound) Stadium. A later move was made to Simonside Hall.

(4): Coincidence was extended unbelievably further when, in 1974, *'this'* South Shields reformed and moved West.... as 'Gateshead (United)'; an act of History repeating itself! Initially this Club played in the North–east Counties League, followed by the Midland, the Northern Counties, the North–east Counties again, and finally the Northern Premier. The 'Gateshead' connection had their high spots, and recorded notable performances in the F.A.Cup. Playing at the East Gateshead Stadium, they recorded a record attendance of 8,000 in their first season, but they, like their predecessors could not command sufficient support, and folded in 1977.

(D): As 'one' South Shields moved away, another arose like the Phoenix from the ashes, in 1974. The first two years were spent in the Northern Alliance, when a move was made to the Wearside League. Apparently living within their means, and playing at Jack Clark Park (in Horsley Hill Road!) they continue to date.

(5): To complete this *'Fact is stranger than Fiction'* story, the fifth Gateshead were created in 1976. Their playing record has been at a high level, with the Club fluctuating between the Northern Premier and the Alliance League. Their matches at The International Stadium can rarely attract crowds in excess of the low hundreds, but in view of the past near Century of football in the area, they can surely have no illusions regarding the fickle local support!

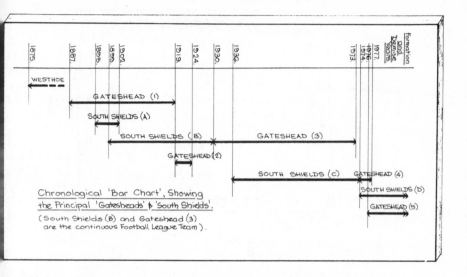

Chronological 'Bar Chart', Showing
the Principal 'Gatesheads' & 'South Shields'.
(South Shields (B) and Gateshead (3)
are the continuous Football League Team).

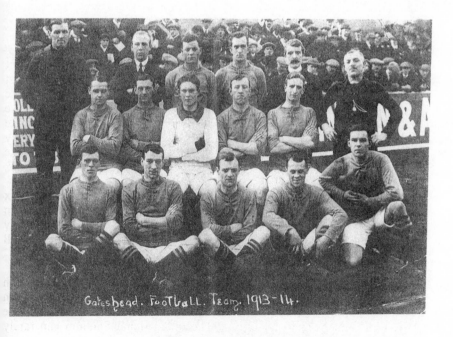

Gateshead. Football. Team. 1913-14.

An earlier Gatehead team

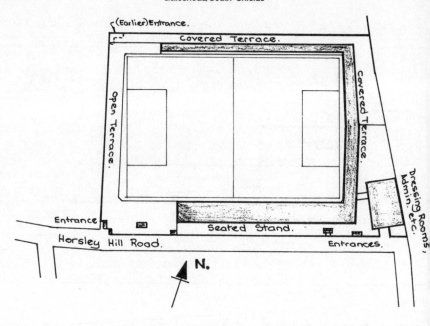

Horsley Hill Road Stadium c.1930
And its location.

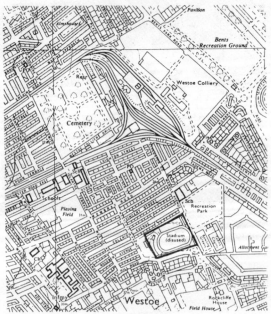

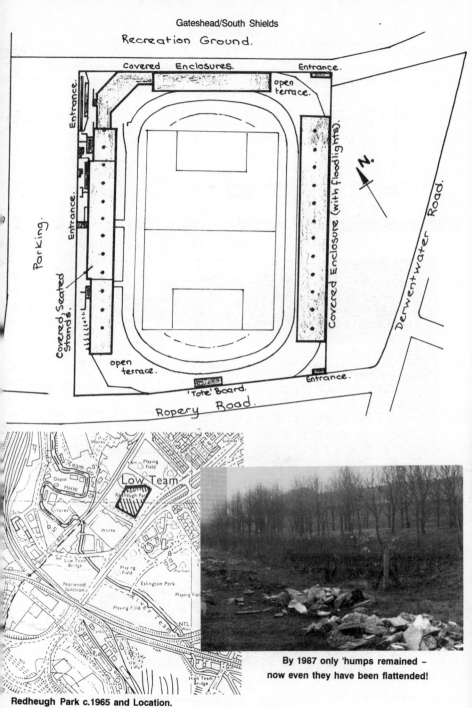

Gateshead/South Shields

Recreation Ground.

Covered   Enclosures.   Entrance.

open terrace.

Entrance.

Entrance.

Covered Enclosure (with floodlights).

N.

Parking.

Covered, Seated Stands.

open terrace.

'Tote' Board.   Entrance.

Ropery   Road.

Derwentwater Road.

Redheugh Park c.1965 and Location.

By 1987 only 'humps remained –
now even they have been flattended!

Glossop.

Back: A. Berwick, A. McFarlane, I. Dearnaley, W. Storer, F. W. G. Morgan, J. McKinley. Centre: J. B. Bowden, J. W. Sykes, A. Sergeant, J. Burleigh, D. McHardie, M. Elliott. Front: J. Hill, O. Farmer, J. W. Dow, J. Frew, R. Orr.

Glossop North End Second League Team.
The Team that gained First Division Honours, 1898-99.

(Rear): ?, Elliot, Orr, Rothwell (Capt.),Williams, J.Gallagher, Paton (Assist.Trainer)
(Middle): Cawson(Trainer), Miller, Sutcliffe,Colyn, Colville, Clifford, Killean, McEwen, Dale(Sec/Man),Oliver (Dir)
(Seated): W.Gallagher, Donaldson, Cochrane, McCosh, Lumsden.

Glossop.

Founded: 1887.
Reformed: 1919 and 1945.
Glossop North End: 1887–1899.
Changed name to Glossop–1899.
Football League:1898/99 – 1914/15.
****

1887 – 1889/90.	Friendly Matches.
1890/91 – 1893/94.	North Cheshire Junior League.
1894/95 – 1895/96.	The Combination.1896/97 –
1897/98.	Midland League.
1898/99.	**Football League Division 2.**
1899/1900.	**Football League Division 1.**
1900/01 – 1914/15.	**Football league Division 2.**
1915/16.	Lancashire Combination (Southern).
1916/17 – 1918/19.	Ceased Activities.
1919/20 –	Lancashire Combination Div.1.
1920/21 – 1938/39.	Manchester League.
1939/40.	Manchester League. *
1945/46 – 1956/57.	Manchester League.
1957/58 – 1965/66.	Lancashire Combination Div.2.
1966/67 – 1977/78.	Manchester League.
1978/79 – 1980/81.	Cheshire League Div.2.
1981/82.	Cheshire League Div.1.
1982/83 to date.	North West Counties Lge.(Div.1).

* Season not completed; disbanded until 1945.

(((((((((((((+)))))))))))))

Football League Record:

	Played	W.	D.	L.	F.	A.	Pts.	Posn.
1898/99.	34	20	6	8	76	38	46	2nd.
Promoted to First Division.								
1899/1900.	34	4	10	20	31	74	18	18th.
Relegated to Second Division.								
1900/01.	34	15	8	11	51	33	38	5th.
1901/02.	34	10	12	12	36	40	32	8th.
1902/03.	34	11	7	16	43	58	29	11th.
1903/04.	34	10	6	18	57	64	26	17th.
1904/05.	34	10	10	14	37	46	30	12th.
1905/06.	38	10	8	20	49	71	28	16th.
1906/07.	38	13	6	19	53	79	32	15th.
1907/08.	38	11	8	19	54	74	30	17th.
1908/09.	38	15	8	15	57	53	38	8th.
1909/10.	38	18	7	13	64	57	43	6th.
1910/11.	38	13	8	17	48	62	34	14th.
1911/12.	38	8	12	18	42	56	28	18th.
1912/13.	38	12	8	18	49	68	32	18th.
1913/14.	38	11	6	21	51	67	28	17th.
1914/15.	38	6	6	26	31	87	18	20th.

Failed to gain Re-election.

Glossop

Summary of Facts.
Grounds:
1887 – 1898:   (Varying periods) Cemetery Road, The 'Pyegrove', Silk Street, Hall Street
1898 – 1952. North Road. (Cricket Ground)
1952 – 1953. Vol Crepe Sports Ground.
1953 to date. Surrey Street.

Nickname: 'Donovans' or 'Peakites'. Latterly 'Hillsmen'.
Colours: To 1898:   White Shirts, Black Shorts.
1898 – 1907:   Black and White Striped Shirts, Black Shorts.
1907 – 1910:   All White. (Blue Collars and Cuffs).
1910 – 1913:   All White. (Purple Collars, Cuffs and 'V' front and back).*
1913 – 1915:   White Shirts, Purple Collars, Blue Shorts.
* First Club to register an All White Strip.
From 1919:   Various including: Black and White Stripes, Red and White Stripes, Blue and White Hoops and Royal Blue with White Trim Shirts.

First League Game: 3rd. September 1898. Versus Blackpool
(Home) Won 4–1.
Last League Game: 24th April 24th 1915. Versus Hull City
(Away).Lost 0–2. Attendance 2,000.
Record Attendance: 10,736. (Receipts £310–7–6) 31st January 1914.
Versus Preston North End.(League)
Football League average attendances: First season 2,625. Last season 1,650. (1899/00 – 4,005)   ....

Main Achievements:
Highest Football League Win – 7–0 v. Barnsley (Home), 1903/04.
Worst Football League Defeat – 0–10 v. Chesterfield (Away), 1902/03.
                                 1–11 v. Birmingham (Away), 1914/15.
International Players: T.Bartley (Wales). A.Goodall (Ireland). J. Raine (England).
F.A.Cup: 4th Round (Quarter Finals): 1908/09.
              2nd Round: 1913/14. (Modern day equivalent to 4th round)
1st or last qualifying Round:
              (Equivalent to 4th round) 1896/97. 1898/99. 1901/02. 1902/03.
              (Equivalent to 3rd round) 1900/01. 1905/06 1906/07. 1907/08. 1909/10.
                                 1910/11. 1911/12. 1912/13. 1914/15.

Football League Division 1:   1899/1900.
Football League Division 2:   Runners–up 1898/1899.
North Cheshire League: Champions and League Cup winners 1893/94.
The Combination: Runners–up 1894/95.
Midland League: Runners–up 1896/97.
Manchester League: Champions 1927/28.
Manchester Lge. Gylgryst Cup Winners: 1922/23. 1929/30. 1974/75.
Cheshire County League Div.2: Runners–up 1980/81.

Number of Football League matches played: 618.

Town with the smallest population (c.25,000) to have a Football League Division 1 Club.

172

At a period in history when Football (both Rugby and Association) was in it's infancy, and was fast being encompassed by the working classes, it is no surprise to find that Glossop, in common with other towns in the North, was the birthplace of several teams. For Glossop North End, it was an initial struggle competing with the 'other' football team, and it was some years before the Association Club triumphed for support, over the Rugby alternative. It is possible that *'Glossop North End'* was the first football Club in the area and they rapidly reached the heights of achievement to the pride of this small Derbyshire Peak District town.

The very first days of Glossop North End tend to be sketchily documented, however the origin of their formation can most likely be attributed to three local lads – T. Pearson Hunter, J. Downing and J. Kershaw who met under a tree at Willow Grove in 1886 and decided to form a football team. Kershaw, inspired by the emergence into prominence of 'Preston North End' (formed some six years earlier), and coupled with the geographical side of the town where they first met, suggested that the team should be known as 'Glossop North End', to which the other two readily agreed. The Baxter brothers were also involved in the Club's formation, their introduction to the game having been generated whilst resident in Darwen and observing at close range the rise of the sport locally and in other nearby Lancashire towns.

The Club's early games brought into prominence a number of other 'locals', namely: Messrs. Partington, Knowles, Warner, H. Hallows, Littler, Hindle, Stopford, Elliot, Garlick and William Hallows – the latter becoming the first Secretary. Matches during those far off days were restricted to 'friendlies', since the first league competition in the World, rapidly followed by other more regionalised competitions, was not to commence for another two years. The team's competitors initially consisted of other local teams – a host of 'Glossops', which included: All Saints, Reserve, Olympic, plus both Glossop South End and West End.

Although only playing as Amateurs for many years, the Club had a reserve team and ambitions, but had to wait ten years before having a properly enclosed base for home games. Matches to this time were initially played in Cemetery Road, followed by the 'Pyegrove' for a short time, then onto Silk Street. A move was made to Hall Street before returning again to Silk Street in 1891. On the 4th of September 1894 yet another move was made, this time to the 'New Pyegrove' (generously paid for by one Mr.S.H.Wood – of whom more later!). Glossop Rugby Football Club, who had an arrangement to play their games within the Town's cricket ground, eventually gave up the eventual unequal struggle with the round ball sport (despite their earlier sporting dominance in Glossop).

Upon their demise – and aided by the influence of Mr.Wood – North End were allowed in their place to play matches at North Road, which became the Club's home for many years.

The early days proved to be a hard struggle, competing in support with the well established Rugby Club, with matches at Silk Street – probably an enclosed ground with some form of spectator accommodation – requiring the expenditure of one or two (old) pence for match entry. Most of the founder–members remained with the Club, with J.H. Downing later in the role of Hon. Secretary, and despite the enthusiasm of the few, there were times when fielding a full eleven were difficult, evidenced with a minute passed at a committee meeting in May 1890:
" Any member being picked and not sending word by Thursday night to the Secretary of their inability to play, unless in a very unfit state of health, or impossible through business, will be fined sixpence. "

The Captain of the team by this time was the later member of Parliament, Mr.Oswald Partington – *" a bustling vigorous full–back with a powerful lunging kick...."*

Frequent changes in the Secretaryship were made and in a period of less than two years the position was filled by T. Nield, J. Hallsworth, E. Garlick – one of the prominent founder–members who was elected in December 1892 but died two months later – the Club Captain for a few months, and finally Mark Elliot. The latter named, another founder–member – gave sterling service to the Club over a long period.

The inaugral season of the North Cheshire Junior League for the 1890/91 season came about following a meeting n March the 29th 1890 at Hyde. Regarding the constitution of this league, Glossop received 19 votes (the second highest number) and along with the likes of Hyde Chapel, Hyde Borough, Hooley Hill Wesleyans, and Glossop Olympic, this gained them an entry into the twelve club competition.

The first match of the 1890/91 season was at home (Hall Street), a friendly fixture versus Dukinfield Onwards, and resulted in a one goal defeat – on September the 20th. One week later an exciting eight goal shared draw (despite the home team, Glossop, scoring after 20 minutes and building up a 3–1 interval lead) was played with Hatherlow in the first ever League game for the two teams. The next three matches were also drawn, including a local derby with the Olympic which was played at Sheffield Road and attended by around 1,000 spectators. The same opposition and venue, plus a similar crowd, produced a 2–4 defeat in the Glossop & District Cup in November.

A move was made back to Silk Street, and by Christmas – after seven league games – the North End lay in eighth position in the League, and finished the season in a comfortable mid–table place.

The next few years saw The Peakites rise to become the major football club in the area, and in their final season in the North Cheshire they achieved the league and league cup double. Although only lying in fifth place at Christmas, an excellent run from then on resulted in a final 4 point lead over runners up Denton Old Boys, with 15 wins, 2 draws and only 3 defeats. The last match resulted in a victory at New Mills, where a number of Glossopians were present; most of the fans walked or cycled, including one exubriant supporter who ran his bike into a brick wall and had to carry the damaged vehicle home on his back! The highlight of the season however was a home friendly match on the 23rd of April 1894, versus Football League opposition – Derby County. A record attendance of 3,000, who paid £23, saw the locals take the lead through Paton after 15 minutes and went on to win by three unopposed goals.

During this period, Mr. Samuel Hill–Wood took a keen interest in the Club, following the disbanding of his own Club, Moorfield. Initially in the team, as an outside right, he went on to become an outstnding benefactor to the Club for many years, and without doubt it was only due to his efforts and enormous cash injections over the years, that the Glossop team reached the heights of success. Professionalism was introduced, a luxury that the Club could not afford from its own resources, with the players wages being paid by Mr. Wood. Whilst it could be argued that he was a millionaire and would scarcely miss such relatively trifling sums, his interests were very much altruistic. However Mr.Wood's involvement was also for political reasons, for he had ambitions of entering parliament, and with his main opponent being another leading Glossop North End personality – the Liberal Member of Parliament and team captain Oswald Partington – what better way to win over the electorate than to lead the fast developing local Football Club.

Hill–Wood's sporting interests were not confined to Football, for he was no mean cricketer having played for and captained the Derbyshire eleven. With the adoption of professionalism, the team's benefactor ensured that prospective players were given a trial in his presence – in these days before team–selecting Managers. One notable case was that of Joe Frail the goalkeeper, in 1895 (who later moved on to Middlesbrough):

" Frail was down on his luck, a tramp, when he came into contact with S.Hill–Wood. He represented himself as a goalkeeper but had never been heard of in Lancashire or Derbyshire football circles; but Mr. Wood with his usual generosity and large heartedness, invited him up to Moorfield, his

residence, where he had a beautifully situated cricket and football ground. Whenever a new player came to Glossop for a trial, the gardeners, coachmen, gamekeepers, butlers etc., connected with Mr.Wood's establishment were called out for a game, and the aspirant for a place in the Glossop team had to undergo a private trial, the sides being formed from the professionals and the house staff. Frail was placed in goal, and gave such a marvellous display in the practise game that he was immediately signed on..."

Mr. Wood presented a new ground to the Club – The New Pyegrove (in Sheffield Road) – and the opening match saw a visit, from Sheffield, on September the 4th, 1894, and well over 1,000 spectators were entertained to a friendly 3–3 draw. This season also saw an entry into the Combination, just four years after its inauguration. This league was a big step up the ladder since Clubs such as Buxton, Northwich Victoria and Stalybridge Rovers were also members. On the 22nd of September the first league match was played at Ashton North End, with 3,000 spectators attending, including a special train containing 170 Glossop supporters on board, who returned in high spirits following the 3–2 win. Two goals were shared at Stalybridge where hundreds of Peakites swelled the crowd to create a record attendance of 5,000.

The Club entered the F.A.Cup for the first time and proceeded on a memorable run. Early rounds were won over Tonge of the Lancashire Alliance (4–0 before 2,000 spectators at The New Pyegrove), a 5–0 victory at home to Barnton Rovers, and an excellent away victory by 2–1 at Wrexham. The end came in the 4th, and final, qualifying round. Meanwhile successes were also being made in the league, and the locals were beginning to take a real interest for attendances at home had by now increased to around 2,000.

The return league match with Ashton North End produced record – to that time – gate receipts of £33. Although only 6th position (out of 11 teams) was held by Christmas, the Club stormed through the latter half of the season to finish in the runners–up spot, having scored no less than 114 goals in the total 44 matches played.

This success was repeated the following season, when third place was achieved, and having proved their worth as a senior Club outside of the Football League, they were accepted into the Midland League for the 1896/97 campaign. Twenty seven games were played that season, under the captaincy of W.Storer – the England and Derbyshire cricketer; 15 games were won, 8 lost and 4 drawn, resulting in the runners–up spot below Doncaster Rovers.

An exit was made from the Manchester Senior Cup at the first round stage, before another 5,000 attendance at Stalybridge Rovers, but better results were forthcoming with the North End's (or *'Donovans'* as they were also known) first entry into the Derbyshire Senior Cup. They reached the semi-final stage, but bowed out to Derby County Reserves at Chesterfield before 3,000 spectators.

The first round of the F.A.Cup was reached with a home draw versus Stoke. At the invitation of the Potteries Club (and a 'consideration' of £100 !) the tie was reversed since a larger crowd was anticipated at their opponents ground. Whilst the result on the 30th of January went Stoke's way – 5–2 after a 4–1 half time score – the financial considerations backfired. Due to heavy snow on the day, barely 1,000 spectators (including a few from Glossop) were present at the kick–off! Earlier, on January the 13th, Glossop had earned their first round appearance due to a final qualifying match replay. An attendance of 700 was treated to what was described as *" The most exciting football contest ever held in Glossop "*. With a few minutes remaining, and the score at 2–1 (1–0 at half time) to the home team, an opposition forward – from Fairfield – missed a sitter.... *" Pomfret positioned almost under the bar with the ball at his toes, shot several thousand yards, more or less, over the bar. "* (!)

As the season drew on, the home attendances started to rise; 2,000 in early January for the visit of Barnsley St.Peter's (a 7–1 victory), the same number in March when Ilkeston came to town, and 3,000 when the current leaders – Long Eaton – were the opponents. The latter crowd equalled the record to that date, and a similar number were present at a Christmas match – for a Reserve game! The interest that had been aroused on this occasion was due to the signing on of ex–England International, Burnup, who was expected to be tried out in the Hadfield game, but in fact did not put in an appearance.

The final game of the season was at home to the leaders Doncaster Rovers, and a record attendance was anticipated, but did not materialise due to an early kick–off. Frew gave Glossop a late goal for a final six equally shared goals result, but the frustrations of the crowd were vented at the visitors team (who only needed the one point for the Championship), and they left the pitch to booing and thrown stones.

Although the following year was not so rewarding, a none the less respectable fourth final position in the League resulted. An exit was soon made in the F.A.Cup when Glossop lost by a single goal at Aberystwyth. The locals whilst not exactly packing into the ground, were at least showing interest.

The first home game with Ilkeston had attracted 2,000 to the Ground, similar numbers being repeated in several other games. The season was memorable in that the Glossop North End centre forward – Tom Bartley – made his debut for Wales; the only occasion that a playing member of the team was ever 'capped' for his country.

An application was made, and accepted, to join the Lancashire League, but with the proposed extension of the Football League Division 2, Glossop along with Barnsley, Burslem Port Vale, and New Brighton Tower were invited to apply. To the delight of the fans and particularly Mr.Hill–Wood, they were elected. The £25 deposit made to the Lancashire League was lost due to them withdrawing from that competition – a small price to pay for such a boost to the town's sportsmen.

A number of well established players were signed on, including goalkeeper Williams and 'Punch' McEwen, both from Luton, Colvin (Liverpool), Colville (ex–Edinburgh Hibernians) and Tinto the ex–Glasgow Rangers player. Additionally a Manager was appointed, Mr.G.H.Dale. The Club's step up in status also coincided with another move to a new home Ground. Mr.Hill–Wood's efforts secured them the enclosure within the Cricket Ground in North Road; a far better equipped arena, which even boasted cover for the Press, an omission for which the Club were previously much criticised!

The 1898/99 season got off to a rousing start, a 4–1 home win over Blackpool on September the 3rd, with T.Bartley gaining the distinction of scoring the first Football League goal for the team. This match was followed by two away draws (versus Grimsby and New Brighton), and a 1–2 defeat at North Road to Newton Heath on the 1st of October. This loss was only a temporary setback, for much to the surprise and joy of their supporters, Glossop North End, victories became commonplace. By the turn of the year an encouraging 7th position was held in the League table. Despite some defeats to established Football League opponents – 0–2 at Manchester City (eventual Champions) before over 12,000 spectators, and 0–3 in mid–January – also in Manchester versus Newton Heath in front of a 10,000 crowd –the second half of the season saw a steady rise up the table, although this period was not without its 'hiccups'.

On February the 4th, the redoubtable Woolwich Arsenal made their first ever visit, but went home pointless having suffered a 2–0 defeat – the attendance though was only a very moderate 1,500. Two weeks later an excellent attendance (on Glossop standards) of some 3,000 witnessed a 1–3 defeat to current second in the table Leicester, the Peakites having also lost one week earlier at Luton.

Overall, it was a relief for the Club to get the February fixtures finished, for from then on there was no stopping the League's newcomers, and they remained undefeated to the end of the season. No less than four, five goal home wins were recorded during the season – three of them without reply. The 5–1 victory over Gainsborough on March the 4th was watched however by only a paltry 1,000 spectators or so – despite the Clubs steady climb up the table. The season finished in fine style with a four goal home victory versus Loughborough on April the 22nd.

Glossop North End had achieved the seemingly impossible, for despite the more experienced challenges from established and famous Football League Clubs, and from those with far greater support, the little town nestling between the hills was promoted – finishing second to Manchester City.

This unprecedented success was not confined to League matches, for a number of victories were recorded in the F.A.Cup. – over New Brighton, Crewe and Stockport County. This put the Peakites into the first round for only the second time in their history, and a plum home draw to Newcastle. The match proved a great attraction, and the North Road ground boasted a record attendance of approximately 7,000 who paid over £195 admission money – £70 more than the previous record. The homesters were defeated but not disgraced, bowing out to a single goal defeat.

Hill–Wood's expenditure – he was still paying the player's wages out of his own pocket – and enthusiasm, had secured for the town of Glossop a 'name' in the football world, a team that had reached the First Division and at the first attempt – a fact that is still spoken about in Glossop to this day, even amongst the non–football fraternity! The Football League team generally consisted of:

Williams, McEwen, Rothwell, Colville, Clifford and Killean plus
forwards Colvin, Gallagher, Donaldson, Price and Lumsden.

Mr. Hill–Wood again dug into his wallet and honoured each man with £25. But the National Newspapers were quick to undermine the newcomers who had reached the highest echelon in the Football League, and were quick to voice their opinions that a team such as Glossop, with poor home gates – due to the small population of the town – were unlikely to remain in such company for long. *"One of the wonders of the Football World"*, was the comment from one daily journal. The population of Glossop was in fact approximately 25,000 at this time – a lower total than some First Division teams could command at their home matches! It was clear that maintaining this new standard was going to be difficult even with the continued financial backing of Mr.Hill–Wood, the largest employer in the district and who by now was also the local Mayor.

The Club, by now, had been formed into a Limited Company with 200 shares of £5 each – significantly Hill–Wood purchased 194 of them! The choice of name of the Club had been influenced by that of the once invincible Preston North End. However, since the Glossopians had now joined the Lancashire team in the same competition, it was felt that there was no need to treat their opponents with such awe, and they dropped the 'North End' to become plain 'Glossop F.C.'.

In preparation for the hoped for increased crowds at North Road, work was undertaken during the close season to cater for same. A large embankment was formed along the railway side increasing the capacity from three to seven thousand standing spectators, and a small covered enclosure was added. The East embankment was also enlarged, whilst turnstiles were added at the entrance to the ground. Few changes to the successful team were made, although Colvin left for New Brighton and Donaldson also left, while the only newcomers were Monks from Preston North End and Evans. And so with a squad of 23 players – the Reserves playing in the Lancashire Combination – the Peakites kicked off the 1899/1900 season on the 2nd of September, a home match with Burnley. When the two teams came out on to the pitch, the 6,000 crowd gave Glossop a prolonged ovation. Just four team changes had been made from those that had received Mr.Hill–Wood's end of season bonus: Orr replacing Rothwell, and forwards Connachon, Monks and Evans in place of Colvin, Donaldson and Price.

The first half of the match was fairly even, although Gallacher gave Glossop a 15 minute lead – a disputed offside goal. A second goal was added in the last 45 minutes to give the Derbyshire team an encouraging start. Two days later the team came down to earth in no uncertain fashion when they were demolished to the tune of 0–9 after being six in arrears at half–time, at Aston Villa before an attendance of 15,000. The return at Preston was then lost by a single goal, in atrocious weather, before only 5,000 spectators. However, the second home game, before another 6,000 attendance saw their favourites easily overcome Nottingham Forest by three unopposed goals. Two games won and two lost, an encouraging if not highly dramatic start. But this was not to last, for the next three matches were all lost, including a two goal defeat at home to the mighty Sunderland, a match attended by a near record, 7,000, in which the forwards had been shuffled about to try to form a winning combination. Overall it was a disappointing start, for after seven games, the team were third from bottom in the League, having won only two games and lost seven, with an adverse goal difference of 5–17.

In the F.A.Cup, the Club were undeniably slighted. For the first time ever – and never to be repeated – Glossop (a First Division team), were required to start their campaign in a preliminary round. Manchester City, who had also been promoted, were not made to undergo this indignity. The reason given for this unprecedented situation was that when the F.A.Cup Committee had met, it had not been resolved who would be promoted with the Champions!

The draw for the F.A.Cup, decreed that Stockport would visit Glossop in the 3rd Preliminary round. Only a small crowd assembled at North Round to witness a 2-2 draw, in which the Peakites were considered lucky to survive against their lesser opponents. The replay at Green Lane was a disaster, for after going in at half-time three goals in arrears, Glossop in their frustration resorted to rough play and bowed out of the competition in disgrace.

Things went from bad to worse, and after ten League games the Club were bottom – on goal average – with three teams. Moves were made to strengthen the team with Goddard from Stockport and Davidson from North of the Border, Third Lanark. £260 was paid for the Scot, Glossop outbidding Liverpool for his transfer. The fee was a record paid by the Club, but he subsequently moved on to the Merseyside Club for £460. 17,000 spectators were present at Manchester City at the end of November, and despite their lowly position, the away team were well supported. A 1-4 defeat resulted despite a 1-1 half-time scoreline. One week later a creditable 2-2 draw was recorded at North Road versus – at that time – undefeated Sheffield United.

General dissatisfaction was expressed at the Club, and both Clifford and Colville asked for wage increases – currently they were being paid £2-15p and £2-05p per week respectively. Two days before Christmas a defeat of 2-5 was sustained at Liverpool, before a paltry 2,000 gate, and by Christmas the team were second from bottom in the League – Preston occupying the bottom slot. There was to be no dramatic recovery, and in the second period of the season just one win was recorded – over Blackburn on February the 27th – whilst away from home only three away draws were achieved to their credit, with no wins on foreign soil throughout the whole season.

The season had been a disaster, the 'experts' and foretellers of doom had been correct, Glossop were unable to compete in the First Division and were relegated having finished in bottom place in the League – nine points below their nearest rivals Burnley. One small bright spot of the past year was the discovery of the diminutive full back Herbert Burgess who was later destined for greater honours. Discovered by Club Secretary George Dale, his services were secured from Openshaw United, and engaged at the initial princely sum of five shillings (25p) per week!

The 1900/01 season was to prove the old adage prevalent in Football throughout history; good support is dependant on success. On September the 1st, the initial Second Division game was watched by a 4,000 crowd – albeit around 1,000 from the visitors Newton Heath. An exciting game was won by Glossop with a single second half goal. A good start to the campaign was made with another home victory, and an away draw at Middlesbrough, but halted when the Peakites succumbed to a one goal home defeat to Burnley, which was watched by 2,500 fans.

An interesting friendly match was played in November with the illustrious Amateurs – Corinthians – and resulted in a 1–2 defeat at Queen's Club, London, before a sub 1,000 attendance. By the end of November a mid–table position was held, and on the first day of December the F.A.Cup defeat of one year earlier was avenged. In dismal weather, and in front of a 3,500 crowd (which included over half the number from the visitors), Stockport County were thrashed by six unopposed goals. Another six goal win was achieved in March over Blackpool, but there was overall little to celebrate by the season's end, with a final fifth place in the League. As the season had progressed the support had dwindled, just 1,500 for Lincoln's visit at the end of April, and the Reserves in the Lancashire Combination, in a poor playing season, could rarely muster more than 300 enthusiasts to their games. On the pitch, the year had been marred by the broken leg of Colville.

The 1901/02 started with *'Visions of returning Glory'*, and with the opening 4 victories, two draws and only two defeats this appeared possible. But an indifferent period followed which gave rise to the statement that: *"This vision has vanished into thin air "*. By Mid–January, and following a scoreless draw with tail–enders Gainsborough, it was reported that... *" The gate was only of small dimensions, a large number having lost all heart and doings of the Club. "*

In the F.A.Cup the high flying Forest from Nottingham visited North Road, but with heavy snow the day before, the attendance produced disappointing receipts of only £65 – the lowest of the round – in comparison with the highest 'gate' of £1,643 at Non–league Tottenham! Glossop lacked skill in the match, and their enthusiasm and energy where insufficient to avoid a 1–3 defeat. By now the Glossop fans, in decreasing numbers, were allowing their frustrations to be expressed at the home matches:

> *" A certain class of visitors to North Road are making themselves a general nuisance by shouting objectionable language to the referee, or as is more often the case, inciting the players to resort to unnecessary and undesirable roughness. "*

Crowd trouble is not a new phenomena !

Following a dismal period which included the Club's worst Second Division defeat to that time of 0–5 (at Middlesbrough) a mini revival was made with two consecutive wins over Burton United and Doncaster Rovers, but no glories were forthcoming. A four goal defeat was suffered at Plumstead versus Woolwich Arsenal, two Easter draws were achieved (including that at home to Barnsley before only 2,000), although the 'double' was secured over Doncaster with a 2–1 win at the Intake Ground on the last day of March. The season finished on a low note with a single goal home defeat to lowly Burslem Port Vale, attended by only 1,500. The Reserves fared worse, finishing as wooden–spoonists in their League. The former International Johnny Goodall was entrusted with the Manager's position following the retirement of Dale.

The glory days of Glossop were never to return, and problems plagued the Club, despite the continuous financial support of Mr. Hill–Wood. Three defeats started the 1902/03 season (two at home) and on January the 17th an uncompromising thrashing of no less than 0–10 was suffered at Chesterfield. This amazing result was not characteristic of the Club however, for the goals against in this one game represented over one sixth of the total for League games that season! By now support had dwindled even further as illustrated by the 18th of October attractive visit of Woolwich Arsenal. At the kick–off there were barely 300 spectators present, and this only later increased to approximately 1,000. Little better was the 1,200 attendance on January the 3rd for Burton United's visit.

The F.A.Cup exploits showed some improvement however. Qualifying round victories were achieved before 3,000 fans at Crewe on November the 1st (Glossop's first win of the season), 4–0 over Wrexham and by five goals at a poorly attended game at North Road versus St.Helen's Recreation. The first round proper brought Stoke to Glossop, and despite the homesters scoring first, they collapsed in the last ten minutes to lose 2–3.

The final 11th placing (of 18 teams) was good compared to one year later when Glossop had to seek re–election for the first time, finishing in 17th position, just four points above bottom placed Leicester Fosse.

The most surprising aspect of this latter campaign was that whilst only two bad defeats ensued (both by five goals – at home to Manchester United and at Bristol City), some surprising home victories were achieved; 7–0 over Barnsley in February, 6–2 versus Burnley and 5–0 wins against both Leicester and Lincoln! Problems were not limited to the field of play, for two of the Club's Officials – Messrs. Oliver and Scarratt – were suspended following illegal approaches to players with other Clubs.

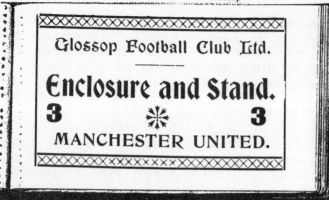

Glossop Football Club Ltd.

Enclosure and Stand.

3 ✳ 3

MANCHESTER UNITED.

Impressive opposition in the 1905/06 season. (An unused match voucher from a season ticket book).....

..... and the cover of a fixture card from this period.

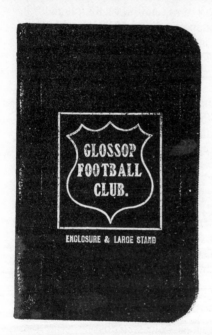

GLOSSOP FOOTBALL CLUB.

ENCLOSURE & LARGE STAND

As if this wasn't enough, and following an attempt to retain some worthy team members, in January 1904 the Club were fined £250 for paying those players, second signing on fees (No more than a single sum was allowed).

As an economy measure the Reserve Team had by now been abandoned. When all the facts are considered, it is perhaps surprising that Hill–Wood's support was to continue for another – largely unsuccessful – decade, and that the team were able to retain their League status during this period.

A moderate recovery was made and final League placings of 12th, 16th (by now in a table of twenty Clubs) and 15th followed. The 1st round proper of the F.A.Cup was reached in 1907 – the first time for four years.

The final qualifying round match was won at Newhall Swifts by 2–1, and was followed by the long trip to London to meet Southern League Brentford. On January the 11th, the Griffin Park gates were opened at 1–30 p.m., and before a final attendance of some 10,000 (£290 receipts), Glossop took the lead, but ran out final 1–2 losers.

By the turn of the year, Glossop were 4th from bottom in the League, a not unfamiliar position, when the team was strengthened when J.T.Robertson, a Scottish International, was signed from Chelsea. But the Club's poor placing hardly improved for apart from a 3–0 home win over Clapton Orient (watched by barely 1,000), several bad results followed; 0–4 at Wolverhampton, 0–5 at Manchester United, and a depressing 2–3 defeat at home to Stockport – after taking a two goal half–time lead.

Fortunately some later victories were achieved and a final place of fifteenth was the final outcome. During the season 41 players were registered with the Club, 22 having played in League games. Callaghan was an ever present, whilst top marksman was Napier with 16 goals.

Although the Club were unable to better themselves over this period, they were able to discover a number of good players. But unfortunately their stay in Derbyshire was normally shortlived, for having made the grade, for financial reasons they were transferred. Irvine Thornley to Manchester City for £600, Joe Lumsden who left for Sheffield and a £500 fee, Joe Hodkinson who commanded a £1,000 transfer to Blackburn and Jimmy Moore to Derby for £750. Players, who if they had remained at Glossop over the years, may well have provided an uplift in Glossop's fortunes.

Another season, and another bad start. After five games no victories had been recorded and the Club were bottom. Whilst attendances were rarely more than 2,000, away support occasionally boosted the crowds, particularly the local derbys with Stockport – 5,000 to see the 1–1 draw on this occasion. The Peakites maintained a lowly position throughout the 1907/08 season, and succumbed to some heavy defeats. These losses included 0–4 results at Grimsby, Stoke and Blackpool, a five goal defeat at Wolves, and 1–6 to Fulham, before some 8,000 spectators – many of whom were unable to see much of the game due to thick fog! There were however a few shock victories including 7–1 at Chesterfiled and 5–1 (after a three goal half–time lead) to second placed Hull in early November.

The F.A.Cup produced little apart from a three goals in eight minutes victory at West Stanley. The Durham side were offered £20 to reverse the venue, but in view of the eventual 5,000 plus attendance, it is unlikely that it would have been bettered at Glossop. The first round was lost to Manchester City with a 0–6 thrashing following a very creditable scoreless home draw.

In the League a slight drop over the year to 17th was the final discouraging outcome. A definite upturn in the team's fortunes occurred during the 1908/09 season, which was shown by the end of season 8th League place and the best ever run in the F.A.Cup. After several years of such indifferent results, the supporters – passionate even if they were few in number –

inevitably blamed the Directors (without fully appreciating the money that had been ploughed into the Club by Hill-Wood) and considered that they should have a say in the running of the Club. Their passions got out of hand with the two goal home defeat at the hands of Bolton on November the 28th, and matches on the North Road Ground were suspended until January following crowd violence; it was ironic that this should happen in the Club's best season for years.

In the F.A.Cup, the 1st round produced a two goal win at Chesterfield – when a special train was chartered but only 23 Glossop supporters travelled on it! This was followed with a local game at Stockport; a 'huge crowd' were present and in the crush several barriers were broken down. This time the Glossopians travelled in great numbers and various vehicles crowded the road between the two towns. Two goals were shared and the midweek replay produced a single goal home win after extra time before several thousand spectators – when it poured of rain for all 120 minutes. This took Glossop into the third round, and an encounter which was afterwards billed as 'Glossop's greatest match'.

Around 1,500 Peakites fans were present in the 30,000 plus crowd at Sheffield Wednesday to see the David and Goliath battle. In a ragged first half Stapley, a home forward, had the ball in the net only to be ruled offside, and this effort was followed by a shock Glossop goal from Greechan. An early second half penalty was awarded to the homesters but was saved by goalkeeper Butler, followed by another spot kick for handball – the resultant shot hit the bar and was cleared by the Glossop defence. In the last 15 minutes, the visitors continued to fight strongly, and held on to their lead, to produce the shock result of the day.

The 4th round on March the 6th was expected to produce a record attendance with the visit of First Division Bristol City, but with heavy snow all day the crowd only numbered some 5,000. Despite clearing the pitch and spreading tons of sand, continuous snowfalls produced an extremely heavy surface. The first 45 minutes saw a number of missed chances by the home forwards, whilst the second period put Glossop under pressure throughout with the wind behind the visitors.

It was a desperate struggle but Glossop held out and earned a replay at Ashton Gate. On the 10th of March a crowd of 15,932 (receipts of £582) including 150 from Derbyshire who had travelled the 235 miles. Glossop held out for 84 minutes despite their more skilful opponents, but the strong defence and excellent goalkeeping of Butler finally succumbed and gave Bristol a somewhat fortunate one goal win.

This best ever Cup run spurred Glossop on, and a steady improvement in League matches in the latter half of the campaign produced a healthy table placing. Even the attendances improved somewhat, typically 3,000 for Wolverhampton's visit, but almost inevitably these tailed off by the season's end. Amongst the 27 players used during the season, two were Amateur Internationals.

The 1909/10 season brought with it a new Manager – none other than the Club's benefactor Samuel Hill–Wood. No doubt wanting to ensure that his many donations were well spent, he confidently predicted the season to be one of the most successful, and this prediction proved to be correct. A first round F.A.Cup defeat was meted out by First Division Bury, but it was in the League that the success came. A good start commenced with a 3–0 victory over Barnsley, and after four games the Club were in 6th position. Sensing the possibility of a return to the First Division, 5,000 spectators were at North Road to see Burnley beaten by two goals in September. This crowd was topped with the visit of third placed Leicester and a one–nil win took Glossop into the top spot.

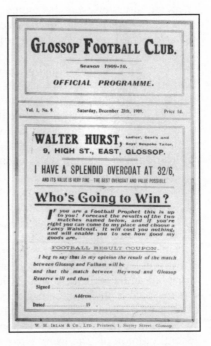

1909/10 season League programme, versus Birmingham. (December 25th).

After twelve games they were two points clear, which was increased by one point after a 2–1 home victory (4,000 crowd) over Hull. On Boxing day the best League crowd for years – 6,000 – also produced the best win of the season, a 6–2 demolition of Oldham.

By the end of the year the Club were three points clear over second placed Derby. But the impetus was not sustained and a gradual slip down the table ensued, aided by four home defeats (including 0–3 to Champions–elect Manchester City) and a 0–5 thrashing at Stockport. The bubble had burst, the crowds once again disappeared, but none the less a worthy final placing of 6th was achieved.

It seemed that at last Glossop were on the way to better things, but in fact just the opposite was the result! A plunge to 14th in the League was their lot by the end of the 1910/11 season (with three defeats on foreign soil of 0–4 and by six goals at Bradford Park Avenue) and a first round F.A.Cup exit at Middlesbrough. But worse was to follow one year later when re–election was only avoided on goal average over 19th placed Leeds City, and another 1st round Cup exit, ironically to this same team. By now the financial situation was becoming desperate, and with the Club's poor showing, attendances at North Road seldom reached 3,000, indeed on three separate occasions barely 1,000 turned up.

One year later the same final place was reached, this time though six points clear of 19th placed neighbours Stockport. Yet again an early F.A.Cup exit was made, this time by two goals at Crystal Palace of the Southern League. The 1913/14 season was one of contrasts. In League battles there was little to celebrate, in fact after the Christmas period things looked very bleak, when the Club were placed a dismal second from bottom and a re–election application was looming once again.

A worse start could hardly have been possible with four straight defeats in September (including 0–3 at home to Clapton Orient and the same score at Leeds City). The first win, at North Road on October the 4th, however did not signal better things to come. Two incredible matches were played on December the 25th and 26th. After being thrashed by six unopposed goals at Birmingham City, the return, just 24 hours later, produced a complete turnabout and a 4–1 home win. A late recovery and a final placing of 17th, was reasonable in the circumstances, and one of the few bright spots in the League programme were the matches with Lincoln City, which were won by Glossop to the tune of 4–0 at home, and 5–1 in the return. However, the general opinion of *'The worst game ever seen at North Road'* was expressed after the 1–1 draw with Stockport, but was watched by a crowd of 5,000, which included many from the County.

The late recovery on the pitch was no doubt aided by two exciting F.A.Cup matches, which also produced an all time record home attendance. The first round game, at home to First Division Everton, was confidently expected to produce a record gate, however as had happened so often in the past, the climate did not favour the Peakites and less than 5,000 were present – receipts produced £138–14. The first 30 minutes saw Glossop somewhat shaky and overawed by the opposition, and it was a true reflection of the play to see the homesters go in at half–time one goal in arrears. However the second half was a different proposition, and Glossop fought back with determination to win the game 2–1. The team went back to the changing rooms in the pavilion to tumultuous cheering at the end.

At last the Gods were in Glossop's favour for the second round game, weatherwise at any event, and with Preston as visitors, 10,736 paid £310 for the privilege. The game did not live up to expectations, and was marred by numerous free kicks – most of them against Glossop. With the wind behind them Preston were one up at the interval, having missed several other simple chances. Although having more of the play in the second period, the Peakites could not score and so the half–time result also became the final one.

Financially things were getting desperate, for not only was the Club the worst supported in the Second Division (the 7,000 crowd at wooden spoonists Nottingham Forest match serving as a good example), but support at Reserve matches was almost non–existent. While the first team were losing at Bury on March the 21st before 8,000 spectators, the Reserves were playing the same opponents' second string before 100 diehards at North Road.

The 1914/15 season was to be the last for several years, and also the last ever for Glossop in the Football League. With the news of War in the air, depression set in amongst the fans. The first home game in September drew the lowest ever League match crowd to North Road, consisting of just a few hundred. On the field things were very wrong, and after 5 games the Club lay in bottom place. An improvement for a short time – at least at home – raised the fans spirits and increased the numbers for a while. But by the time the 6th qualifying round of the Cup was played – and won – at home to Coventry, the crowds had again sunk to less than one thousand.

The next Cup match took Glossop to London, where they lost by 1–2 to Southern League Queens Park Rangers at the White City – despite through injury the Rangers being down to ten fit men in the second half. Back in the League things were looking grim, and after the Christmas Day match (watched by now a good attendance of 2,000), which was lost to Leeds City, Glossop were rooted firmly on the bottom rung of the League ladder. January the 6th was perhaps the bleakest day of all, when Glossop succumbed to one of the highest defeats of all time in the League, with a 1–11 (half-time 1–7) away demolition at Birmingham – and Glossop missed a penalty! And so it went on. By April the question was asked of whether the Club would even bother to stand for re–election, it being taken for granted that this would be required.

On April the 17th a paltry 500 were present at the last home match, versus Stockport – which mostly consisted of away supporters – and the result ended in a 1–1 draw. In the past their benefactor had pulled them round, but now things were different.

With severe disruption with regard to football imminent, Mr.Hill–Wood (by now a prominent Member of Parliament), announced that he must withdraw his financial backing as all efforts should be concentrated on the war effort. In reality the circumstances probably provided the perfect excuse for him to cease giving the enormous sums of money that he had provided over many years. No doubt, he was disenchanted with the lack of success of the Football Club, and the sure knowledge that even his wealth could not bring back success to the Club. Equally money could hardly be asked of the local populace, due to economy measures that were being endured at that time. It had by now become apparent by those that cared, that until that time, Glossop F.C., **was** Mr.Hill–Wood. At the season's end the Club announced an enormous deficit over the season of £3,000.

The last match in the Football League was enacted on April the 24th 1915 at Hull, where before a crowd of 2,000, Glossop succumbed lamely to a two goal defeat. The Club finished bottom in the League, six points below their nearest rivals, Leicester Fosse. Glossop went through the formalities of applying for re–election, but even most of their – by now few – supporters realised that it was a lost cause. The voting took place on the 19th of July at which Glossop received just one solitary vote, the lowest in the poll. In the event Football League matches did not recommence until the 1919/20 season, and the Peakites were not part of that scene.

The first season of Wartime football saw Glossop placed in the Lancashire Combination – Southern Division – and with no wages for players, it was football run on a tight shoestring – which was reflected in the virtually non–existent support. The first match was lost at Altrincham by 2–4 on September the 4th. Although results were reasonable, attendances plummeted; initially less than 100 at home matches, which dropped to 50 for the Eccles game and the ultimate low of just 20 hardy souls at the end of 1915 for the home victory over Denton. It was obviously pointless to struggle on, and so their few assets were auctioned off and the Club disbanded. At the conclusion of the War, a number of sportsmen met to discuss the reformation of Glossop F.C., and a further meeting with Hill–Wood's old political adversary, and one time player Captain Partington produced a £250 donation from him – a large and generous sum at that time – but hardly compared in size with the amounts given by the Club's previous benefactor.

Hill–Wood was destined to become a famous man, being later Knighted, and his footballing interests changed to more successful pastures, for he became the renowned Chairman of Arsenal F.C. in 1927; this Glossop born man died in London in January 1949, aged 76 years.

The reformation meeting was held on the 18th of March 1919, and was poorly attended, which once again demonstrating the apathy amongst the general public. None the less there was a determination to start again, particularly since substantial financial promises had been given. At the meeting it was resolutely stated that the new Club, would be: *" A Democratically owned and managed Club "*.

The 1919/20 season saw the, *"newly revived Glossop Club"*, albeit at a much less senior level than the former, commence their fixtures on August the 30th in the Lancashire Combination, Glossop being one of three Clubs voted in from the 29 applications! This first home match, 'home' still being the North Road Ground, produced an exciting victory over Great Harwood; two down at half-time, the locals pulled back to win 4-2, before a 'fair' crowd – but lower than that hoped for. Even a Reserve team was run, in the Lancashire and Cheshire Federation, but as ever there was little support for the seniors – 300 to 400 being the norm.

The stay in the Lancashire Combination was a brief one, for just one season, and the 1920/21 season resulted in a move to the far more regionalised Manchester League where they remained until 1939. The revised Club's first season in the Manchester Competition brought the Manchester Junior Cup to Glossop and a reference to.... *" The Club's large and ever increasing following "*, and regarding a Cup match versus new Mills, a big crowd (around 3,000).... *" Reminiscent of the Football League days "*.

But it didn't last, despite some high final placed seasons – and the Championship in 1928. The support never returned during this period, even though in the run-up to the Second World War, the runners-up place was achieved for five consecutive seasons. Matches commenced in the League for the 1939/40 season, but in common with the rest of the Country, the uncertainty and rapidly diminishing male population who were joining the armed forces, saw the crowd figures take a nosedive. Acknowledgements were given to the work of the Supporters Club by the Directors, but even the former couldn't raise attendances to more than 100 or so. With no forthcoming financial aid, the last game was played on December the 9th at North Road, when before 120 spectators – half of whom were from the visiting team – the Peakites lost 0-3 to New Mills in the Derbyshire Senior Cup. It was emphasised however that the Club were not disbanding, and the Supporters Club vowed to organise Dances, Socials etc. to wipe off the debts that had accrued.

The post war years were first spent in the Manchester League again. The first season, 1945/46, saw the team heading for the Championship with good support at the gate – including 5,000 for the Dick Kerr's Ladies Eleven versus Lancaster County Ladies, Charity match – but with the last six matches all resulting in defeats, fourth place had to suffice. New colours were introduced for the 1946/47 season, that of Blue and White Hoops, but there was no change in luck for the team on the pitch.

Although no major honours came the Club's way during the ensuing years, a step up in status was realised in 1957 when Glossop rejoined the Lancashire Combination (Division 2) where they remained for nine years before trying their luck in the Cheshire League, also in Division 2. After three seasons with this new company of approximate equal status to their former league, promotion came their way when they finished as runners–up. However the 1981/82 season was to be the last of the Cheshire League, and along with many of that league's teams, Glossop joined the North–West Counties League where they have remained to date.

Only the keen football enthusiast is aware that Glossop F.C. once graced the First Division of the Football League, however talk to any descendant of the townspeople of the year 1900, and they will proudly inform you that their team once took its place amongst the top football teams in the land!

****

THE GROUNDS.

In some respects a visit to Glossop – the town – somewhat off the main highway and presumably insular in its outlook, is like a walk back in time; many of the houses and other structures remain as they must have been during the Football League days of their Football Club – even some cobbled streets have not changed. Armed with the exact locations and a little imagination, most of the venues used by the Club, back in time some 100 years, can still be viewed to varying degrees. The grounds (in the distant past probably little more than roped off fields) can be traced at Pyegrove (which was a fenced enclosure, and at least for a period shared with the town Rugby Club), Silk Street, Norfolk Street, Cemetery road and Hall (now Manor Park) Road; even more remarkably these locations have all, at least in part, escaped the ravages of progress, and to this day football is still played thereabouts – perhaps even on the very same pitches!

But most rewarding of all is the North Road Ground which was still in use by Glossop F.C. until 1952. The Ground has been for the past 150 years the home of the Cricket Club, and this has ensured the preservation of at least some remnants of the Football Club also. Enter through the gates in North Road – possibly the self same bastions that guarded Glossop F.C. in the late 19th century. Pass the turnstile enclosures, they too have seen the passage of time for many decades.

The North Road Cricket Ground in 1987 (Photos Dave Twydell)
(Top) The entrance gates, and to the left the turnstile enclosure.
(Bottom) The pavilion, superficially changed, but the same as used at the turn of the Century.

The Pavilion was also that used by the Club, at least from the latter days of the Nineteenth century, including the Dressing Rooms that have been occupied by the teams of yesteryear. The Football Pitch remains (but in total only during the football season) and is now used by only local teams. During the heady days of the Football League, an uncovered wooden seated stand was erected behind the Cricket pitch goal – but for the duration of each football season only, for it had to be removed as Summer approached. The large, near triangular, embankment alongside North Road is however no more, but that adjacent to the railway still forms a boundary.

For one year, Glossop F.C. used the Company of Vol Crepe's Sports Ground before moving, in the 1952/53 season, to their present Ground in Surrey Street – which was purchased with the help of a legacy from W. Bramall. The official opening occurred on the 7th of October, and 2,000 attended the Manchester League match versus Ball Haye Green – a 1–0 victory. The old timber stand from North Road also made the journey, but alas was burnt down in March 1979. At the Surrey Street enclosure one final reminder of the old Glossop F.C. remains, the turnstiles, almost certainly the same as those that were installed when the Club were making their rise to fame back at North Road.

PROGRAMMES:

The situation in the early years was unusual, perhaps unique. Initially there were no programmes, however following public demand a team sheet was pinned up in a Public House en route to the North Road Ground from which the fans could obtain their information, and no doubt the Landlord increase his custom! Around 1903 however, individual team sheets were available, but not at the Ground. These could be purchased on the day of the match, from the Printers workplace only ! In the latter Football League seasons, the more conventional programme – and means of buying same – was available, but very few have survived the passage of time.

Season ticket book with match vouchers.

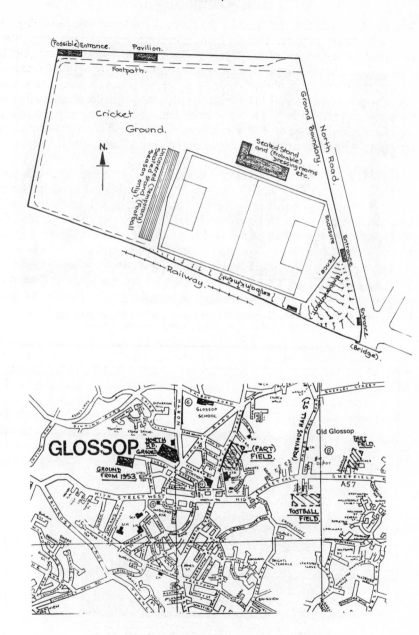

**The North Road Ground c.1900
and location.**

Loughborough.

LOUGHBOROUGH TOWN F.C. 1889:
(Back) W.Coltman, T.Vessey, G.Bosworth, W.Cockain (Umpire). (Middle) W.Cross, W.Cockain (Capt.)
T.Ashmole, W.Kellam. (Front) G.Spiby, W.Gibson, H.Griffen, A.Peters.

Loughborough F.C. 1897/98 season: (Back) H.Dunn (Sec.), Clifford, Hardy, Mumford,
Stenson(Comm.), Bailey, Mee (Trainer). (Middle) Johnson & Clarke (Comm.), Parry,
Hodgkinson, Roulstone, Elliot & Fearn (Comm.) (Front) Parker, Pegg, Culley, Pike.

Loughborough.

Founded: 1886. As Loughborough Football Club.
(Merger of 'Loughboroughs' – Athletic and Victoria)

Football League: 1895/96 – 1899/1900.

1886 – 1890.	Friendlies.
1890/91.	Midland Alliance.
1891/92 – 1894/95.	Midland League.
1895/96 – 1899/00.	**Football League Div.2.**

* First team also played in United League 1896/97 – 1897/98 *

Football League Record:

	Played	W.	D.	L.	F.	A.	Pts.	Posn
1895/96	30	9	5	16	40	67	23	12th.
1896/97	30	12	1	17	50	64	25	13th.
1897/98	30	6	2	22	24	87	14	16th.
Successfully re-elected.								
1898/99	34	6	6	22	38	92	18	17th.
Successfully re-elected.								
1899/1900	34	1	6	27	18	100	8	18th.
Failed to gain Re-election.								

Summary of Facts.
Ground: Athletic Ground, Nottingham Road.
Nickname: The Luffs.
Colours: (Football League Period)
Black and White Striped Shirts. Dark Blue Shorts.

First League Game: 7th September 1895. Versus Newcastle United (Away) Lost 0–3.
Attendance 6,000.
Last League Game: 28th April 1900. Versus Gainsborough Trinity (Home) Lost 1–2.
Record Attendance (Probable): Approx. 10,000, 7th October 1893.
Versus Leicester Fosse (Midland League) Won 1–0.
Football League average attendances: First season 2,175. Last season 1,750.

Main Achievements:
Midland League Champs: 1894/95.
F.A.Cup 1st Round: 1892/93. (equivalent to modern 4th round)

Representative Player:
George Swift, Football League versus Irish League 1895/96.

Number of Football League matches played: 158.
Best League Win: 1898/99, 10–0 v. Darwen (Home).
Also: 1896/97, 8–0 v. Woolwich Arsenal (Home).
Worst League Defeat: 1899/1900, 0–12 v. Woolwich Arsenal (Away).
Also: 1898/99, 0–9 v. Barnsley (Away).

1899/1900 season: (34 League Matches) Gained only eight points – Football League record low. Won only one match – Football League record. Scored only 18 goals total, 12 at home and 6 away – Each Football League record 'lows'. Lost all 17 away matches, of which 8 were by four clear goals or more. Despite the solitary one home win, only three of the ten home defeats were by two clear goals or more.

The former Headquarters of the Club still remains. The alleyway was the main entrance (North-west corner) to the Athletic Ground. (Photo Dave Twydell)

Poster for a reserve match in September 1894, discovered in 1958 on a wall during alterations to a building in the cattle market. (Loughborough Library)

In Leicestershire, Loughborough was the pioneer town of Association Football, and after the amalgamation of the three senior teams in the town, they were also one of the instigators of the Leicestershire Football Association. Yet for many years, the town has not had a Football Club of senior status in it's confines.   Football was originally played in Loughborough before the emergence of several recorded Clubs in 1880. The principal teams at this time were the Victoria, Olympic, Alliance, Brittanic and the Athletic. Of these five Clubs, the Athletic and the Victoria emerged as the two senior outfits, with the former playing on the Bromhead or Hubbard (each name referring to the current Landlord) Cricket Ground behind the Greyhound Hotel, whilst the latter used the Recreation Ground in Redmoor Road.

These early days were difficult ones, for the Loughborough townspeople were reluctant to support the new emerging sport, consequently few spectators were present at the friendly matches played by the two teams. In 1886 the Athletic and the Victoria decided to pool their slender resources and merged to become 'Loughborough Football Club'. In November 1887, the local Athletic Club, was purchased by the football team and the combined organisation was from then on known as the 'Loughborough Athletic and Football Club'. The combined Club now had 135 Members, all of whom were allowed to use the Gymnasium at the Corn Exchange, that had formerly been for the sole use of the Athletic Club.

On the first of December, it was announced that the Ground – at that time known as Hubbard's Ground – would be changing hands of Ownership. The Midland Brewery Company were to take out a 7 year Lease on both the Ground and the adjacent Hotel.   The Company avowed to make improvements to the field in order to make it suitable as the centre for Athletic Sports in the town.   Most references give the Club's name as 'Loughborough **Town**', however there appears to be no documentary evidence to substantiate this specific title; but with the Club now being the sole representative of senior football in the town, frequent references are made to the 'Town Club', and hence the football team being referred to as 'Loughborough Town'.

The first year of Loughborough F.C. showed little improvement in respect of spectator attendances, although with only friendly matches to watch a stimulus was needed to attract support. With the emergence of football as a major sport, County bodies were forming throughout the country to regularise the activity, and Loughborough F.C. were one of the main instigators in the formation of the Leicestershire Association; two of the Club's players, Cockain and Gadsby, being the main driving force in this venture.

It was fitting that the first Representative match under the newly formed Association was played at Loughborough's Athletic Ground, a game between the North and the South of the County, with Walter Cockain keeping goal for the former. That same day Loughborough F.C. lost by 3–5 at Grantham – without their first choice goalkeeper. The first formal match played by Loughborough F.C. was contested on September the 25th 1886, and resulted in a one–all draw with Derby County Wanderers. The Loughborough team included in their line–up:

> Walter Cockain, Will Cockain, Stubbs, Smedley, Coltman, Gadsby, Onions, Simpson and Rogers,

> With Colins being the first goalscorer for the team.

Other friendly games played in this first season included those against Loughborough Liberals (an 8–1 victory), ten goals shared at Sheepshed (note the spelling!) plus a home victory and away defeat in the first two meetings of many battles to come, with Leicester Fosse.

The 1887/88 season saw the first Leicestershire Senior Cup Competition, and in the first round the Loughborough team soundly disposed of Kegworth to the tune of 6–1, but a complaint by the loser's was upheld, and the game had to be forfeited by the Luffs; Shannon who had played in the team had previously turned out for Derby Junction that season and was ineligible. A friendly match arranged with Aston Villa Reserves aroused great interest in the town, but the spectators were dismayed when the Birmingham team turned up with only nine players! There was no great satisfaction obtained when the Luffs ran out as 8–1 victors, and a strong letter of protest was sent to their opponents to the effect that with the respected name of the Villa at stake it was considered that they should have sent a full team. The Villa agreed to send another squad for a second friendly match – this time a full eleven – and on this occasion the visitors won by 4–1, before a 1,000 crowd; a great improvement on the 300 who attended the earlier Derby County Reserves fixture. At last the game was catching on in the town, and with the Club's first professional – the Scot, McKay – signed on, the Club were determined to become a force in at least local football.

The highlight of the 1888/89 season was the winning of the County Cup Final, when Mill Hill House were defeated by 3–0 at Coalville. Earlier victories had been achieved over Leicester Wanderers by 8–2 (attendance 300), and a two goal win over Leicester Fosse before an 800, Athletics Ground crowd. The next season saw the Club and the first Leicestershire team's entry into the F.A.Cup, but this initial venture into the competition also turned sour. Following the 2–1 beating at home of Derby St. Luke's it was found that the Luffs player – Bosworth – was ineligible and the match was ordered to be replayed at Derby; the second match ended up as a 0–2 defeat. A few miles away, the other senior Club in the area (who were formed in 1884) were beginning to make their mark – Leicester Fosse the forerunner of Leicester City. The two teams played each other in the Senior Cup semi–final at Coalville in 1889. The honours this time went to the Fosse by four goals to one and they went on to win the Cup and retain it one year later. However in this competition, the Luffs once again came to the fore and captured the trophy in 1893 and 1894.

With the formation of the Football League in 1888, other regional Leagues quickly followed suit, and the formation of the shortlived Midland Alliance included the Luffs in their line–up for the 1890/91 season – the first Club from the County to be elected into a League. On September the 21st the Club's League matches got off to a poor start with a four goals, without reply, defeat at Doncaster. However, shortly after a 7–2 home victory was recorded over the Sheffield club. Attendances varied considerably at the Athletic Ground; 300 and 1,000 for the Derby Junction and Long Eaton Rangers games respectively at league matches, 800 for a Friendly with Burton Wanderers and a new record crowd of 2,500 (£23 receipts) for a friendly with the Fosse. Overall the season could be considered a success, for a final placing of third, in a League comprising of eight teams was the outcome. Sixteen points were obtained, with a goal difference of 35–23. There was also some success in the F. A. Cup, for the final qualifying round was reached when Derby Midland were beaten, following a second qualifying home victory over Burton Wanderers by 8–1.

Although the next game was scheduled to be played at Loughborough, the venue was reversed and played at Sheffield United's Brammall Lane – for monetary reasons – where the Luffs were defeated by 1–6. For the first time ever cup 'fever' had taken a hold of the town, and a Football Special train was run for the Luffs supporters. The Yorkshire team subsequently met their match in the first round proper when they were defeated at home to Football League opponents Notts. County to the tune of 1–9!

In all matches during the season, 33 games were played of which nineteen were won and five drawn – whilst 102 goals were scored with only 59 against. Perhaps more importantly the inhabitants of the town were aware that they had the makings of a successful football team in their midst, and Loughborough was entering a period when interest in the game was at it's highest.

Along with Leicester Fosse, the Luffs were accepted into the Midland League for the 1891/92 campaign – there was great competition with the Midland Alliance to attract suitable clubs and many teams interchanged between the two competitions, before the final demise of the Alliance.

The local enthusiasm could be judged by the unprecedented attendance for the home League win of 6–2 with their nearest rivals at the Athletic Ground, when a crowd of 8,000 was present; but the return at Leicester ended in defeat – a bitter pill to swallow. A notable victory was that of the 11–2 home thrashing of Doncaster Rovers. The league contained eleven teams – including: Rotherham Town, Gainsborough Trinity, Burslem Port Vale, Burton Wanderers, and Doncaster Rovers – who, along with the Fosse were all destined to eventually achieve Football League status. Lougborough's final placing in the table was eighth. Eight games were won, just one drawn and eleven lost.

There was however little progress in the F. A. Cup competition when a 0–7 defeat at Brierley Hill put paid to ambitions in this direction, although Hereford Association had been overcome by the same score at Loughborough in the previous round. Within a League of only a few Clubs, friendly games continued, and for the match versus Newark, over 1,000 fans were present.

Coupled with their new found favour in the eyes of the public, the Luffs responded with their best season to date, which saw them finish in third place in the League in 1893; just one point separated them from runners–up Burton Wanderers, whilst the Champions Rotherham Town (who were then elected to the Football League) obtained eight points more. By now thirteen teams formed the Midland League, and the Luffs had lost only six of their 24 games.

The home win, of 2–1 – versus Leicester – attracted another large attendance of 7,000, and for the return match these numbers were increased by 1,000, a game at which a programme (card) was issued, one of the earliest mentions of a match publication. More typical of the team's home support was the 2,000 attendance for the Derby Junction (who finished bottom) game, a number that was in general, by no means poor at this time. By now the Club were wholly professional, and fittingly they won through to the first round proper of the F.A.Cup for the first time. The early rounds required victories over Riddings (8–1), Heanor (3–1), Kettering (2–1) and finally a 3–0 win at Buxton – the latter match had been ordered to be replayed, following the Luffs earlier 6–0 success!

There was, however, no further progress when the home match, attended by an enthusiastic 5,000 crowd (receipts £94), was lost by the odd goal in three to Second Division Northwich Victoria. For the second time the Club were the winners of the County Cup, a success that was to be repeated one year later. Ward, the Club's long serving goalkeeper 'hung up his boots' at the season's end. Running a professional team was an expensive outlay.

During the season the total wages bill amounted to £572, and although this was virtually balanced with gate money – just £2 more received – the day to day running costs had to be paid for – rent on the ground, travel, etc. and with only £185 taken on subscriptions from members there was little money, if any, left over.

The records show a near identical repeat performance one year later – third in the League and the Senior Cup win – however somewhat galling was the Fosse's superiority as they finished as runners–up in the League, with just two points more than the Luffs. On the 7th of October the home game with their great rivals drew a (probable) all time record crowd of 10,000 to the Athletic Ground, to see the Luffs triumph once again, this time by the only goal. Revenge was sweet for the Fosse in the return for the Luffs were crushed by six goals.

By now typical home attendances were the 2,500 for the visit of Mansfield Greenhalghs (who combined with Mansfield Town at the season's end), 3,000 when Burton Wanderers came, and a Friendly match with Middlesbrough Ironopolis which also attracted 3,000 to see six goals equally shared. The F.A.Cup 4th qualifying round was reached, but the Luffs bowed out by a single goal to their near neighbours – Leicester Fosse.

Arguably the biggest shock result ever for Loughborough occurred in the Birmingham Senior Cup. The visitors to the Athletic Ground were Aston Villa, and this time they brought their full first team for the Cup match! It was a prestigious competition at this period, and the visit of the Villa – frequent winners, current Football League Champions and top of the First Division at the time – generated great excitement in the town. 6,000 noisy fans assembled for the game, and the Luffs surpassed themselves by holding their illustrious opponents to a one all draw after the full ninety minutes. Extra time was played, and after ten minutes the Loughborough right winger, Carnelly, scored the winner. Although the Cup was not eventually won by the Luffs – they lost by 1–6 to West Bromwich in the semi–final – they had already had their 'Cup Final'.

With the improved performances on the field, interest in the town reached an all time peak, for during the season a record (not subsequently exceeded) £1,005 was taken in gate money; although members subscriptions increased by 50% over the previous year, a similar additional expenditure percentage was required for the players wages. Leicester's playing records at this period coincidentally matched those of Loughborough which added to the keen competition between the two geographically close Clubs; the two were in the same League – they were bottom in 1892 (when the Luffs were eighth), fourth to their rivals third one year later, and now just one place separated the two teams. In addition the Fosse had also passed the qualifying rounds of the F.A.Cup (1893/94) just once, whilst their County Cup Final wins amounted to two compared to the Luffs three! Even the two Clubs entries into the Football League followed one another with Leicester's election in 1894 and Loughborough's one year later. Loughborough also attempted the upward move in 1894, but their application only received eight votes (Leicester obtained twenty), and so it was left for the Club to prove themselves in the Midland League – which they did in no uncertain terms.

The 1894/95 season got off with a visit to London, where Millwall Athletic were the hosts for a pre–season friendly match, which was lost by 0–2 before over 4,000 spectators. With several new signings and their great rivals in the Football League, the Luffs were tipped to win the Midland League by a comfortable margin. This prediction soon appeared likely as a string of victories ensued, including an eight goal thrashing of Newark and 6–1 victories over both Rushden Town and Doncaster Rovers. By Christmas the record showed nine wins, two draws and no defeats – and a comfortable lead in the table.

Meanwhile in the F.A.Cup, fellow leaguers Kettering were beaten by four unopposed goals at the Athletic ground, followed by a 4–1 home win over Hucknall St.John's, then a single goal thriller at Newark in which the Luffs goalkeeper – Rose – was outstanding. There then followed three matches with 'the old foe', Leicester, yet again. On December the 15th, two goals were shared at the Fosse before a 10,000 gate (£369 receipts) whilst at the replay the next Wednesday four goals were divided equally – the latter game would probably have produced a new record attendance had it not been for the game being played midweek. A few days later a second replay was held in Leicester, when, in appalling weather, the Luffs lost by 0–3.

Despite this set–back, the team's winning ways continued in the League, and after their first defeat, a run of 10 victories plus two drawn games followed. The victories included that at Gainsborough Trinity, despite the Loughborough team playing throughout the match with only eight players as the rest missed the Gainsborough train! 9–0 and 7–1 beatings were dished out to Chesterfield and Rushden respectively, whilst the home victory over Ilkeston in March drew a healthy 3,500 attendance. The Championship was assured with only two games remaining, and surprisingly these were both lost.

The final record placed the team seven points clear of runners–up Stoke Swifts with a goal difference of 84–25. An interesting second visit was made to London in January, when at Caledonian Park, Holloway, London Caledonians were held to a 1–1 draw.

A total of 47 matches were played throughout the season, and Edge missed only one (he was also the top, all matches goal–scorer with 29), whilst Berry was present for 45 games.

In April a meeting was held in the pavilion at the Ground to decide the financial position and the Club's future. Democratically it was decided that the views of the members should be heard and not just those of the Committee. However, it was announced that before taking the bold step and applying for Football League status – for which election was very likely in the circumstances – a number of salient points should be recognised. Although regional, in League games alone the team had travelled 2,075 miles, this would increase if admitted to the Football League and £50 extra would be expended in extra travelling costs; despite the Championship win, both gate money and subscriptions were slightly down on the season, yet wages had leapt to £920 – this added up to a loss on the year of £258; even so very reasonable home gates that averaged just under 2,000 (£32) – Reserve matches attracted less than 500 – but these numbers could be considered acceptable in the higher sphere with proposed increases in entrance money to home games from 4d.to 6d. (2.5p) and season tickets doubled to 50p. Therefore before taking a decision, these facts had to be seriously considered, but the meeting voted unanimously to apply for Football League status again.

In preparation of their hoped for elevation, improvements at the Athletic ground included the fencing in of the same at a cost of £30. Over the years, the Luffs were not surprisingly aggrieved with the loss of promising players to Football League Clubs from which they received no compensation. This led to Loughborough repeating the exercise in reverse, notably with Wolverhampton Wanderers. This of course in turn upset the Wolves and in retaliation they had sent 'spies' to watch the Luffs and decided to make approaches towards both Edge and Owen. The feud between the two Clubs was resolved when Edge was eventually transferred, on the somewhat unethical condition that the Wolves would wholeheartedly support the Non–leaguers application to join the Football League! In late May 1895, Loughborough F.C. were elected to the Second Division of the Football League in place of the relegated Walsall Town Swifts. With this elevation in status, the Club advertised for a Trainer, for which there were 200 applications! Richard Prince the ex–Preston North End player was appointed. By the time of the Club's Football League debut they had signed 17 Professional players. On September the 9th, the first Football League match was played, at St. James Park, Newcastle where the Luffs were represented by:

Monteith, Swift, Berry, Rose, Middleton, Hamilton, A.Ward,
Clarke, Cotterill, W.Ward and Bull.

The match, before 6,000 spectators, started well for the visitors, but Newcastle soon took over a commanding role. With only a few Loughborough attacks, the homester's defence easily coped, and by half–time Newcastle had taken a two goal lead. As the game wore on it became apparent that overall the Luffs were outclassed, and they did well to only concede one more goal – almost with the last kick of the game.

The Club and it's supporters were not downhearted over this poor start, and seven days later at the Athletic Ground a crowd of over 2,000 assembled in brilliant sunshine to witness the same line–up home debut in the League, with Newton Heath in opposition. Amidst tremendous cheers, W.Ward scored for the newcomers after only eight minutes and nearly added a second immediately after the resultant re–start. Loughborough continued to have the better of the encounter up to half–time by which time Clarke had added another goal. The second half was a different story for the Luffs were under far more pressure, and the final result of the encounter was a satisfactory 3–3 draw. At least the entertainment value had been proved for the next home game, on the 23rd of September, showed a £10 increase in the gate receipts, to £60 (approximately 2,500) when Liverpool were the visitors; the result was a disappointing 2–4 defeat.

On the following Tuesday, a visit was made to Burton when the Swifts entertained the Luffs before a 'large gate' and the visitors achieved their first win by 2–1. The match that all of Leicestershire was waiting for occurred the next Saturday when old foes in the shape of Leicester Fosse played host to Loughborough. An attendance of 7,000 was present for the local derby which turned out to be a disaster for the Luffs when after trailing by two goals at half–time the final tally was 0–5. The commencement of the F.A.Cup trail brought Nottingham League club, Bulwell United to Leicestershire, and although the home team ran out easy 5–2 winners, only a small crowd was in attendance. Although the second qualifying round was won, the next Cup match resulted in an embarrassing 1–2 defeat at Non–league Kettering.

November the 16th saw the return League match with the Fosse, and a 'great crowd' – which included the Mayor – witnessed a one–sided game when the visitors ended up as 4–1 winners, after leading by three clear goals at the break. Leicester City rubbed 'salt into the wound' when they were also the victors in the Leicestershire Senior Cup Final at Coalville with a win by four unopposed goals.

Whilst League results were generally going against the team, they had a boost when it was announced on the 12th of December that a project was underway – a private venture – to provide a new Ground for the Club; the intention was to build stands – accommodation for spectators was poor at the Athletic Ground – with free use to the Club for the first year. Despite the high hopes the scheme never materialised!

With only two wins, two draws and eight defeats by Christmas, the Luffs were placed third from bottom in the League table. The six goal defeat at Woolwich Arsenal – attended by only 4,000 due to the nearby Rugby International at Blackheath – made things even worse. In mid–January the local newspaper stated that:

> " Football is at a low ebb in Loughborough this week as far as the Town Club is concerned; indeed it almost seems as though the Town does not possess a Club at all of any importance. "

How things had changed in just one year!

Results for the second half of the season continued in an overall poor, but eventually improved, vein, although the situation remained grim before it got better. To add to their problems, cash flow became difficult, since for the period January to March only four home League games were played, although at least these brought in six valuable points, including the 2–1 victory over the Arsenal on February the 29th.

Two games were played in the Birmingham Senior Cup competition during January, bringing with them mixed fortunes. Long Eaton were first defeated with a single goal at the Athletic Ground – before a healthy 2,500 crowd – followed by defeat at Burton Wanderers, where only 800 spectators were present at Derby Turn.

If Loughborough F.C. thought they had troubles, then pity the financial fortunes of Darwen; for the match against the Luffs on February the 22nd, the condition of the pitch was so poor that an alternative one had to be set out within the Barley Bank Cricket Ground – and only 300 fans were present to witness a two goals shared draw. The return match was a very welcome 4–1 victory for the homesters, although the first goal had reputedly gone round the outside rather than the inside of the post! A crushing 5–1 defeat was experienced at Manchester City before 2,000 spectators and after 24 games the Luffs were rooted in bottom but one position in the League.

A rare away win was achieved on April the 3rd, when the hapless Crewe (destined for the wooden spoon) were beaten 2–1 at their ground in Sandbach, the victory aided no doubt by the illness of the opponents goalkeeper who was replaced at short notice by the Crewe trainer! Previously the home game saw a crowd of 2,000 at the Athletic Ground. The final run–in to the season was a big improvement over the preceding months to such an effect that the final position in the League was twelfth of sixteen.

During the season, Loughborough gained the distinction of providing a player in a Senior Representative game – George Swift – who played for the Football League versus their Irish counterparts. With nine victories and sixteen defeats in the 30 League matches things were not, at the final count, too bad on the pitch, but a different story was told on the financial front. Although the entrance moneys had increased, spectator support fell and a loss on the season of £250 was announced at a meeting on the 8th of May. Whilst the income at the gate showed a marginal rise to £970, the players wages had leapt to over £1,250, about a 30% increase, over a year earlier. A proposed Midland Counties Athletic meeting at the Ground at which it was hoped to raise £300 had to be abandoned when it became likely that a loss on the event was probable!

A meeting was called, to decide on the Club's future. Their first season in the Football League had been a great disappointment and those at the meeting were asked whether the Club should stay in the Second Division, revert to the Midland or even run only an Amateur team! Points to take into account was the running costs of the Club, now at £36 per week – £6 more than a year earlier – with the additional expenses of Agents fees of £130 which had been paid for the securing of suitable players; Bull and Owen had cost transfer fees of £40 and £50 respectively. Football people throughout the decades being what they are, decided that despite the difficulties and with the firm conviction that better times were on the horizon with anticipated larger home gates, a unanimous vote ensured their continuing in the Football League.

Nine players re–signed for the Club. The 1896/97 season started with four straight defeats, leaving the Club one off the bottom of the League from Darwen, who had also lost all of their opening matches but had an inferior goal average. Whilst the two goal defeat at Woolwich Arsenal attracted an 8,000 attendance on September the 19th, a disappointing figure of under 5,000 were present for 'the' game of the season – the 0–2 defeat to visitors Leicester one week later. Already the Luffs were becoming a 'Cinderella' Club when it came to home gates; the £53 receipts (approximately 2,000) for the visit and defeat by Notts. County was by now a 'high' for League games – and this gate was only achieved by the 1,000 or so 'away' supporters! It was not until the 3rd of October that the first victory came, at Lincoln, but this was only a brief interlude in the gloom. The following weeks produced the (above) Notts. County result, a 1–2 defeat to Walsall at Loughborough, and a 1–8 thrashing at Grimsby. To compound their problems the closure of the ground was ordered for a period due to the behaviour of the Luffs supporters at the Walsall defeat – which was blamed by the locals, on the standard of the refereeing!

By mid-November the team were anchored to the bottom of the League, relieved only by their second win (first at home) when one goal against Gainsborough was enough – aided no doubt by only a ten man visiting team, as the absentee had missed the train!   The final ignominy occurred when the Club were unceremoniously dumped out of the F.A.Cup when a very poor display produced a 1–2 defeat at Mansfield – a Club in the lowly rated Notts.County League.   The Executive of the Football Club had had enough, and several players were suspended, resulting in difficulties in raising a full team at Newcastle on November the 28th, and the resultant 1–4 defeat.

Although the return match at Gainsborough was then lost, the most amazing result of the season – and arguably in Loughborough's brief Football League career – occurred on December the 12th; a result which to this day stands as perhaps the greatest embarrassment to the redoubtable Arsenal in respect of their Football League match results. A peculiar arrangement of fixtures and rules at this time, required the Gunners to also play an F.A.Cup match on the same day! None the less it was virtually a full first team that visited Loughborough, and were then demolished by the Luffs eight goal to nil victory. An local epitome of the day gloated:
" Eleven little lads in a deep red hue, Came to show
Loughborough a thing or two. But the Luffs they said nay. It is
our turn today. And the Reds returned thoroughly worsted."
The weather was very poor by kick-off time, so much so that the two Captains tossed for ends whilst still in the dressing rooms.   Quite unexpectedly the Luffs put on a display of far better quality than any previous games, and by half-time they were four goals to the good, the best of which being the third by Ward. With the wind behind them in the second half, a 'cricket score' could have been anticipated, however, it was some time before the tally was increased. Despite a noticeable relaxation by the homesters, they still managed to double the half-time score after ninety minutes; a match that was to be vividly remembered by those present for a very long time afterwards. Even after this outstanding defeat it did not alleviate the Club's overall position – 3rd from bottom in the League – and a current deficit of some £500.

However, the good form continued seven days later when Small Heath were beaten, but suffered on Christmas Day when the short trip to Leicester was undertaken. The revitalised Loughborough team were well supported in the 11,000 (£220 receipts) crowd, but all to no avail for a 2–4 reversal ensued. The team's fortunes from then on to the season's end were very mixed. The remaining seven home games were won, including a six-nil goal feast over Burton Wanderers and a two goal victory over Newton Heath in April, their latter opponents' first defeat of the year.

Meanwhile the games on foreign soil were a different proposition, with just one victory being recorded, the completion of the 'double' over the Wanderers of Burton. Once again the second half of the season recovery saved the Club, with a final 13th position in the League table.

But once again it was a sorry tale on the money front, with the Club getting ever further into debt; gate receipts were marginally down, season tickets just two thirds the revenue of a year earlier, and despite a 20% drop in Players wages a loss was again made on the season. The start of the 1897/98 season was for the Club better than the two previous ones, but albeit not good. The 'big' match versus the Fosse finished all square in what was a very disappointing contest at the Athletic Ground on November the 13th. With 4 wins, 1 draw and 8 defeats the Luffs were placed fifth from bottom by Christmas. From then on it was one long drawn out disaster with the team consisting by now of mostly local players, the coffers being insufficient to buy suitable imports. The latter half of the season produced just one home win, 2–1 over Grimsby in April, whilst elsewhere not a single point was won. With continuing cuts in the wage bill, the Club suffered some humiliating defeats with an ever increasingly inexperienced team – 0–7 to Luton, 3–9 versus Burnley, and four goal losses at Blackpool, Gainsborough, Woolwich and (on Christmas Day) Leicester. So bad had been the Gainsborough home match that spectators were seen leaving well before the final whistle!

On February the 12th this dire statement was made:
" Loughborough F.C. are feeling the financial strain of the Second Division in a manner scarcely expected before, and so acute has the situation become that the various rumours circulating have gained currency ". With one of the worst goal averages ever in the Football League, 24 to 87 against, the Club finished bottom with the same number of points as Darwen. Gate receipts and season tickets were well down and with a further loss, despite severe pruning in costs, the future looked bleak – and so it was! The Club were duly re–elected into the League, and were allowed to desperately try to pull themselves out of the doldrums.

On September the 3rd 1898, the Luffs started the playing campaign in the worst imaginable manner, by losing their first game – at Walsall – by seven unopposed goals. At the next game, at the Athletic Ground, some recompense was received when Burton Swifts were beaten in the only goal of the game. Any hopes that a recovery was on the way was dispelled over the next few months for it was not until the following March that another home victory was recorded. Away matches were no better with just one win from a 1–0 scoreline on December the 3rd at Darwen – a Club whose record was even worse than the Luffs.

Just one more point, two goals shared at Burton, proved to be the only other success on the Club's travels. Up to Christmas there were some further heavy defeats in store; in October the match at Newton Heath was lost 1–6 and Lincoln City provided the fireworks on November the 5th with their 6–0 win. After the 0–3 home defeat to the Fosse at the end of November, Loughborough were languishing in third from bottom in the League with one win and two drawn matches from the nine played. Despite a 4–0 win at home to Mansfield, this was the limit of progress in the F.A.Cup competition!

By the New Year the situation and position in the table had not changed, for although the win at Darwen had been achieved a further, four defeats had also been conceded. By now things had reached a critical level and a meeting was called for at the Ground, on January the 12th, to discuss the dire position the Club were now in. Before a reasonable attendance the first point to consider was whether the Club could carry on, or whether they should immediately resign from the Football League. On this point it was agreed that the Club should at least continue to the end of the season if possible, since to resign then would mean not only the end of their Football League membership but the end of Loughborough F.C. in total. Another matter of particular concern was the lack of Committee members present, just two (although one arrived after the start of the meeting). This absence was no doubt due at least in part by some questionable movement of money following the Leicester home game and the £100 received for the transfer of Bosworth. With the Club in debt, payments outstanding, and a Bank Loan, the moneys from these sources had been paid into the Bank, whilst some of the outstanding Bills should have received preference.

With the state of the Club being what it was, and no apologies from the absentees, the Club's Members demanded the resignation of the Committee – en–bloc – which the Secretary, Mr. Harriman, acceded to forthwith! Mr.Dunn was elected new Secretary, and it was decided that the Club should somehow continue with their fixtures. Any hopes of a revival were soon shattered when the rest of the League fixtures that month were lost in no uncertain terms – by 0–3 at home to Burslem Port Vale, 0–6 at Small Heath (a match which by all accounts should never have been played due to a waterlogged pitch) and worst of all a nine goal hammering at Barnsley on January the 28th.

As if things were not bad enough, another bombshell hit the Club on January the 23rd when the Leicestershire Football Association ordered that the Athletic Ground should be closed until the 6th of February! A few days earlier, during the Reserve match at home to Colville, there were alleged crowd disturbances (from presumably just the handful that were present!), with these spectators disagreeing in no uncertain terms, to many of the decisions of the Referee (who happened to be the Secretary of the Leics. Association). The Referee informed the Gateman, without reference to the Clubs Officials, that if these malcontents were not controlled he would abandon the game – which he subsequently did. There was conflicting evidence later from the Referee, who first claimed that the abandonment was due to the state of the ground and later the "misconduct of spectators" ! In any event the punishment was meted out, and was sufficient to call for another crisis meeting at the Club, on January the 30th.

In all the events this could have well been the 'last straw', however, with the new Secretary reporting that the finances were now on a smoother path, and in view of the sympathy aroused near and far, for the apparent highanded attitude of the local Association, the meeting concluded that they should once again grit their teeth and struggle on. Notts.County had sent the Luffs a cheque for £10 – *"We have every sympathy with your Club in the troubles you are passing through"* – a similar unsolicited amount was received from Manchester City, and Leicester Fosse offered two free transfer players to the Club until the season's end. The Fosse went further in helping their near neighbours by offering the use of their Filbert Street Ground for the Luffs one first team 'home' game during the ban. This support from such diverse sources gave the Club's Officials the encouragement to soldier on.

Ironically the punishment to the Club backfired on the Association for this one 'home' game produced receipts considerably more than if the match had taken place at Loughborough! The game followed a Fosse Reserve fixture, and with good support locally from the curious, the match attracted nearly 4,000 spectators with receipts approaching £100; after expenses there was £62 left for the Luffs! The one sour note was that of yet another defeat, 1–3 to Blackpool. In contrast the Reserve match at Loughborough's true home, seven days later, produced the paltry sum of under £4 at the gate.

By March the playing situation had not improved and by now with no more wins, four draws and eighteen defeats the team lay second from bottom in the League. From this point on, as in the past, the Club's fortunes on the field at last took a turn for the better – at least at Loughborough – for the final six home games resulted in just one defeat. Of these remaining results there were two amazing scorelines.

On April the 1st, a poor chance of date for the opposition, Darwen were the visitors to Leicestershire. Although it is difficult to imagine, the 'Darreners' were in an even worse situation than the Luffs; with no money, the opposition were operating an unpaid team, and could only raise ten men for the match; with the homesters situation little better a collection raised nearly

£2 at the end of the match for which to provide a tea for their impoverished foes! Never before had such a one sided match taken place at the Athletic Ground, although Loughborough went in at half-time only two goals up. An early effort had been ruled offside, but Pegg opened up the scoring after 15 minutes, followed by another offside 'goal' before Pegg added a second to his tally. With Bailey injured, the second period was played with ten men per team, but this ironically signalled the start of a scoring deluge. Darwen had brought in an outfield player after half-time to perform in goal, which turned out to be a poor choice, for within five minutes the Luffs were five up – Pegg having completed his hat-trick aided by Parker and Hodkin on the score sheet. From then on the floodgates opened, the Darwen defence completely broke down and Loughborough ended the match as 10–0 victors. If this wasn't encouraging enough for the Club's members then the surprisingly high gate of over 1500 was the 'icing on the cake'.

The euphoria over this win was shortlived however, for the next two home games brought trouble, not only by way of the results but by the behaviour of the home fans. The no score draw with Gainsborough was ruined as an entertainment due to a poor and inconsistent Referee. The players bad tempers were not quelled by the Official and the crowd showed their disgust to the effect that the Referee was hustled as he left the pitch at the end of the match. This led to a report to the F.A. from the mistreated Official. Two weeks later, however, yet another alleged poorly controlled game, led to more spectator problems – aided no doubt this time by the Luffs 1–3 defeat to Grimsby! Another shock result occurred on April the 29th when earlier promotion contenders New Brighton Tower (who finally finished in 5th place) were overwhelmed to the tune of 6–0. This new found form was not reflected away from home, and the Athletic Ground victories were insufficient to raise the team above 17th in the League at the final reckoning, although nine points over wooden spoonists Darwen.

The team's last match was a promotion clincher for Glossop North End at North Road, but before an attendance of only a paltry 1,900. With the re-election meeting due, the Club's end of season meeting revealed at last some good news. The Secretary reported that the deficit of £670 in January had been reduced to £300, and with the team capturing eight of the last fourteen points on offer, it was a unanimous decision to apply for a continued presence in the Football League. However it was recognised that despite poorly attended home matches, misconduct by spectators at some games had closed the ground once and was nearly repeated on two further occasions, providing yet another problem to be overcome. The other Football League Clubs were obviously impressed with Loughborough's efforts, both financially and on the field of play, for they were confidently awarded the highest votes (28) of the three Clubs who were elected.

In contrast to the Luffs problems over the year, another team from the town were making the headlines locally, that of Loughborough Corinthians; although only in the District League, they were the new Champions, and despite the princely sum of just under £5 total gate money for the season they were able to announce a profit, after all expenses, of nearly £3!

The start of the 1899/1900 campaign, despite all the optimism within the Club, commenced in an all too familiar fashion – three defeats. However there was a glimmer of hope on the horizon when newly relegated Sheffield Wednesday were the attraction on September the 23rd. For a locally well advertised fixture, a last minute rush swelled the attendance to nearly 4,000 and the Luffs were more than happy with a scoreless draw against a team that had not until then dropped a point. This result was, however, no more than the lull before the storm for immediately afterwards the results then adopted the normal pattern. A 2–3 defeat at Lincoln before 3,000 spectators on September the 30th took the team down to the bottom rung of the ladder, a position from which they never arose. For a short period the fans kept faith with the Club despite their poor showings, and attendances of around 2,000 were present at the Small Heath and Grimsby matches – the latter producing a rare point for Loughborough from a scoreless draw. However, this faith was irreparably broken after a humiliating defeat to Hinckley of the County League in the Leicestershire Senior Cup.

Seven days later at the Athletic Ground a crowd of only 500 saw the Luffs miss many scoring chances before another final scoreless draw, this time with lowly Barnsley. In contrast, match receipts of £147 (approximately 6,000 spectators) were taken when Leicester were the visitors, but there were a minority of Loughborough fans amongst the crowd to see the Luffs lose 0–2. By Christmas Day not a single game had been won, and a further disaster occurred when the return with the Fosse was lost by five unopposed goals before an attendance of 7,000. January the 6th was a red–letter day for Loughborough, a win was at last achieved, when Burton Swifts were defeated 2–1, but this was but a brief respite as the Club were to sink further into the mire.

The match one week later versus Newton Heath, a normally well attended fixture, could provide a good indicator of the Clubs chances of surviving – but despite good weather, an approximate attendance of only 600 were present! Whilst throughout the season only one heavy defeat was suffered at home (0–4 to Chesterfield), and only two other games lost by two clear goals, it was a different story on their travels. High scoring losses followed relentlessly – 0–7 at Bolton, 0–5 at Sheffield, a six goal defeat at Small Heath and another seven goal hiding after the visit to Barnsley. The position was so dire for the Small Heath game that in order to fulfil the fixture, the Luffs had to rely on a loan for fares from the host Club! The Barnsley match also turned out to produce a farcical situation. Three first team players refused to make the trip (wages were owing to them), and the team left with only eight players, intending to pick up two Reserves en-route. There was one 'no show', and so the team took the field with nine players – in a borrowed kit as the Club's Trainer, complete with playing strips, also did not turn up!

By now the Club, to put it mildly, were in a precarious position, for finance – like points – was virtually non-existent. On February the 9th the Club's Officers were sued for, amongst other items, the unpaid rent of the Ground for the previous season! The end, to all intents, came on March the 3rd when Woolwich Arsenal were the victors by 3-2, the winner a hotly disputed goal. The referee's decision which gave the game to the visitors incensed the crowd – they may have been few in numbers but they were loyal, in a destructive way – causing them to invade the pitch during which time the Official was struck.

The outcome of this unfortunate incident was the death blow to the Club; the Ground was once again suspended – for one month – with no 'home' games allowed within six miles of the town. The Club's Officials were fined by the Courts, and Mr. Dunn whose efforts as Secretary had kept the Club going was also suspended from his duties. With the affairs of the Club in complete disarray, most of the Playing staff walked out, non-payment of wages adding to this decision. Loughborough F.C. at this time all but gave up, declaring that they would endeavour to retire gracefully by fulfilling their remaining Football League fixtures. Woolwich Arsenal came to the Luffs aid by sending a cheque to cover fares for the fixture at Plumstead on March the 12th.

The 'down and nearly out' Club managed to raise a team which consisted of just four regular first-teamers and seven Amateurs some of whom had not played a game for several weeks. Watched by a small crowd, Loughborough were never in the game, and were completely overwhelmed in the 0-12 defeat they suffered. Hence Arsenal completed a unique all-time Football League double in which they have recorded both their highest win and their biggest defeat (0-8) against the same opposition! True to their promise the Luffs continued to fulfil their fixtures. For their one 'home' fixture during their suspension, the Reverend J.W.A. Mackenzie generously offered the use of a pitch at his Vicarage in Leicester Road, Whitwick! An attendance, attracted by the novelty value once again – of approximately 1,000 – turned up to see a 1-2 defeat to Burslem Port Vale. Loughborough were not the only Club with problems for the visitors had debts of some £900!

The three Easter games were all at home and coincided with a return to the Athletic Ground. In view of the Club's appalling season the two points from two drawn games was reasonable, but the support did not return with the team, for there were only 800 present for the visit of Middlesbrough, 500 to see Chesterfield win by four goals, and a pathetic 300 souls for Luton's visit. The last ever away game for the Luffs was played in the return at Chesterfield – a respectable single goal defeat – leaving just two home games left, and a total of five matches played at Loughborough in April. On the 21st it was again not possible to raise a full team, and the Club took the field with just ten men; included in the line–up were the Trainer and three Reserves. The public had by now given up as there were barely 100 spectators present to see the local team lose yet again. One week later, it was much the same story. And so, on April the 28th 1900, Loughborough F.C. played not only their last ever Football League match but their last ever game when Gainsborough Trinity provided the opposition and went home happy with their 2–1 (half–time 1–0) away win.

The end of season meeting was a sorry affair. A miserable attendance, including only two Committee members, met to decide the future of the Club – if in fact there was to be one! Ironically at a time when many Football Clubs were financially struggling, (has there ever been a time when this was not so ?) it was revealed that the Club were only £219 in debt, a figure probably better than most of their contemporaries. However, as to the future, coupled with the team's pathetic showing on the pitch – just one win in 34 games – the ground had been suspended on two occasions and the precarious financial straits that they had found themselves in had resulted in them virtually begging for help from other Clubs; hardly a recipe for confidence. On the assumption that they would not be re–elected – although they decided to make the attempt – the meeting decided that they should apply for a return to the Midland League. On May the 21st Loughborough F.C. obtained just three votes of support (Blackpool were the lowest of those voted in, with 24)

Unbelievably Loughborough's troubles were still not over, for on June the 9th they failed to send a representative to the Midland League meeting at which fixtures were to be arranged. The old Committee had retired and a public meeting had not been called to elect a new body of men; problems were by now being allowed to drift. At last on June the 21st a meeting of the Club's members was called, with just one volunteer willing to stand for election! This prompted the comment in the local press, " *It seems that the Loughborough Football Club is dead"*. Eight days later another meeting, very poorly attended, decided that the Club was defunct; attempts it was said would be made to form a new Club, but with several in the area already it would require a supreme effort.

The F.A.Cup draw had already paired the Luffs and Hinckley, but the game was never played.

Loughborough F. C. were never resurrected. The final irony revealed that at their demise the Club's finances were no longer in the precarious state as in the past! In that most able of abilities – hindsight – many said that the Club had advanced too quickly; their leap into the Football League after such a short period of Non–league success should have required a longer look. However, other Clubs had started with less and achieved far more. Nearer the truth is the apathy generally shown by the town towards Senior football in Loughborough. A Football League team had tried but failed, now it was the turn of another to win support from the public......

Loughborough Corinthians were formed in 1896 as an Amateur team, their first match being played against Loughborough Park which they lost 0–4. For the first four years the home games of 'The Blues' as they came to be known were played at Forest Road, but in 1900 the opportunity arose for this ambitious Club to become the premier outfit in the town. Although only playing in the Loughborough and District League, albeit a leading Club therein, they took over the lease of the Athletic Ground vacated by the now defunct Loughborough F.C. The winning of the Leicestershire Junior Cup in 1901 made the locals sit up and take notice, and although still Amateurs, they attracted large crowds to their home games – surplus money from their endeavours being given to local charities. The 1903/04 season saw the Club elevated to the County League where they remained until the Great War. During this period they achieved arguably their greatest achievement by reaching the final of the Leicestershire Senior Cup Final. Defeat came by only a single goal, to the strong Fosse Reserve team.   This stage was surpassed when as a stronger club they won the Cup on five occasions during the 1920's and '30's. With the 1914–18 war over they entered a new field of battle, that of the Central Alliance where in the 1924/25 season they achieved their highest position of Runners–up.

For eight seasons, from 1925, the Blues were members of the Midland League, but this competition eventually proved too strong and a downward move was made to the Central Combination. The 1933/34 season was to be the last for the Club as they, like their luckless predecessors folded, due to lack of money.   At this time there was a suggestion that the old 'Loughborough F.C.' should be reformed, but the idea never progressed.

In 1908 the Athletic Ground had been sold for redevelopment by the owners – a brewery – and the Blues had to find another Ground. The last match on Nottingham Road occurred on March the 28th when the biggest crowd for several years saw the locals beat Coalville 3–1 in what was described as both one of the finest and roughest (a collar bone was broken by one player) games ! Eventually an enclosure was found for the Blues at Glebe Street – with a pitch better than that at the Athletic Ground – but this venue only lasted until 1921 when the lease ran out.

The remainder of their days were spent at Brown's Lane, where their first match attracted an attendance of 3,000 ....

Another Loughborough team formed in 1879, even earlier than the two previous Clubs, was Falcon Works. The large Company of *'Brush'* (electrical rather than cleaning type) formed a Football Club and by 1919 were known as 'Brush Works', and playing at the old Falcon Works Ground. By the mid–1930's, following the demise of the Corinthians, the Club were the natural successor to wear the 'crown' of the *'Town Team'*; they changed their name in 1939 to become 'Brush Sports'. For some years Loughborough did not have representation in the Senior football 'World', but the winning of the Leicestershire Senior League once and the County Cup several times during and soon after the Second World War rectified this situation. With the vacation by the Corinthians of the Brown's Lane Ground, they became worthy occupiers of this eventually well equipped venue. Brush Sports despite their commercial background had become the team to represent the town, but in 1960 at a public meeting a decision was taken on whether a truly representative Loughborough Club should be formed. With the involvement of much of the Brush Sports organisation, 'Loughborough United F.C.', were created with several members of the Brush organisation helping to form a Committee.

The United had no connection with the Junior team of the same name from the early 1900's. It was decided that the past experience of Brush Sports should get the new Club going before creating a new 'Brush Amateurs Football Club'. From the Central Alliance in 1960/61 the newly named outfit made upward progress to the Midland League where they soon became Champions, in 1963. In 1973, a Local Council decision was made to create a Sports centre in the town and the Brown's Lane Football Ground was chosen as the site. Once again the football apathy of the town came to the fore, and with insufficient interest locally to find and establish a new 'home' for the United they folded; although this last season was disastrous for the team for they finished bottom in the League, with a goal difference of 24 –167! 300 Faithfulls were present for the United's last match on April the 21st, a surprising 2–1 victory over Bridlington Trinity.

And so to date there has been no football representation at a senior level in Loughborough. The question must once again be asked, does anybody in the town really care?

There has been little change over one hundred years or so; to quote a newspaper statement of 1899:

"We must come to the inevitable conclusion that Loughborough people do not want a Second Division football team ".

One notable absence here has been any reference to Loughborough Colleges, who have had their degree of prominence, particularly in the F.A.Amateur Cup. However they are by inference a non–indigenous Club, and therefore hardly 'qualify' as a team for the locals.

FOOTBALL MATCH AND BICYCLE RACES
BY
ELECTRIC LIGHT :

ON WEDNESDAY Evening. November 27th, a FOOTBALL MATCH between the Leicester Alert F.C. and the Loughborough F.C., will take place on Bromhead's Cricket Ground. Loughborough.

On the same Evening, Prizes will be given for a ONE-MILE HANDICAP BICYCLE RACE (open to all Amateurs). 1st Prize value £3 : 2nd Prize value £1 10s : 3rd Prize value 10s. Entrance Fee 2s. 6d. Entries. giving name. address. colours. and height of machine, to be sent to T. B. CARTWRIGHT. Forest road. Loughborough. on or before Monday. November 23rd.

The Ground will be illuminated with a GRAND DISPLAY of the ELECTRIC LIGHT. by Messrs. Welch and Scott. Electrical Engineers. Manchester, with two Siemens' Machines' producing lights equal to 12,000 Candles.

Admission to the Ground. One Shilling. and Sixpence.

Bicycle Races commence at 7 o'clock ; Football Match commences at 7.30 p.m.

Floodlight football comes to the Bromheads (Athletic) Ground.....
On the 21st November 1878! (Loughborough Advertiser)

THE ATHLETIC GROUND.

The venue was originally referred to as the Greyhound Athletic Ground, but did not have any allegiance to the canine sport as the title suggests. The ground was in fact situated immediately behind the Greyhound Hotel in Nottingham Road, both being owned by the Warner Family, and were leased out to the Midland Brewery Company in 1887. The Ground was originally for the sole use of Cricket and, at different times, became known as either Hubbards or Bromheads Ground – each title referring to the current Landlord at the Greyhound Hotel. During a particularly cold spell in the winter of 1871, the Ground was sprayed with water and used as an Ice Rink for several weeks! The name of the Ground was finally changed to the 'Athletic Ground', probably in 1878.

Details relating to the Ground (which disappeared in 1908) are somewhat sketchy, but there appears to have always been a close association between the Hotel and the Ground, and particularly during the days of Loughborough F.C. The teams' dressing rooms were located in a rear extension of the Greyhound, since it would seem that the Athletic Ground had few facilities. Raised banking was unlikely, although there was a pavilion (probably located near to the Greyhound), and in the early 1890's a Grandstand was built, located probably on the opposite side of the pitch to the pavilion. Another structure existed, opposite the Grandstand, that could have been a small standing enclosure and/or a Tea Bar.

Just prior to the demolition of the Ground in 1908, a storm in February blew down several hoardings around the Ground and caused the collapse of 'one of' the Stands; the match in progress was suspended, but there were no injuries. The main entrance to the Ground was located between the Greyhound and an adjacent building in Nottingham Road, with most likely a second entrance (probably to the 'Reserved section and Stand') located in the South–West corner.

Nothing remains of the Ground today, houses and side roads have long covered the site, but The Greyhound, located near the Queens Road junction with the Nottingham Road, is still standing and much of the structure is as it was 100 years ago; the dressing rooms extension has long since gone, but there is an alleyway to the side of the premises – the former entrance that led to the Ground. In addition parts of the original wall in the South–West corner also remain.

In the true traditions of folklore history, the indomitable cricketer W. G.Grace is said to have once honoured the Ground with his presence. Appearing in a Charity match, he was bowled out on the first ball – or so the story goes – in apparently identical circumstances to his appearance at the Glossop F.C. Ground in North Road! On this occasion too, he allegedly refused to leave the wicket, with the wry comment that the spectators present had paid to see him bat and not to see a an unknown bowler dismiss him with the first ball!!

PROGRAMMES.

It is very unlikely that Loughborough F.C. ever issued programmes either pre-1895 or during their brief flirtation with the Football League. During the Midland League days, a few Clubs issued team-sheets at matches, and although the idea was mooted at Loughborough there is no evidence to suggest that this occurred. Loughborough Corinthians, at least in their Senior football days, did issue a match programme, but surviving copies are very rare. More common, but still fairly unusual are surviving Brush Sports programmes, whilst Loughborough United editions are relatively easy to obtain.

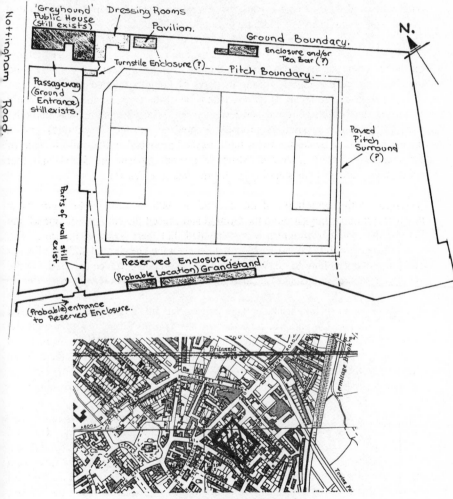

The Athletic Ground c.1900, and its location.

Nelson.

Back Row (*players only*) : RIGG, BRAIDWOOD, ABBOTT, BROADHEAD, CRAWSHAW.
Front Row : HUTCHINSON, HOAD, BLACK, WOLSTENHOLME, EDDLESTON, McCULLOCH.

Third Division (Northern Section) Champions 1922–1923

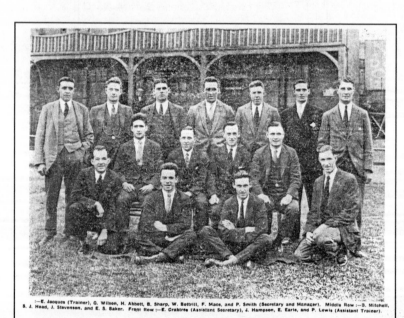

:—E. Jacques (Trainer), G. Wilson, H. Abbott, B. Sharp, W. Bottrill, F. Mace, and P. Smith (Secretary and Manager). Middle Row :—3. Mitchell, S. J. Hoad, J. Stevenson, and E. S. Baker. Front Row :—E. Crabtree (Assistant Secretary), J. Hampson, E. Earle, and P. Lewis (Assistant Trainer).

Team Group for the 1926/27 season

Nelson.

Founded: 1881.

Reformed: 1899, 1919 and 1936.

Football League: 1921/22 – 1930/31.

****

1881 – 1888/89.	*Friendly Matches.*
1889/90 – 1898/99.	*Lancashire League.**
1899/1900 –	*North-East Lancashire League.*
1900/01 –	*Lancashire League.*
1901/02 – 1906/07.	*Lancashire Combination Div.1.*
1907/08 –	*Lancashire Combination Div.2.*
1908/09 – 1915/16.	*Lancashire Combination Div.1.*
1916/17 – 1918/19.	*Ceased Activities.*
1919/20 – 1920/21.	*Central League.*
1921/22 – 1922/23.	***Football League Div.3 North.***
1923/24 –	***Football League Div.2.***
1924/25 – 1930/31.	***Football League Div.3 North.***
1931/32 – 1935/36.	*Lancashire Combination Div.1.*
1936/37 – 1938/39.	*Nelson Colne & District League.*
1939/40 –	*West Lancashire League.***
1946/47 – 1965/66.	*Lancashire Combination Div.1.*
1966/67 – 1967/68.	*Lancashire Combination Div.2.*
1968/69 – 1981/82.	*Lancashire Combination Div.1.*
1982/83 – 1988/89.	*North-West Counties League Div.3.*
1990/91 –	*West Lancashire League Division 2.*

* *Disbanded January 1899, League record expunged.*
** *Only 2 games played. Disbanded until 1946.*

(((((((((((+)))))))))))

Football League Record:

	Played	W.	D.	L.	F.	A.	Pts.	Posn.
1921/22.	38	13	7	18	48	66	33	16th.
1922/23.	38	24	3	11	61	41	51	1st.

(Promoted to Second Division)

	Played	W.	D.	L.	F.	A.	Pts.	Posn.
1923/24.	42	10	13	19	40	74	33	21st.

(Relegated to Third Division North)

	Played	W.	D.	L.	F.	A.	Pts.	Posn.
1924/25.	42	23	7	12	79	50	53	2nd.
1925/26.	42	16	11	15	89	71	43	8th.
1926/27.	42	22	7	13	104	75	51	5th.
1927/28.	42	10	6	26	76	136	26	22nd.

Successfully Re-elected.

	Played	W.	D.	L.	F.	A.	Pts.	Posn.
1928/29.	42	17	5	20	77	90	39	15th.
1929/30.	42	13	7	22	51	80	33	19th.
1930/31.	42	6	7	29	43	113	19	22nd.

Failed to gain Re-election.

Nelson

Summary of Facts.
Grounds: 1881 – 1889: Barrowford Cricket Field, Nelson.
              1889 – 1970: Park Ground, Seedhill, Nelson, Lancs.
              1970 to date: Victoria Park, Lomeshaye Way, Nelson.

Nickname: 'Seedhillites'.

Colours: Royal Blue Shirts, White Shorts.

First League Game: August 27th 1921. (Home) Versus Wigan Borough.
(1–2 Defeat). Attendance approx.9,000.
Last League Game: May 2nd 1931. (Away) Versus Hull City
(0–4 Defeat)
Record Attendance: Approx. 14,000. Versus Bradford. (League)
(Receipts £685). April 10th 1926
Football League average attendances: First season 8,275. Last season 2,375.

Main Achievements:
Best League Win (All Home) 7–0 v. Crewe Alex. 1924/25 v. Tranmere Rovers 1925/26
plus Accrington Stanley and Wigan 1926/27.
Worst League Defeat (Away) 0–8 v. Stockport County 1927/28.

Total Number of Football League Matches Played: 412.

International Player (Wales): J. Newnes. (1925/26)

F.A.Cup: (Football League period never past equivalent of 2nd round)
2nd Round: 1930/31. 1950/51.
1st Round: 1932/33. 1951/52. 1953/54.

Football League Div.3 North.Champions: 1922/23. Runners–up: 1924/25.
Lancs.Combination Champions: 1949/50. 1951/52. (1925/26–Reserves)
              Runners–up: 1947/48. 1950/51. 1960/61.
Cup-winners: 1949/50. 1950/51. 1959/60.
Lancashire League Champions: 1895/96.
Runners–up: 1897/98.
Lancs. Challenge Trophy Winners: 1907/08. 1954/55.

Virtually nothing remains of
the Seedhill Ground .....
The West boundary wall being
the sole reminder.

224

The origins of Nelson Football Club can be reputedly traced to a group of townspeople who, in 1881, on witnessing a local football match between Burnley and Blackburn were inspired to form their own team. However, it was to be some eight years before Nelson F.C. became a force in Lancashire football.

The 1889/90 season was the first in which the Club competed in a Senior Competition, in the Lancashire League. It was also the first for season for this League – thereby following closely behind the Football League – and therefore establishing itself as one of the first Leagues for Non–league teams. Just twelve Clubs were members, including Bury, Blackpool (later to combine with South Shore) and Southport Central who together with Nelson were later to become members of the Football League. Until 1889, the Club had used the Barrowfield Cricket Field as a home venue, but on entering senior football, a move was made to the New Park Ground Cricket Club – an enclosed area, with football being played on the southern side of the field.

The first three seasons proved successful when, despite not winning any honours, satisfactory final league placings were achieved; 4th in 1889/90, repeated one year later and 6th in 1892. The 1892/93 season however proved to be a disappointment when in a League of still only twelve Clubs, Nelson were placed second from bottom having recorded only 4 wins and 2 draws. The next two seasons showed a gradual rise in the team's fortunes first to 5th, and then to 3rd. Challenging for the Championship in April 1895, hundreds of 'Seedhillites' travelled to Raikes Hall to boost the crowd to around 3,000 and see their team achieve a one goal victory over table topping Blackpool. This lifted Nelson to second place, but a disastrous 1–5 defeat at Fairfield (the eventual Champions) produced a one place drop in the table.

The Championship however was finally captured one year later when the Club scored – for the first time – more than a century of goals (105) whilst conceding only 39. In a League which had by now increased to 16 teams, the Club's excellent record produced 22 wins plus 4 draws and only 4 defeats. Nelson had reached the number one spot by Christmas, and with average gates approaching 2,000, the biggest crowd of the season, 5,000, attended the top of the table win over Blackpool – in three inches of snow – and paying £99 gate receipts for the privilege. The second best gate of the season was 3,500 for the game versus Fairfield.

The 1896/97 season was a disappointment for the large number, and enthusiastic supporters, and a slip to 6th place ensued. But there was a return to former glories one year later when the Championship was only just missed, and the runners–up position became the final outcome. The Club were heading the League – on goal average – at the start of 1898, when a top of the table clash with second club Chorley attracted a 5,000 crowd to Nelson and a single goal home victory resulted. A few weeks later one of the best matches ever seen in Nelson was enacted, despite being scoreless, when New Brighton Tower (whose own home attendances averaged only some 1,000) were the visitors and the fans paid over £70 at the gate. A poor run followed including a defeat at Stalybridge Rovers (attendance 3,000) in the League Cup, which resulted in a drop to 5th in the League by early February. However, a good final run–in ensured the eventual runners–up place. The best victory was the eight goal thrashing at home over Ashton North End – yet ironically the return match produced the worst defeat (0–3)! A good run in the F.A.Cup ended with a 1–3 defeat at Wigan County.

The following season results did not emulate those of a year earlier and the 1898/99 season proved the most traumatic for the Club to date. The start of 1899 saw the Club in a mid–table position but having played less games than their opponents. The unplayed games were the result of the Club's suspension following incidents earlier in December. The reason for the suspension has been clouded in the mists of time but appears to have stemmed from the Club's Secretary not replying to letters from the F.A. The suspension was regarded as a somewhat severe punishment and the Club received much sympathy, not only in the locality but from the Lancashire F.A. President and other Clubs. None the less the Nelson fans had already 'blotted their copybook' following incidents at Mornington Road station after the Club's F.A.Cup defeat at Southport Central. More reminiscent of the 1980's rather than the 1890's, Nelson youths aged 17 to 23 – most of whom were drunk –were accused of; *'disgraceful conduct and using abominable and filthy language'*.

But worse was to follow after the 12th of January when the suspension was lifted, for what became the Club's final match, was played at home to Ashton North End. Due to the late notice given for the game, support at the gate was poor, although sympathetic, but did not prevent a 2–3 defeat. No further matches were played, and at the end of January the President – Councillor Wooliscroft – announced that there was no possibility of Nelson F.C. completing their fixtures and the Club were forced to disband. Heavy debts had mounted, due to poor attendances, which resulted in their inability to pay the players wages. Director disputes had also added to the financial problems. In the hopes of re–forming the Club, Mr. Wooliscroft became the saviour of football in Nelson for he purchased the Club's effects, and aided by circulars around the town which started in mid–February, funds were raised to wipe off the debts left by the former Nelson F.C.

Just a few months after their demise, Nelson F.C. were reformed and accepted into the North–East Lancashire league for the 1899/1900 season. The town's football team problems were now behind them, as was the further suspension that had been imposed on the former Club, not only by the Lancashire League but also by the F.A.Directors and Council. The new Club commenced battle on September the 2nd when Accrington Villa were the visitors before, 'a fair gate', and they witnessed a 3–2 victory which was secured by two late goals for the homesters. Victories continued and the team's first defeat did not come until the 1st qualifying round of the F.A.Cup at Oswaldtwistle – this followed an earlier local derby victory over Trawden Forest, that was watched by around 2,000 spectators at Nelson. Included in the North–East Lancashire League was Accrington Stanley, at that stage a Junior Club, prior to their rise into the Football League.

A successful new start for Nelson F.C. led to a return to the Lancashire League the following season. A one year stay produced only a moderate showing with a final mid–table placing when four matches were drawn and eight games were won, and eight lost. Defeat had come in the 1st qualifying round of the F.A.Cup by three goals at Darwen of the Football League.

Running in parallel with the County League was the Lancashire Combination – formed two seasons later than the former – which over the years gradually became the dominant Competition. In 1901, Nelson were accepted into the Combination, just one season before the Lancashire League finally became defunct.

In 1905, the football pitch had moved a very short distance away, in order that the Ground be completely divorced from the now independent cricket field. The New Park Road Ground had by now become Seedhill Cricket Ground, and the new Football Ground was similarly prefixed.

On the pitch, the next fifteen years did not produce the hoped for progress of the Club, flanked as they were on all sides by other football teams, and Nelson were barely able to mark time. Just one major achievement was accomplished, the winning of the Lancashire Junior Cup (later changed to the Challenge Trophy), in 1908. A taste of the apathy that was shown for the Club, was to come to light more forcibly twenty years later, and was also experienced in 1916. With the Club barely making ends meet, the Bailiffs were called in and Nelson F.C. were forced to close down for the duration of the First World War, and with little hope of revival after the hostilities. Liquidation was avoided through the generosity once again of the President Mr.Wooliscroft who, out of his own money, purchased the Stands plus the Fixtures and Fittings that were owned by the Club.

The end of the War brought with it a new spirit to the Country as a whole, and this was reflected at such organisations as Nelson F.C., for with a new determination to succeed, a move was made near the end of 1918, to put the Club on a sound financial footing. Willie Hartley along with other enthusiasts formed 'The Nelson Football Club Debt reduction Scheme', that set out to raise the £1,500 that was required to bring the Club back into the 'black' and start the football team again. The intention was:
"To put the Club on a thorough sound basis so that football in future will be in keeping with the dignity of the Town."

With these thoughts in mind and despite the austere immediate post–war financial restraints, the £500 in subscriptions received by January 1919, was increased to £1,006 by the end of February. Work had also to be carried out at the Ground which was in a virtual derelict state, whilst the small Stand had become dilapidated. By the time that applications were due for league entries, the Club were confident enough to offer themselves for membership of the Central League, and were accepted. This was a bold move from a Club so near to final extinction just a few months previously, for they would now be in opposition to the reserve teams of Football League Clubs as well as other established senior Non–league elevens.

The first game of the 1919/20 season brought the attraction of Everton Reserves to Seedhill, and a large crowd of around 1,000. The match kicked off at the unusual time of 6–15 p.m. in order that the spectators at the adjacent cricket match could be cleared from the area, there being no separation barriers at this time between the playing areas of each sport! A poor, but by no means desperate start was made, which by Christmas saw the Club lying in 15th place in the 22 Club league. Even so a new enthusiasm prevailed, which saw a new Company takeover the Club, with the intention of improving both the team and the Ground, with the capability of entry into the Football League. Home gate receipts to the end of the year rarely fell below the breakeven figure of £140 – representing around 3,500 crowds. An improvement on playing performances in the second half of the season ended with a respectable final league placing. Little progress had been made in the F.A.Cup, despite beating Accrington, defeat came in the next round at Lancashire Combination Club, Horwich Railway Institute.

By the new year of 1921, during the Club's second season in the Central League, little in the way of success had been forthcoming, for the team's league placing was a disappointing 16th. None the less an excellent 7–0 home win over Stockport was followed a month later with a 6 goal victory versus Tranmere. On the minus side the worst defeat was a 0–5 defeat at Champions – Manchester United Reserves – a Club whose second string could attract attendances of up to 17,000!

The last game as a Non–league team resulted in a 3–2 win over Blackburn's Reserves, which ended in a poor final 17th league position for Nelson.

The lack of success was not helped by the transfer of Sam Wadsworth to Huddersfield after an offer of £1,600 that was too good to refuse. However it was recognised that the Club required quality players if they were to enter the Football League, and with this objective in view, a start was made with Dave Wilson (ex–Scotland) signing on as player/manager from Oldham. On March the 7th, 1921, at the Football League meeting in London, Nelson's main ambition was realised. The 'Seedhillites' – together with 13 other teams from the Central League – were voted into the premier League competition, along with others, to form the new Third Division North.

Before the start of the Club's debut in the League, a number of experienced players were signed on, principally; Steele (from Third Lanark), Marsh and Wilde from Bradford, plus Halligan, ex–Ireland and Oldham. Despite these 'big' names, it was the Club's intention to rely to a large extent on young unknowns, and 300 players applied for a trial, of which 22 were selected and given a showing. Meanwhile an 'Easy Payment Scheme' was devised to encourage season ticket holders, and improvements were made to the Ground. The covered accommodation was extended and terraced to the Cricket side, which gave cover for 3,000, and provided a total capacity at Seedhill of 18–20,000. This brought the total to over £2,500 that had been spent on the Ground over a period of one year. In addition the Capital of the Club was increased to £5,000.

A new record attendance of over 9,000 paid £360 to be present for the first match in the League, at home to Wigan Borough, an occasion which also saw the first issue of a Nelson match programme. The team that day consisted of:
Hayes, Lilley, Steele, Marsh, Wilson, Wilde, Eddlestone, Andrews, Halligan, Hargreaves and Proctor.

Despite an excellent start to the game which produced a goal from Halligan after only 2 minutes, there was to be no victory, for by half–time the locals were 1–2 down, a score that remained unchanged – despite many missed chances – at the final whistle. This however proved to be only a temporary set–back for by Christmas – aided by a good 'away' record – a mid–table placing of 12th had been achieved. Results up to this period included a surprise win in the return at Wigan by 4–1. In this new prestigious competition other good home attendances were recorded – 9,000 on September the 12th when Stalybridge were beaten 1–0, and the Ground record was broken again when over 13,000 paid £569 to see the local derby with Accrington on October the 15th, which ended in a single goal defeat.

However, these were the exceptions rather than the rule, for within thi
elevated status it was hoped to attract – and budgeted for – such crowds, fo
every match.

Concern was expressed by the Directors over the financial situation, with th
team's mediocre, position coupled with the start of the depression an
consequent unemployment in the area, forming the reasons for an overa
shortfall in expected gates.   To alleviate the money problems, Harr
Hargreaves was reluctantly sold to Wolverhampton Wanderers in Novembe
for no less than £1,200.

The Accrington defeat was avenged in the F.A.Cup with a 1–0 win at Pee
Park on November the 19th when aided by 2,000 Nelson fans a crowd c
nearly 12,000 paid £638 at the gate.   Progress in the Cup was halted ;
Non–league Worksop (5,000 attendance) with a 1–2 defeat in the 6t
qualifying round – a run which equalled the best progress by Nelson to date
The season was not without it's bad reverses which included the 3–5 resu
at home to Durham on Boxing Day, and the heaviest defeat of 1–6 (despit
being one goal up at half–time) at Hartlepools at the end of January.

Overall the season could be considered as one of consolidation, but a fina
League table place of only 16th of 20 was the disappointing final outcome
however there was to be a surprise turnaround for the Lancashire Club in th
months to come!   The purse strings had had to be watched, but a fina
'respectable' loss on the season of £44 would have been considerably mor
had it not been for the sale of Hargreaves.   Match receipts for the seaso
amounted to almost £6,400.   During the close season, three players wer
transfer listed and seven others freely released.

Despite the Club's poor showing in their first Football League season, th
start of the second was eagerly awaited by the team's supporters, an
encouragingly a 5,000 crowd turned out for the public practise game, t
view the 24 professional players now on the books, and which included te
new signings.   The first League match hardly bode well for the comin
months, when a 2–6 defeat was suffered at – relegated from the Secon
Division – Bradford City.   However, after two home wins over Halifax b
2–0 (attendance only 5,000) and Southport by the same score – before
more encouraging seven to eight thousand crowd – coupled with an awa
win, the Club headed the table.   After seven games first place was retaine
only to be lost after a 1–3 defeat before 8,000 spectators at Ashingto
However, the return match was won before a 7,000 gate producing receipt
of £315.   Despite the good start in the League which continued throughou
the season, the crowds (in common with most other, albeit less successfu
Clubs) actually started dropping – from the low 7,000's to barely 5,000!

The F.A.Cup campaign produced little, for after overcoming Rochdale by a single away goal, before a 10,000 crowd, (the next week Nelson were defeated at home in the League to the same team) the abrupt end came in the 5th qualifying round at Stalybridge before a 7,000 crowd. Meanwhile by the New Year, with the Club topping the table (11 wins, 1 draw and 5 defeats – one point ahead of Bradford City), the locals started talking seriously about promotion. The Seedhill Ground was acknowledged as one of the best equipped in the Northern section of the Third Division and was capable of extension, although it was recognised that the gates would have to double to ensure survival at a higher level. It was hoped that additional outside support would be forthcoming, especially from nearby Colne. In November, a Supporters Club had been formed, with the object of raising funds, and relieving the Football Club's Directors of some of the financial burden that was mounting.

Meanwhile, on the pitch, the successes continued with opponents and their supporters recognising that Nelson were worth watching, an example being the record attendance at Halifax on Christmas Day when 18,000 packed into The Shay Ground to see four goals shared. Competition at the top was very tight, and a surprise defeat at Hartlepools by no less than five goals saw the Seedhillites drop to 5th place, but a three goal win at Rochdale one week later bounced the Club back on top again! With the necessary financial restraints it was not possible to buy players that were thought necessary to ensure the Club's promotion, and even the £108 raised by the Supporters Club was a godsend.

In February, home attendances at last improved with 6,500 for the Durham game and 10,000 for the clash with other hopefuls, Wigan Borough. It was still vexing for the Club's Directors to see other opponents supported in numbers – 12,000 at Chesterfield – a 2–1 win there was followed by a four goal return victory (Nelson completing the double) – and receipts of £478 (10,000 crowd) at Accrington, albeit boosted by the estimated 4,000 from Nelson! However the final outcome was a well deserved Championship winning side produced by Nelson, with the title being clinched by the two goal home win over Wrexham on the 24th April. The midweek game had an evening kick-off, with local factories closing early for the workforce to support the team. But this exciting season ended with an amazing and anti-climatic five unopposed goal thrashing at Walsall!

An almost unprecedented step was taken in May when a foreign tour to Spain was arranged. Victories were achieved over Real Oviedo (2–1) and Real Madrid (4–2), plus defeats by 1–4 to the Madrid side and 1–2 to Racing Santander. For the tour, a prolonged and tiring journey had to be undertaken.

In just four years Nelson F.C. had achieved an incredible rise from obscurity to a place in the Football League Second Division, and with a team that cost just £500 in transfer fees. The success put Nelson 'on the map' with the Daily Mail amongst others asking the question – *'where is Nelson ?'* Although finance was limited, the Club were determined to prove that both their team and their Ground were worthy of such status. In the latter department £4,500 was spent on improvements; the pitch was enlarged to 110 x 75 yards, a 45 foot wide enclosure on the Carr Road side was erected, and on the Park Side of the Ground a steel and timber Stand to accommodate 1,500, was added, replacing an unpretentious 400 seater which was sold to Barnoldswick Town F.C. for £200.

With a Ground capacity now of 25,000, the season opened with a near record attendance of 12,500 paying £534 to watch the duel with Clapton Orient. But the enthusiasm of large crowds could not bring victories to the Club, and early disappointments included a 1–5 defeat in the return at Clapton (before approximately 20,000 London fans) and it wasn't until September the 29th that the first victory was enjoyed with the 2–0 win at Seedhill over Stoke City before an 8,000 crowd. The second win arrived in mid–October when 9,000 Crystal Palace were beaten, a victory which raised the Club to 8th from bottom in the League. The team's away record was letting them down with a number of heavy defeats, despite an undefeated home run which lasted well into the season. By Christmas things were far from good with Nelson deep in relegation trouble and laying third from bottom in the League.

There was hope, however, for a slight improvement had been made in the few weeks leading up to the end of the year, and the Club had the distinction of being the first visiting team to score a goal at high–flying Blackpool. The most notable achievement was the home victory over Champions–elect, Leeds – one of only nine defeats for the Yorkshire side during the season. Nelson were one up through Eddleston in the first minute, and increased their lead within the next 15 minutes. Leeds came back strongly after the break, and despite them pulling one goal back, the homesters held on to their slender lead to provide the fans with the best game and win of the season.

January, as a whole, proved disastrous, and by February the 2nd the Club had slipped to the foot of the table. Whilst the home attendances naturally decreased, the Club could still depend on the faithful, and they were well represented within the 10,000 that attended the game at Bury. Nelson's first away victory was not accomplished until mid–March, when middle of the table Manchester United succumbed to the Seedhillites. Even this win still left the Club at second from bottom spot, a position that was not improved upon, and they together with wooden–spoonists Bristol City were relegated to their respective Third Divisions.

The Club's gamble in providing the facilities for a Second Division outfit did not come off, for at the A.G.M. it was announced that they were £5,000 in debt and losing at a rate of £150 per week. Whilst the season had proved a great disappointment, the hardcore supporters still stood by the Club, and a good crowd was present for the pre–(1924/25) season practise game, where six new players – notably new signing, ex–Middlesbrough Captain Ellerington made his debut for Nelson. Player/Manager David Wilson hung up his boots but continued in his Managerial capacity. The campaign got off to a poor start with a defeat at Southport, where an estimated 2,000 'Nelsonites' were amongst the 8,000 crowd. Home wins commenced with a three goal victory before 6,000 fans, versus Ashington, and it wasn't until December that the first point at Seedhill was lost. Once again the away record left a lot to be desired, otherwise a higher placing than sixth at Christmas – 9 points behind frontrunners, Darlington – could have been realised.

The financial situation was questioned by many, and the Directors found it necessary to issue a statement to the effect that the Club were not going bankrupt. Cash injections had been made, but the outlay of £8,000 in ground improvements over the previous five years was proving an enormous burden when each home gate was only producing on average of around £220. Ex–Nelson player and now England Captain, Sam Wadsworth, urged supporters to make cash donations to help the Club out of their plight.

The F.A.Cup record gave little cause for celebration; after an easy 4–1, 5th qualifying round home victory over Non–leaguers Winsford United, defeat came in the next match in a poor game versus Coventry – a team destined for relegation into the Third Division at the end of the season.
A bombshell was dropped, but hardly surprising in the circumstances, when on the 8th of January – for financial reasons – both Phizacklea and Kennedy departed to Preston North End and Fulham respectively. In the other direction, Frank Laycock signed in March from Barrow F.C. His joining Nelson was unique since he signed for the Club during the Barrow versus Rotherham match, leaving the field with an alleged injury; Laycock was severely censured and Nelson fined £5–25 by the F.A. for this unconventional action!

Low attendances continued, not helped by poor weather at several attractive home matches – an example being the sub–5,000 that turned up for the single goal victory over Chesterfield.

None the less the team battled on and recorded some good wins to lift them into second place, seven points – and two games in hand – behind leaders Darlington. With a 4–2 win at well supported Halifax the gap between top and second was closing, only for Nelson to then lose their games in hand over the leaders. On April the 4th, a new ground record attendance was achieved when nearly 14,000 spectators paid £678 to see the top of the table clash with Darlington that finished as a 1–1 draw.

The last few games of the season included two defeats – by a single goal at bottom of the League Rotherham, and at home to Wrexham (the first home defeat) before a crowd of between five and six thousand. Second place, and hence no promotion, was the final outcome. Hardly failure, but none the less disappointing for a Club who had hoped to regain the higher status. 23 Players had been used during the past months, with Abbott and Braidwood being League match everpresents. Some high scoring games had been played, including the 7–1 victory over Durham and an amazing pair of results with New Brighton – 0–5 in November and 5–0 in the home return on March the 7th! May the 22nd saw the departure of David Wilson to take over the reins at Exeter.

The Directors of Nelson F.C. were determined to regain the Club's Second Division status, and another bold gamble caused a sensation in view of the past financial problems and a reported season's lost of £633. A Third Division record transfer fee of £2,500 was paid to Sheffield Wednesday for ex–England Captain George Wilson (with twelve 'caps'), whilst seven players were given free transfers and Percy Smith joined as the new Manager. The high priced capture was acknowledged with an attendance of over 9,000 for the first home game of the season. Despite scoring first, the visitors – Crewe – lost by two goals to one.

The Club's hopes were soon deflated, for after 9 games only a mid–table position had been achieved, and by mid–October they had dropped to 14th. Not surprisingly poor attendances returned; for the visit of nearby Accrington, an expected bumper gate only attracted between 7 and 8,000, despite the good weather. Joe Eddlestone was dropped, for the first time ever, for this game, having missed only six Nelson Football League matches in total. None the less the team's fortunes picked up, aided by four straight wins in November, and by Christmas they had risen to 4th place, just 5 points behind the leaders Bradford City. The season was to produce extremes in home attendances. For the Tranmere match – ironically the best win of the season with seven unopposed goals – only 2,000 turned up, although the weather was very cold; whereas on the 10th of April the Club's record attendance of all time was set when Bradford were the visitors.

The Yorkshire leaders brought with them some 5,000 supporters in 3 special trains and other vehicles, and although by this time the Lancashire Club trailed them by 13 points, a massive 15,000 paid record receipts of £685 to see the game. In a fast and exciting match the home team went in two goals in arrears at half–time, but made an amazing recovery in the second half, and drew the game 2-2.

A fairly poor second half to the season produced a final placing of eighth in the League, the last two games ending in defeat – 1-3 at home to Rochdale, and 2-4 at Tranmere, despite taking a 2-1 half-time lead in the latter match. A favourite with the crowd – Joe Eddlestone – departed for Swindon at the end of the season, and at his Benefit Match (versus an International X1) at Seedhill, 5,000 turned up to say goodbye, raising £225 for the player. Eddlestone, although only five and a half feet in height was a prolific goalscorer recording 98 in 185 League matches; for five seasons he was the Club's leading marksman, with 25 in the 1924/25 campaign being his best.

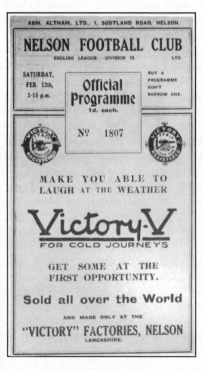

Programme cover for the Bradford (P.A.) game.

(12th February 1927)

An enormous boost to the Clubs funds was made when a Fete was held at the Ground in April and the amazing sum of £3,771 was raised. By August 1926, the Club had 28 players on the books, including 10 amateurs. With early defeats – 1-2 at Wigan (a last minute goal settling the issue), and 1-5 at home to Doncaster, the crowd numbers once again gave cause for concern. But after some early defeats, things came good, and aided by some excellent victories, including the first away victory (4-1 at Lincoln) and a crushing five goal spree at Accrington, the team was once again in contention for promotion. Yet the crowds were still reluctant to attend at Seedhill, and under 7,000 were present for the attractive match with Halifax, which resulted in a 0-0 draw. A 7-1 win at home to mid-table Crewe took the Club to 4th place, a match in which the forwards were described as *"fast, clever and tricky."*

As per normal, little headway was made in the F.A.Cup, for despite an easy 4–1 home win over fellow 3rd Division Stockport before an 8,500 gate, an unlucky defeat came in the next match by the odd goal in three at Ashington, which attracted 5,000 spectators. By the end of the year a 4th position had been maintained in the League – 7 points behind Champions-to-be Stoke, and the final position of 5th was the end of season outcome. At the season's end Manager Percy Smith left Nelson to take over at Bury and six players were transfer listed, including three 'frees'. A profit of £365 had been made in player transfers, but an overall loss of £1,136 on the season resulted.

Jack English who had spent 10 years as Manager at Darlington moved to Nelson in the same role and no less than twelve new players signed for the Club. With (lack of) money inevitably to the forefront, exasperated by poor results and low gates, Jimmy Hampson left for Blackpool, making Nelson £1,000 the richer; Hampson had scored 42 goals in 63 League matches following his move from Bolton in 1925.

After tasting the fruits of Second Division football, and always having maintained high placings in the Third, the 1927/28 season was an unparalleled disaster for the Club. Things went from bad to worse, and in January an Emergency Meeting was held to try to find a way out of the Club's financial worries. Reluctantly the Directors were given the power to consider bids for any of the Nelson players. A further meeting was held during the next month when it was announced that the Club were £6,500 in debt, and an appeal fund for Nelson F.C. was set up by the Mayor of the town. Even a change of Manager in March, when Buchanon Sharp was appointed, failed to stop the rot – his first game in charge ending up with a 1–3 home defeat to Lincoln City. Further efforts were made to boost the Clubs funds. Burnley, in a good neighbourly gesture, switched a home friendly with Hamilton Academicals to Seedhill, and at the end of April a match between the current team and the 1923 Championship winning side was staged which raised £200.

Following the four goal home defeat to Stockport, the team were firmly rooted to the bottom of the Third Division North League table, from where they never moved, with five defeats and one drawn game in their last matches. Re-election was necessary for the first time, 3 points adrift at the bottom below Durham City. If this ignominity wasn't enough, the team also suffered the humiliation of having conceded 136 goals (an average of over 3 per game), an all-time record for any Division of the Football League. Having been re-elected at the Football League's end of season meeting, only six players were retained and it was obviously impossible for the Club to do any worse.

A new appointment was made with Albert Tulloch joining as Trainer following his 18 years at Blackpool. As it transpired an improvement was made in the 1928/29 season, albeit only to a final 15th position. The potential money making F.A.Cup revenue was lost since the Club's entry was barred following their omission in applying to partake in the Competition by the required date! An inevitable loss on the season was made – this time of £785 – and six players were given end of season free transfers.

Belts had to be tightened even more as the Club's financial plight worsened, and although losses at the seasons ends were being contained, the financial constraints gave the Directors no chance to raise a successful team. Attendances continued to fall and on January the 14th 1930, only £27 was taken at the gate for Rochdale's visit. Crowds averaged around 4,000 for each home game, producing just £124 per match – a figure well below 'break–even'. It was perhaps almost a relief when losses of 'only' £458 were revealed at the end of the 1929/30 season. On the field of play things were no better and a 19th final placing was the outcome.

The 1930/31 season became the worst in the Club's history, and the final death for Nelson as far as the Football League was concerned. After five years on the field, George Wilson retired, but stayed on at Seedhill as Coach, and ten new players were signed on in an attempt to halt the decline of the Club on the playing front.

The team got off to their customary bad start, losing the first match, four–five at Rochdale, and apart from a home win in the third game, the next victory did not arrive until Darlington were the visitors on October the 25th. Defeat followed defeat, punctuated by only the occasional home win, and some of the losses were substantial – 1-7 at Tranmere, 1-8 on New Year's day at Southport, a repeat on March the 14th at Carlisle, and a five goal defeat at home to Chesterfield on April the 4th. The debacle at Carlisle was matched with a seven goal home thrashing of the Reserves on the same day when Clitheroe were the visitors – the second string finished in bottom but one place in the Lancashire Combination. Meanwhile the F.A.Cup sortie came to an abrupt end at York with a 1-2 defeat following the abandoned match one day earlier (due to thick fog) when the Seedhillites were two down after 52 minutes.

At the end of January, Jack English left to try his hand at Northampton, and seven days later Albert Tulloch retired to become a Publican. Nelson dropped to bottom position in the League on Boxing day, and remained there to the season's end. In line with the team's performances, the attendances dropped further, with less than 3,000 present for each of the two

Christmas home matches, and even lower –to around 2,000 over Easter – traditionally, each Holiday period being the time to attract the best crowds. With the Club unable to keep the better players and a shortage of money, it was necessary in March for the Directors to assure everybody that the Club would continue at least until the end of the season.

Even a fund–raising Carnival at Seedhill in March was a disaster when a loss of £20 was made! Admittedly the Club were not alone with their financial worries, for only 2,000 spectators were present at the match at Accrington (a 1–3 defeat), and an end of season visit to Wrexham attracted only around 1,000. The last game of the season, and in the final event the last as a League Club, came at Hull on the 2nd of May. Nelson were represented by:

> *Ingham, Shuttleworth, Waterfield, Naylor, Witton, Roberts,*
> *Wilkinson, Duckworth, Hargreaves, Chadwick and Marsden.*

An inevitable defeat resulted, to the tune of four clear goals – the Club having completed the season without one single away victory.

In a last desperate bid to remain solvent a fund was started by the Mayor, and for the last few matches the players continued without wages; Manager Jack English had by now already left the Club. Twenty–nine players were used through the season, Raisbeck leading the goalscorers with 14.

With cap in hand, the Directors of the Club desperately sought re–election, but in view of the past few seasons and Nelson's financial plight it could hardly have come as a surprise when they were voted out. The initial re–election application, along with Rochdale's, had to be made to the Third Division North Committee Members, at which Nelson, Rochdale, Chester, Mansfield and Manchester Central received 14, 18, 4, 2 and 0 votes respectively. On this basis Rochdale and Nelson were recommended for re–election to the full Third Division Committee. The latter meeting was held on June the 1st, and whilst Rochdale were successful, the voting resulted in both Nelson and Chester obtaining 27 each. This tie necessitated a new vote between the two at which Chester received 28 and Nelson 20. Chester replaced the Seedhillites, with Nelson's Directors making the rather lame excuse that it was all a conspiracy on the part of the rest of the Football League Clubs, who wanted Chester in since they were interested in this Club's players! None the less the result was without precedent since it was the first time that the Full Committee had not acted upon the recommendations from the initial voting.

The Nelson F.C. A.G.M. was a dismal affair with only 37 Shareholders present. The Club President – Alderman J.H.S. Aitken – resigned, along with all the Directors, and only three stood for re–election.

Perhaps the saddest man of all was retired Director Woolscroft who had twice saved the Club and had been a loyal follower for 37 years.

With much reduced expenses, the Club managed to carry on, with the first team playing in the Lancashire Combination – the league previously occupied by the reserve team. Surprisingly the first League game produced a gate of over 2,000 – better than some of the latter Football League attendances – when Horwich were beaten 2–0. In view of this good monetary start, it was inexplicable that despite being placed second in the league at the turn of the year, the gates had slumped again, this time to around 1,300; the Reserves meanwhile could rarely attract more than 150 to their home games, when four times this number was financially necessary.

Nelson F.C. struggled on, without the winning of any honours, until 1936. This last season started well, but was followed with a bad run in November, with the worst result coming at Lancaster when nine goals were conceded without reply. The Supporters Club was still active and announced that:

"We still have a vision of the good old days. We do hope that our efforts will be renewed to raise the status of the Club and once more place it on the map."

But those efforts came to virtually nothing.

Attendances had inevitably dropped to a low level, and the 1,500 present for the 1–3 home defeat to Barrow Reserves was by now good, more typical were crowds of less than one thousand. The first win since November the 29th was achieved on the 14th of February when Southport Reserves were surprisingly beaten by five clear goals followed the next week with a 6–0 thrashing of Great Harwood. However, this was only a temporary respite as the following week the Seedhillites lost at Clitheroe by 4–9.

The final outcome was a not–to–bad 10th place in the Lancashire Combination with 15 wins, 9 draws and 14 defeats – but it was not good enough! The end of season announcement that a big loss had been incurred over the year came as no surprise, and with the Directors generously deciding to wipe out the £302 deficit, additional Share Capital was to be issued. But with only 130 of the 500 ten shilling shares taken up, the Directors had had enough, and with this public apathy shown towards the Club, they resigned en–bloc. There was still a last ditch effort, and with new players having signed for the Club, the Supporters Club made a house to house effort to raise funds.

Sufficient moneys were not forthcoming however, and on the eve of the 1936/37 season, on the 7th of August, it was announced that the Club was to disband. Another Club immediately arose from the ashes, *'Nelson Town'*, who continued to play at Seedhill, competing in the – albeit minor – Nelson, Colne and District Amateur League. The entrance cost was now down to 2d.– boys free – and there was a surprisingly good turnout of 700 for the first game of the new Club – a 2–3 defeat to 'J.Nelson Sports' on the 1st of September, at what must obviously have been by far the best Ground in this league.

Following the last match of the 1938/39 season, against Gargrave, and still in the local minor league, the Club announced that it would be attempting to get into a higher competition. As a prelude to the final ambition of Lancashire Combination status, the West Lancashire League was entered. With match entrance costs now doubled, just two games were played – the first at home to Netherfield Reserves in front of a low attendance – before the outbreak of World War Two brought about the decision to cease activities.

The desired rise in status came just seven inactive years later when the Club, once again under the name of *'Nelson F.C.'*, were accepted into the First Division of the Lancashire Combination. Honours came to the Club in a surprisingly short time, with the runners–up spot in 1947/48 and again in 1950/51, and the ultimate – the League Championship twice – in 1949/50 and repeated two years later.

These were without doubt the post–Football League glory days, for two League Cup wins were also added to their achievements, and in 1952, Nelson were on the brink of regaining that former premier League status. With the two Club increase in numbers to the Third Division North membership in 1952, Nelson along with twenty other Clubs applied, and they only narrowly missed out, coming fourth in the poll.

Post-war glory – Oldham Athletic are entertained in the F.A.Cup.

Those early post-War heydays were never repeated – apart from another runners-up spot in May 1961 and a League Cup win in 1960, and the end of the 1965/66 season saw their relegation to the Second Division of the Combination. When the lower Division disbanded, Nelson were once more accepted into the First Division, where they remained – without winning any major honours – until the end of the ninety-one year old competition in 1982. Due to a poor latter period in the Lancashire Combination, which itself in it's last years had lost it's former highly rated status, Nelson joined the North-West Counties League – at the bottom, in the Third Division. But a poor playing record, coupled with difficulties of Ground grading has resulted in yet a further drop in status, to the West Lancashire league.

The population of the town has remained fairly constant over the years (around the mid-30,000's), and with the vast selection of both Football League and Senior non-League teams in the area, it is difficult to imagine that Nelson F.C. could ever regain it's former Football League status.

SEEDHILL.

After the first few years playing at Barrowfield Cricket Field, the Club took up residence at The Seedhill Cricket Ground – or the New Park Ground as it was formerly called. Being very much the tenant of the Cricket Club, there was little to offer spectators in the way of facilities. The pitch was located on the Southern perimeter of the Ground – overlapping the Cricket pitch – and far removed from the Pavilion. In 1905, a separate Football Ground was created, when Nelson F.C. moved slightly South, retaining part of the Cricket Ground and taking over a portion of the adjacent Recreation Ground in the process. Initially there was no physical barrier between the two Sports pitches, but a small seated stand was erected on the Southern side of the pitch. In 1921, major improvements to the Ground were undertaken, and further extended in 1923 – as detailed previously. With the Club's exit from the Football League, they were left with a fine Ground, which remained more or less intact – and far superior to most of their contemporaries – until the Ground was finally demolished, to make way for a Motorway, around 1980. By this time, the Football Club had moved out to a very basic Ground at Victoria Park, whilst the Seedhill Ground had been used for a number of years, principally, for Stock-Car Racing and Speedway meetings.

Virtually nothing is left now of the old Football Ground. All the enclosures have been removed, and the former embankments levelled. The Motorway runs over what was the East end of the Ground. The only remains, are the West boundary Wall – approximately three metres high – with wording referring to 'Nelson' and 'Visitors' (probably relating to the Speedway) – and the wall which formed the boundary with the still existing Cricket Ground.

PROGRAMMES.

It is believed that Programmes were first issued at the Club's entry into the Football League in 1921. No doubt, they were regularly produced over the years, at least until their re-formation in 1936. Such examples are extremely rare, for very few appear to have survived the passage of time.

(Right) The large seated Stand, seen from Carr Road.

(Below) A Panoramic view of Seedhill shortly before its demolition ..... and an aerial view of the Ground.

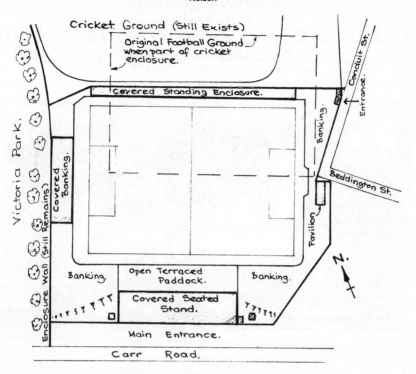

Cricket Ground (Still Exists)

Original Football Ground when part of cricket enclosure.

Conduit St.

Entrance.

Covered Standing Enclosure.

Banking.

Victoria Park.

Covered Banking.

Enclosure Wall (Still Remains)

Beddington St.

Pavilion

N.

Banking.

Open Terraced Paddock.

Banking.

Covered Seated Stand.

Main Entrance.

Carr Road.

The Seedhill Ground c.1925, and its location.

NELSON

SCOTLAND

81

M65 Motorway

82

OMESHAYE

MANCHESTER ROAD

Stalybridge Celtic

CELTIC'S DEBUT IN FOOTBALL LEAGUE

STANDING : J. S. Johnston (Secretary-Manager), Tyler, Carney, Barton, Lonsdale, Dennis, Lockett, Duckworth.
SEATED : Dance, Thompson, Gee, Petrie, and Benson.
[*Reporter* Photo.

6 — THE REPORTER, SEPTEMBER 3, 1921.

A TENSE MOMENT AT BOWER FOLD

Mitchell (Chesterfield's goalkeeper) fists away just as Petrie endeavours to head through from a well-placed corner by Benson.
[*Reporter* Photo.

244

Stalybridge Celtic

Founded 1906.
Football League Division 3 North. 1921/22 – 1922/23.

****

1906/07 – 1908/09	Friendly Matches.
1909/10 – 1910/11.	Lancashire & Cheshire League.
1911/12.	Lancashire Combination Div.2.
1912/13 – 1913/14.	Central League.
1914/15.	Southern League Division 2.
1915/16 – 1918/19.	Lancashire Combination (South).
1919/20 – 1920/21.	Central League.
1921/22 – 1922/23.	**Football League Div. 3 North.**
1923/24 – 1939/40.	Cheshire County League.
1940/41 – 1944/45.	Ceased Activities.
1945/46 – 1977/78.	Cheshire County League.
1978/79 – 1981/82.	Cheshire County League Div.1.
1982/83 – 1986/87.	North–West Counties League Div.1.
1987/88 –	Northern Premier League Div.1.
1988/89 – to date.	Northern Premier League Premier Div.

((((((((((((+))))))))))))

Football League Record:

	Played	W.	D.	L.	F.	A.	Pts.	Posn.
1921/22.	38	18	5	15	62	63	41	7th.
1922/23.	38	15	6	17	42	47	36	11th.

Resigned from Football League, May 1923.

Summary of Facts.

Ground: Bower Fold, Mottram Road, Stalybridge, Cheshire.
Nickname: 'Celtic.'

Colours: Royal Blue with White Sleeved Shirts, White Shorts. (Later changed to all Blue)

First Football League Game: August 27th 1921. (Home) Versus Chesterfield. (6–0 win)
Attendance: 6,000.
Last Football League Game: May 5th 1923. (Away) Versus Halifax Town (1–2 defeat)

Record Attendance: Club Match: 9,753. (Receipts £550).
Versus West Bromwich Albion. F.A.Cup 1st Round replay.(January 13th 1923)
Football League average attendances: 1921/22 – 5,250. 1922/23 – 3,465.

Ground Record: 10,400 (official), estimated 12,000.
Dick Kerr's Ladies X1 v. Rest of Lancashire. (February 8th 1921)

....

Main Achievements:

Best League Win: 6–0 v. Chesterfield. August the 27th 1921.
(The Club's first Football League Game)

Worst League Defeats: 1921/22: 0–4 (Home and Away) to Stockport.
0–4 (Away) to Chesterfield. 1–5 (Away) to Crewe.
1922/23: 0–4 (Away) to Hartlepool.

Due to such a brief Football League career (two seasons), some unusual facts emerge:
Best and (Joint) Worst League results occured in consecutive games (the first two)!
(Joint) Worst League result – against the same team (Stockport) –
Home and Away, same season!
First League and last League game against same opponents – Halifax T.!

Total Number of Football League Matches Played: 76.

International Player (England):M. Webster. (After being transferred to Middlesbrough).

F.A.Cup:
1st Round: 1922/23. (Modern day equivalent, 3rd Round)
2nd Round: 1935/36.1st Round: 1932/33. 1934/35. 1936/37. 1938/39. 1945/46.
*   1947/48. 1984/85.*

Cheshire League Div.1 Champions : 1979/80. Runners–up: 1977/78.
North–West Counties League Champs.: 1983/84. 1986/87.
Lancashire & Cheshire League Champions: 1910/11.
Lancashire Combination Div.2 Champions: 1911/12.
Cheshire Senior Cup Winners: 1952/53.

Wide angle view of the ground in 1987 – The Stand on the left existed in the Club's Football League days
(Photo Dave Twydell)

COMPLETE RECORD (FOOTBALL LEAGUE PERIOD).

Season 1921/22:

August	27th	Chesterfield	(Home)	6–0.
September	3rd	Chesterfield	(Away)	0–4.
	10th	Grimsby Town	(Home)	3–0.
	12th	Nelson	(Away)	0–1.
	17th	Grimsby Town	(Away)	1–1.
	24th	Walsall	(Home)	2–0.
October	1st	Walsall	(Away)	2–2.
	8th	Halifax Town	(Away)	3–2.
	15th	Halifax Town	(Home)	2–1.
	22nd	Tranmere Rovers	(Away)	1–4.
	29th	Tranmere Rovers	(Home)	4–0.
November	5th	Rochdale	(Away)	1–2.
	12th	Rochdale	(Home)	1–0.
	26th	Wigan Borough	(Home)	0–0.
December	24th	Southport	(Away)	1–5.
	26th	Hartlepools Utd.	(Home)	1–3.
	27th	Nelson	(Home)	2–0.
	31st	Stockport County	(Home)	0–4.
January	2nd	Hartlepools Utd.	(Away)	1–0.
	7th	Wigan Borough	(Away)	2–0.
	14th	Stockport County	(Away)	0–4.
	21st	Crewe Alex.	(Home)	2–2.
	28th	Crewe Alex.	(Away)	1–5.
February	4th	Accrington Stan.	(Home)	3–1.
	11th	Accrington Stan.	(Away)	1–4.
	18th	Darlington	(Away)	0–3.
	25th	Darlington	(Home)	1–0.
	28th	Southport	(Home)	0–0.
March	4th	Lincoln City	(Away)	1–2.
	11th	Lincoln City	(Home)	2–0.
	18th	Ashington	(Away)	3–2.
	25th	Ashington	(Home)	2–0.
April	1st	Barrow	(Home)	3–0.
	8th	Barrow	(Away)	1–2.
	14th	Wrexham	(Away)	0–2.
	15th	Durham City	(Home)	4–3.
	22nd	Durham City	(Away)	1–3.
	29th	Wrexham	(Home)	4–1.

F.A.Cup.

November	19th (4th Q.)	Carlisle Utd.	(Away)	0–0.
	22nd (Replay)	Carlisle Utd.	(Home)	3–2.
December	3rd (5th Q.)	Hartlepools U.	(Home)	2–0.
	17th (6th Q.)	Ashington	(Away)	0–1.

Season 1922/23.

August	26th	Tranmere Rovers	(Away)	1–1.
September	2nd	Tranmere Rovers	(Home)	4–1.
	9th	Nelson	(Away)	0–1.
	16th	Nelson	(Home)	2–0.
	23rd	Lincoln City	(Away)	1–1.
	30th	Lincoln City	(Home)	0–1.
October	7th	Southport	(Away)	0–0.
	14th	Southport	(Home)	1–0.
	21st	Durham City	(Away)	0–0.
November	4th	Ashington	(Home)	2–1.
	11th	Ashington	(Away)	3–0.
	18th	Bradford (P.A.)	(Away)	0–1.
	25th	Barrow	(Home)	2–0.
December	9th	Wrexham	(Away)	1–2.
	23rd	Wrexham	(Home)	3–2.
	26th	Bradford (P.A.)	(Home)	1–0.
	30th	Darlington	(Home)	4–2.
January	2nd	Barrow	(Away)	1–0.
	6th	Darlington	(Away)	0–1.
	20th	Hartlepools U.	(Home)	1–1.
	27th	Hartlepools U.	(Away)	0–4.
February	17th	Chesterfield	(Away)	0–1.
	20th	Wigan Borough	(Home)	0–2.
	24th	Chesterfield	(Home)	1–2.
March	3rd	Crewe Alex.	(Away)	1–4.
	10th	Crewe Alex.	(Home)	0–1.
	17th	Grimsby Town	(Home)	3–2.
	24th	Grimsby Town	(Away)	0–3.
	30th	Durham City	(Home)	1–0.
	31st	Accrington Stan.	(Home)	1–0.
April	2nd	Rochdale	(Home)	0–0.
	3rd	Rochdale	(Away)	0–2.
	7th	Accrington Stanley	(Away)	0–1.
	14th	Walsall	(Home)	2–0.
	18th	Wigan Borough	(Away)	0–3.
	21st	Walsall	(Away)	1–2.
	28th	Halifax Town	(Home)	4–3.
May	5th	Halifax Town	(Away)	1–2.

F.A.Cup:

December	2nd (5th Qual.)	Nelson	(Home)	1–0.
	16th (6th Qual.)	Bristol Rovers	(Home)	0–0.
	20th (Replay)	Bristol Rovers	(Away)	2–1.
January	13th (1st Rd.)	West Brom.Alb.	(Away)	0–0.
	17th (Replay)	West Brom.Alb.	(Home)	0–2.

Stalybridge had representation in the senior football world from 1895, when the Stalybridge Rovers Club entered the Lancashire League, in which they had an unremarkable existence apart from claiming the Runners–up position in the 1899/1900 season. The Rovers fortunes dipped after the 1903/04 campaign – when they played in the Lancashire Combination – until they became defunct in 1907. They had a well appointed Ground, located off Northern Road, with spectator facilities that included at least a covered, seated stand.

It is generally recognised that Stalybridge Celtic, a completely separate Club from the 'Rovers', was founded in the Spring of 1909. However, records exist showing that an amateur club was formed under the name of Stalybridge Celtic in 1906. The formation of this Club having taken place in Harry Bayley's Billiards Room. 'This' Celtic's first match being played in September of that year, on Joe Walsh's meadow at Spring Hollows. The Club was represented by:

Webb, Smith, Storrs, Manwood, Mallalieu, Ridyard, Watts, Hall, Lofthouse, Knott, and Rhodes.

Further matches were played during that season, including that at Droylesden Corinthians on the 29th of September (a 0–5 defeat), and with Worsley Wanderers, Monton Amateurs and – a local club – Woodlands. The latter game – producing a four goal defeat – was contested on the 17th of November at Millbrook, and had been: *"Eagerly looked forward to by both Clubs "*. All of these matches were Friendlies against minor opposition, therefore it can be assumed that the Club was at that time a 'low key' outfit. Scant mention of the Celtic can be found until 1909, and it is probable that after a 'reportable' start, the Club played only further minor friendlies for three years or so. It is possible of course that this earlier Celtic folded, and a new, more dominant Club appeared later, however one point of particular significance is the player named in the outside left position for the first game in 1906 – Rhodes. A further significant point with regard to the 'two' Clubs, is that players named 'Storrs' and 'Manwood' played in both 'first' games.

In 1909, there was one main driving force behind Stalybridge Celtic, that of the Club's outside left, Herbert Rhodes, a vice–President, who over the years not only provided loyal service – in addition to his Captaincy of Stalybridge Cricket Club – but expended considerable sums of money during the Celtic's formative years. A field was found at Bower Fold, where £100 was spent by Mr.Rhodes on levelling the pitch area and erecting strong enclosure barriers.

For a time this venue had been used by both Stalybridge United and Stalybridge Christ Church for their home matches in the localised Hooley

Hill League. The first competitive game played by the Celtic in 1909 was the September fixture versus Manchester South End at Whalley Range, when a 'fair crowd' witnessed a 2-2 draw after a 0-1 half time score.

On September the 25th the first game in the Lancs. & Cheshire League was played at Bower Fold when Xaverian College attracted an attendance of several hundred (gate receipts of £7). The indomitable Rhodes at outside left (and also Captain) had a good game and with a half time score of 1-1, no further goals were scored in the second period. The other players that formed the team that day, all locals, were:

> Whyatt, Manwood, Crossland (the latter later had trials with
> Manchester City), Buckley, Saxon, Storrs, Thorneycroft, Harrop,
> Wood and Goldthorpe.

The second league match was won by four unopposed goals at Droylesden, and by Christmas a satisfactory 3rd place in the table was reached after the eight games played. Whilst no honours were won that season, one year later the Celtic triumphed by becoming League Champions and were also losing finalists in the Ashton Junior Challenge Cup.

In the Summer of 1911, the Club turned professional and secured the services of ex-Southampton, Bury and Stalybridge Rovers player - J.S. Johnston as Manager. This forward thinking was backed up by entry into the Lancashire Combination Division 2, the Celtic's acceptance being gained in preference to Hooley Hill who were in conflict with the Manchester League. The first match was scheduled to be a home fixture versus Tranmere Rovers Reserves, however, the pitch was not ready for play and the first game was played and lost at St.Mark's Field in nearby Dukinfield. Despite a slow start the Celtic gradually became the masters and recorded an unbeaten run from November the 11th until March the 9th - a defeat at South Liverpool. The Celtic became Champions, with a record of 23 wins, 2 draws, 5 defeats, and a goal difference of 110-39; late season victories included a nine goal thrashing of Lancaster and 10-2 (3-2 at half time) over Tyldesley in which Woodcock scored 5 goals - on May the 12th - before he signed for Manchester United.

Another notable achievement was the Club's progress through to the final of the Cheshire Senior Cup - the first time an appearance had been made by a team in the locality. The route included the beating of Altrincham in a replayed semi-final. The final versus Crewe was lost following an initial drawn game. The ambitious Mr.Rhodes decided that the Central League was the next goal, and this was achieved with an entry for the 1912/13 campaign. Just one year earlier it had been unthinkable that the Club could achieve an elevation to this most Senior League in the North - outside of the Football League - but they now had the team and an enclosed Ground worthy of such ideals.

The reigning league runners–up, Burslem Port Vale, were easily overcome at Bower Fold on September the 3rd, by five goals to nil, where, despite the bad weather a *'good attendance'* was reported. Although admission to matches had increased from 4d.to 6d.(2.5p.), matches were well supported with crowds of four to five thousand being common.

The Club, whilst not winning any honours at the season's end, gave a good overall account of themselves, and finished in 4th position in the Central League. The following season led to greater successes in the League, when the Championship was only narrowly missed.

The ultimate target was aimed for, with the Club's application for membership of the Football League (Second Division) in 1913, but with no sustained record behind them it came as no real surprise when they only polled six votes – none the less the second highest of the five aspirants. One year later, however, the somewhat surprising decision was made with the team's entry into the Southern League for the 1914/15 season! This League was generally accepted as the most senior Non–league competition, and the Club were accepted into the Second Division. Yet the League attracted Clubs from a very wide geographical area and as the name suggested the Southern part of the Country was the supposed catchment. But the Celtic found themselves in the in company of Stoke and Coventry, together with nine South Wales Clubs in the 13 team League.

From past achievements it came as no surprise when the Celtic's efforts were rewarded with the runners–up spot, to Stoke, with 17 wins, 4 draws and only 3 defeats. This achievement would have resulted in promotion to the First Division, however with the First World War in progress, the Club had to look to nearer horizons.

The majority of Football Clubs ceased activities during the War years, but the North–West continued to provide a senior competition. Not deterred, despite criticism from those that considered the playing of sport during hostilities to be in poor taste, the Lancashire Combination continued; Stalybridge entering a team in the Southern Section. Under Wartime conditions many matches were left unplayed, and therefore the final League tables did not always reflect a club's precise ability; however with the games split into two separate sections, the Celtic became the 1915/16, '2nd Competition' Champions. Further changes were made in the ensuing years, culminating in Liverpool and Manchester sections for the final 1918/19 Wartime competition, with the Celtic becoming Champions of the latter.

The Club, not surprisingly, opted for the Central League once again, after the War, and there followed two unremarkable seasons within this Competition.

Despite only finishing in 13th place in a League of 22 teams in May 1921, support was apparent with attendances normally between 4,000 and 5,000 for home games, including the last match, a two goal win over Blackpool. However these figures were considerably exceeded when a Charity match was arranged on Tuesday the 8th of February 1921. An unprecedented gathering of 10,400 (receipts of £569), but an estimated actual figure of 12,000 including advanced ticket holders who crammed into the ground; the match being a contest between Dick Kerr's Ladies and the Rest of Lancashire!

One year earlier a Third Division was formed within the Football League, with Clubs from the first division of the Southern League being voted in en-masse. In the Summer of 1921 a similar situation was enacted with a near total move of all Central League Clubs into the new League – the Third Division North. In a surprisingly short period of time the Club had climbed from nothing to the threshold of fame, but in this respect, Mr.(by now Councillor) Rhodes cannot be ignored, for it was only through his continual enthusiasm and the injection of a staggering £25,000 into the Club over those years that the Club had prospered. The Club's first line-up for a Football League match consisted of:

T.Lonsdale, W.Barton, W.Dennis, J.Carney, H.Tyler, H.Lockett, T.Dance,J,Thompson, A.Gee, C.Petrie and G.Benson.

The match, versus Chesterfield on August the 27th, was played in front of a total crowd of around 6,000 enthusiastic supporters of both teams. Although the visitors played well for the first 20 minutes, it was Petrie who opened the scoring for the Celtic. Thompson added a second before half time, but in the second period further goals by Carney (penalty), Petrie and two more from Thompson ensured a 6–0 thrashing of the Derbyshire team. The win was unique, since it was to become the Club's Third Division record score – in their first ever Football League match!

Surprisingly the return game, seven days later, produced a 0–4 defeat before an attendance of nearly 10,000. Good results in the main were achieved which provided the club with a 4th from top placing after 7 games. Although some useful wins continued up to November, notably the 'double' over Halifax, December was a poor period with a single 2–0 home victory over Nelson and three defeats. None the less by this time a creditable 7th position in the League had been realised. 1922 started with two away wins – over Hartlepools and Wigan Borough – but it was not until March that a consistent record was established, when 4 straight victories were recorded. A high final placing in the League could have been possible, but once again an indifferent run, in April, led to a somewhat disappointing, but none the less very respectable final position of 7th.

A good run in the F.A.Cup, the best to date by the Celtic, saw a win over Carlisle by 3-2 before a 5,000 crowd – after a scoreless draw in Cumberland – followed by a two-nil victory over Hartlepools at Bower Fold before 6,000 spectators who paid £250 gate money. Entry into the first round proper was thwarted by Ashington, where Stalybridge lost by a single 28th minute goal. Little progress was made in Local Cup Competitions, since the first round of the Lancashire Cup was lost at home to Nelson and their Manchester Senior Cup progress was halted at Bolton despite an earlier and excellent 2-1 home victory over Oldham. The somewhat lesser Ashton Senior Cup saw the Club lose at Hurst Cross to Ashton National (fielding a near complete first team) in a semi-final replay.

The Club had started with a massive playing staff of 37 players, and no less than 28 had made at least one appearance in the Third Division North games. Goalkeeper Tommy Lonsdale, and Herbert Tyler, were 'ever presents', whilst Charlie Petrie led the goalscorers with 17 in League matches of the 62 total – a figure that he no doubt would have increased upon, were it not for his transfer to The (Sheffield) Wednesday on February the 10th; Jimmy Carney had seven successes of which six were penalties. Twenty-one year old Maurice Webster who had only joined the Celtic during the season, moved on to Middlesbrough at the end of March, and later won three full England International Caps. A new record (club match) attendance of 7,475 was realised with the visit of nearby Stockport County to Bower Fold on the last day of 1921, producing match receipts of £350. This first campaign in the Football League was seen as a success, and further progress was hoped for the forthcoming season.

An indifferent start was made to the Celtic's second, and as it transpired last, season in the Football League. An undefeated home record soon came to an end with the single goal defeat versus Lincoln City on the 30th of September. This following on just one week after Stalybridge's joint worst defeat in the League – 1-5 away to Stockport County (Several other 1-5 and 0-4 defeats were also suffered by the Club, only one of which was recorded at home). A good League match run however started with the October the 7th scoreless draw at Southport, and extended up to early January, resulting in 8 wins, 2 draws and only 2 defeats, and which saw the Club rise to 4th in the table. Attendances began to give cause for concern however, with crowds seldom rising above 5,000, and on the 30th of December – despite the Club's current good run – only 3,000 were present, although the poor weather obviously had an affect.

The F.A.Cup though should have provided a stimulant to the team and its supporters, since for the first time ever the 1st round proper was reached. Qualifying round wins were achieved over Nelson (1-0 at home) and at Bristol Rovers by 2-1 (following a no score home draw, which produced a new Club record attendance of 8,800 and gate receipts of £428). The biggest game ever for the Celtic came on Saturday January the 13th when a visit was made to one of the leading First Division teams – West Bromwich Albion.

Although support for run of the mill games was poor, the glamour of 'The Cup' encouraged a large number to travel to Birmingham, including a special excursion train, and so the Celtic were represented with around 500 supporters in the 24,182 crowd – the biggest attendance that the Club was ever to play before. Seats in the stands cost 2 and 3 shillings (10p and 15p) and the total gate money produced £1420 – Stalybridge's share providing a lifeline for the Directors who were trying to balance the books. With the Celtic playing in a changed strip of Red Shirts and White Shorts, they shocked the football world by holding their illustrious opponents to a 0–0 draw. A full house was confidently expected for the replay on the following Wednesday, and despite the 2.15 p.m. kick-off, the first spectators started arriving at 9.30 a.m., although the gates were not opened until midday. The final total present for the match amounted to 9,753 (£550), a new club match record, but less than that anticipated. Once again the Third Division side contained the opposition, and by the 81st minute with the match goalless, a shock second replay looked on the cards. However the Albion finally showed their superiority by scoring two goals in those last nine minutes, to bring to a halt any ambitions that the Celtic may have had as giantkillers.

The departure from the F.A.Cup signalled the start of a poor run in the League, to the extent that apart from a home draw with Hartlepools on the 20th of January, the next six games all resulted in defeat. It was March the 17th before the next victory occurred, 3–2 at home to Grimsby. The run was matched with decreasing gates, which had by now slumped to around 3,000 average.

On March the 12th, a Public Meeting was held at the Town Hall, at which the plight of the Club was explained to the 1,200 or so supporters in attendance. In order to continue in the Football League, an immediate cash injection of £2,000 was required plus a substantial increase of numbers at home matches. Mr.Rhodes, the undisputed Benefactor of the Celtic, had spent enormous sums of money to get the Club thus far, and it was now realised that other financial help was required. The proposal was made to form the Club into a Limited Company. It was also recognised that a more centralised Ground was required in order to provide easier access, and for which an estimated £10,000 was needed. The most surprising fact was conceded that no real blame could be levelled at the local townspeople in not supporting the team; with a total population of 24,000, and an average attendance to the end of February of 3,830 plus 700 season ticket holders.

these numbers represented approximately half of the town's adult male population – the section considered to form by far the majority at games. It was therefore obviously necessary to attract support from a greater area.

However the next few weeks proved that the Town was not big enough to sustain a Football League team, and when put to the real test, the locals were not prepared to offer their monetary support in sufficient numbers. A proposal had been made to form a Supporters Committee, but events overtook the Club before this came into being and the Limited Company formation failed, when less than £500 was raised. Although a moderate recovery was made on the pitch, by now apathy had set in amongst the Club's followers to the degree that the one goal home win over Accrington Stanley could only attract 2,000 to the Bower Fold, with a further decrease to around 1,500 (£47 receipts) when Walsall were the visitors on the 14th of April. Perhaps in the knowledge that the locals were about to witness the last ever Football League game in the town, a boost to 3,000 spectators were present for the last home game on April the 28th. The Celtic quickly built up a two goal lead after only 15 minutes, with the visitors Halifax pulling one back before half–time. The final result was an entertaining 4–3 home win. One week later the last ever League match was played in the return at Halifax. Before an attendance of 6,000, the Celtic were defeated by 1–2 with Fryer scoring this last League goal, and the home Club's goalkeeper getting on the score sheets with a penalty.

In Local Cup competitions, Stalybridge had mixed fortunes. The Cheshire Senior Cup competition was soon lost with a 1–5 away defeat to Stockport in September, and the Lancashire Senior Cup efforts were little better with an early exit following the 1–3 home defeat to Blackpool, despite a previous round victory over Nelson. However a good run was made in the prestigious Manchester Senior Cup, with victories over Manchester United Reserves (2–1 at Old Trafford before a 3,000 attendance), 5–1 at home to Manchester University, and the 2–1 defeat of Hurst in the semi–final at Bower Fold.

The last ever game as a Football League Club was played at Hyde Road, Ardwick, when the Celtic lost by two unopposed goals to Stockport County in the final of the Manchester Cup Competition. During this second and last season as a League Club, a total of 28 players were used – this number perhaps being indicative of the Club's inability to remain financially viable. Tommy Lonsdale played in all but one of the League matches, whilst Jimmy Carney was an everpresent. Carney was once again the leading converter of penalties with 7 out of 8 successes, and Joseph O'Kane and Chris Sambrooke led the goalscorers with ten goals each in all competitions – Sambrooke scoring the most, just nine, in League games only.

The Celtic's final placing in the League table was a healthy 11th of 20 Clubs, a situation that for many others would have been considered satisfactory with plenty of hope for improvement. However, the Directors, in their wisdom (in view of their slender resources), took the not unreasonable stance that the Club would never be able to become financially secure as a Football League outfit. And so, immediately following the Manchester Senior Cup Final, the Club formally announced its decision to resign from the Third Division North – a very rare decision taken by a member club of the Football League. It is open to conjecture whether such a move was the right one, for as years went by it became nigh on impossible to join the 'elite' and it could be argued that the Celtic had, perhaps lamely, relinquished their status that had been comparatively easily achieved, whilst others have fought for decades for a comparable position. Conversely the Club, reasonably decided to compete in a competition that they felt they could financially cope with, and so they applied for, and were accepted into, the Cheshire County League for the 1923/24 season.

All the players on the Celtic's books were given free transfers; Stafford and Dennis signed for Manchester United, Tetlow for Nottingham Forest, whilst several joined Third Division teams. Holt, Lockett, Mace and Carney however re-signed for Stalybridge; the latter had experienced the unusual situation of appearing for two clubs in their final Football League seasons, his other Club being Glossop.

With the prospect of several exciting local derbys, Stalybridge commenced the next season with a home game versus Stockport County Reserves. A paltry attendance of 1,200 was present for the 1–1 draw, but this crowd was improved upon by 300 for the next fixture at Bower Fold, when the reserves of Tranmere were thrashed by four goals. The Club proved their worth to the league, for after 8 games they led the table and for the home game versus Whitchurch in mid–October a 3,000 attendance was present, but for a disappointing scoreless draw. A 1–3 defeat at Walsall in the F.A.Cup came as no real surprise, but by Christmas the team lay in third place in the league – with fewer games than others having been played – and over the Holiday period, matches versus Macclesfield (in the County Cup), and Mossley, attracted 4,000 attendances to each home games. The Club however did not feature in the end of season honours as hoped for.

In 1935, the Celtic became a limited Company, a move which had failed 12 years earlier. The period coincided with one of their best years when they finished in third place in the league – separated only on goal average from the Champions, Wigan Athletic. Despite being a consistent prominent member of the League, the Celtic had to surprisingly wait many years for another commanding league position as it wasn't until the 1977/78 season that their highest placing was realised, that of runners–up.

Even the League Cup eluded the team, other than in 1922, when ironically it was the Celtic's Reserve Eleven that carried away the trophy. It was fitting, in view of the Club's past, that in the 1979/80 season they at last won the Cheshire League Championship, 7 points clear of runners–up Winsford United and with a goal difference of 94 – 46; C.Skillen scored 36 league goals, 8 more than his nearest competitor, from Rhyl.

In 1982, the North–West Counties League was formed, composed almost in total by the amalgamation of the Lancashire Combination and the Cheshire County Leagues, the latter providing the majority of Division 1 Clubs in the new competition.

Once again Stalybridge Celtic appears to have let their chances slip by, for the Northern Premier League was open to top Cheshire County League clubs in its formation in 1980, but with the Ground not reaching the required 'A' classification this league was denied to them; this competition being one step from the top rung of the 'Pyramid' in Non–league football.

The Celtic became Champions of the North–West Counties League in 1983/84 – the second season of this new Pyramid feeder league, and they were also the League Shield Winners, but with promotion to the more senior competition not being automatic, it was very frustrating for the Club to have their application for a move up turned down. However recent years of success, first into the Northern Premier League First Division, and finally the Premier Division, has seen the Club become a dominant non–League force in the North–west.

Over the years the Celtic have produced few shock results in the F.A.Cup, for apart from several appearances in the 1st round in the 1930's (and the 2nd round in 1935/36), twice in the 40's, and in 1984/85, they have yet to get the better of a Football League opponent since their own days in such company. But the support has been there when the Club has staged a big match, including 6,641 in 1932, 5,869 two years later and a massive 8,776 for their 1935 second round appearance.

Stalybridge Celtic parted from the Football League as they were unable to justify their existence on gates of around 4,000. Although such numbers were repeated in the 1940's, they, like their contemporaries, have now had to come to terms with running a part–professional Club, but coupled with relatively poor support at the turnstile. Until their elevation into the Northern Premier League, it was a rare occurrence to see more than 400 spectators at the Bower Fold, although recent years of success have seen the numbers more regularly approaching four figures.

BOWER FOLD.

Stalybridge are one of only three Ex–League Clubs – the others being Gainsborough Trinity and Northwich Victoria – that still exist, and whose home venue has not changed since they entered Senior level football. Ignoring the first few years when the Club was questionably the same as the later Stalybridge Celtic, then the Club can claim to have had the same Ground since the start – in 1909.

Being located in a still rural area on the outskirts of the town, Bower Fold has changed relatively little since the early days when the shortlived venture was made into the Football League, and it is probable that without the pressing ravages of so called progress, their surroundings are probably much the same too. It is most likely that, that same 'progress' caused the redevelopment of Stalybridge Rovers Crookbottom Ground – located between Northend Road and Wakefield Road (near the centre of the town) – soon after this Club's demise in 1907. If this had not been so then it is very probable that the Celtic could have quite easily taken oven this already well developed enclosure.

Until the Celtic's development at Bower Fold, the site was no more than a vacant field. The field was turned into a Football Ground due to the principal monetary efforts of the Club's benefactor Herbert Rhodes. Initially the main feature was the wooden covered stand that seated around 500 spectators and was present by the time the Club entered the Football League. It is quite surprising to discover that this stand (and open paddock in front) is one and the same as that which still stands today! The early years also saw the formation of banks to all four sides of the Ground. These were not, in all probability, initially constructed of concrete since some areas of the surrounds are now flat or only grass banked; possible additional evidence for this conclusion lies outside the North–west corner of the Ground. Near a low stone boundary retaining wall (probably part of the original enclosure wall) are scattered around several large timber railway sleepers – conceivably originally used in forming the Ground's 'terracing'. At the South–west corner there is a section of brick wall that may well have been part of the original boundary walls – these have undoubtably been rebuilt relatively recently. The present covered enclosure opposite the main stand does not date back to the Football League days since it is now deeper, but the original (which was approximately the same length) probably remained until the early 1950's. The covered enclosure behind the goal with its curved roof, is however of modern construction, the original probably being longer, (but later part removed), and remained also at least until the 1950's. The original enclosure was not built until after the Club's entry into the Football League, and this date may well have coincided with an area of concrete terracing (no longer remaining) that was introduced at the South–east corner of the Ground. Initially the main, or only, entrance to the Ground was via a narrow enclosed strip off of the Mottram Road, but by the early 1930's the Club's land was extended to provide ample parking and access to the whole frontage of the Seated Stand side.

The Ground today complete with its modern extension to the North of the Seated Stand, presents a compact and neat football arena, and with apparent space for development, it is quite possible to visualise Bower Fold once again hosting Football League fixtures.

PROGRAMMES:

Post–Football League programmes are of course easily available, and although they are known to have been issued during the two seasons in the Third Division North, suffice it to say that any remaining copies are now extremely rare!

1966/67 season, the Celtic versus Wrexham ....
.... In the 1920's the match would have been between both Clubs first teams!

Bower Fold c. 1921, and its location.

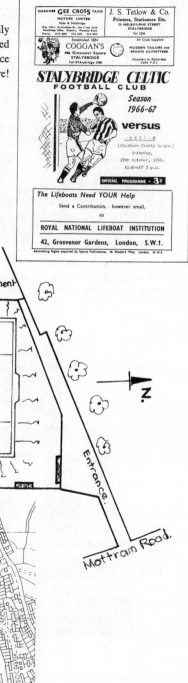

Workington.

THE WORKINGTON SQUAD WHICH BEGAN THE 1965-66 SEASON —

Back Row (left to right) — George Ainsley (manager), John Lumsden, John Ogilvie, Ian Ower, Mike Rogan, Bobby Brown, Tony Geidmintis, Clive Middlemass, George Aitken (trainer).

Front Row (left to right) — Peter Foley, Ken Oliver, Kit Napier, Dixie Hale, Jimmy Moran, John Chapman.

At the end of the 1965-66 campaign Workington attained 5th position in the 3rd Division — their highest placing in twenty six seasons of League football.

The flag goes up for the last home League match
(14th May 1977 versus Newport County)

Workington.

Founded:1884 Disbanded: 1911 Reformed: 1921.
Football League: 1951/52 – 1976/77.

****

1884 – 1889.	Friendly.
1889/90 – 1900/01.	Cumberland Association.
1901/02 – 1902/03.	Lancashire League.
1903/04	Cumberland Association.
1904/05 – 1906/07.	Lancashire Combination Div.2.
1907/08 – 1909/10.	Lancashire Combination Div.1.
1910/11.	North Eastern League.
1921/22 – 1938/39.	North Eastern League.
1939/40 – 1944/45.	Ceased Activities.
1945/46 – 1950/51.	North Eastern League.
1951/52 – 1957/58.	**Football League Div.3.(North)**
1958/59 – 1963/64.	**Football League Div.4.**
1964/65 – 1966/67.	**Football League Div.3.**
1967/68 – 1976/77.	**Football League Div.4.**
1977/78 – 1987/88.	Northern Premier League Premier Division.
1988/89 –	Northern premier League First Division.

<<<<<<<<<<<<<>>>>>>>>>>>>

Football League Record:

	Played	W.	D.	L.	F.	A.	Pts.	Posn.
1951/52	46	11	7	28	50	91	29	24th
Successfully re-elected.								
1952/53	46	11	10	25	55	91	32	23rd
Successfully re-elected.								
1953/54	46	13	14	19	59	80	40	20th
1954/55	46	18	14	14	68	55	50	8th
1955/56	46	19	9	18	75	63	47	10th
1956/57	46	24	10	12	93	63	58	4th
1957/58	46	14	13	19	72	81	41	19th
Founder-members of Fourth Division.								
1958/59	46	12	17	17	63	78	41	17th
1959/60	46	14	14	18	68	60	42	16th
1960/61	46	21	7	18	74	76	49	8th
1961/62	44*	19	11	14	69	70	49	8th
1962/63	46	17	13	16	76	68	47	10th
1963/64	46	24	11	11	76	52	59	3rd
Promoted to Third Division.								
1964/65	46	17	12	17	58	69	46	15th
1965/66	46	19	14	13	67	57	52	5th
1966/67	46	12	7	27	55	89	31	24th
Relegated to Fourth Division.								
1967/68	46	10	11	25	54	87	31	23rd
Successfully re-elected.								

1968/69	46	15	17	14	40	43	47	12th
1969/70	46	12	14	20	46	64	38	20th
1970/71	46	18	12	16	48	49	48	10th
1971/72	46	16	19	11	50	34	51	6th
1972/73	46	17	12	17	59	61	46	13th
1973/74	46	11	13	22	43	74	35	23rd

Successfully re-elected.

1974/75	46	10	11	25	36	66	31	23rd

Successfully re-elected.

1975/76	46	7	7	32	30	87	21	24th

Successfully re-elected.

1976/77	46	4	11	31	41	102	19	24th

Failed to gain Re-election.
* Fixtures versus Accrington Stanley deleted.

Summary of Facts.
Grounds:

1884 – 1909:	Schoose Close. Workington Cricket Field. Ashfield.
1909. (Two games)	Recreation Ground, Whitehaven.
1909 – 1937:	Lonsdale Park.
1937.	(Temporary Ground) Ellis Sports Ground.
1937 – to date:	Borough Park.

Nickname: The Reds.
Colours (Football League):
1951 – 1966: Red Shirts, White Trim. White Shorts.
1966 – 1968: All Red.
1968 – 1977: Red Shirts. White Shorts.

First League Game: 18th August 1951. Versus Halifax Town (Away) Lost 1–3.
Attendance: 11,000.
Last League Game: 17th May 1977. Versus Newport County (Away) Lost 0–1.
Attendance: 8,313.
Record Attendance: January 4th 1958. Versus Manchester United (F.A.Cup) –
Attendance: 21,000. Lost 1–3.
Football League average attendances: First season 6,679. Last season 1,338.
Lowest League Attendance: 1973/74. Versus Exeter City – 693.

Main Achievements:
Promotion to Third Division (3rd in 4th Div.): 1964.
Football League Cup 5th Round (Quarter Finals): 1963/64. 1964/65.

F.A.Cup – As a Non-league Club:
4th Round: 1933/34.
1st Round (equivalent to modern 3rd round) 1908/09. 1909/10.
3rd Round: 1935/36.
2nd Round: 1932/33. 1934/35. 1947/48.
1st Round: 1926/27. 1927/28. 1930/31. 1937/38. 1938/39. 1946/47. 1948/49. 1977/78.
1978/79. 1979/80. 1980/81. 1981/82. 1982/83.
(As a Football League Club, didn't progress beyond 3rd Round)

North-Eastern League Runners-up: 1938/39.
North-Eastern League Challenge Cup Winners: 1934/35. 1936/37.
Cumberland County Cup Winners: 1887–1891 incl. 1896–1899 incl. 1907.
1908. 1909. 1925.1935. 1937. 1938. 1950. 1954. 1968. 1986.

Number of Football League matches played: 1,195.
(Incl. Accrington Stanley, away, 1961/62)

Best League Win: 1965/66. 7–0 versus Swansea Town (Home).
(The return result, 6–1)
Best (major competitive game) Win: 1933/34. 16–1 versus Chopwell Institute (Home)
– North-Eastern League.
Worst League Defeat: 1953/54. 0–8 versus Wrexham (Away).

Most Football League Appearances – 419 by Bobby Brown. (1956–1968)

1976/77 (Last Season) Recorded only 4 wins (Football League 4th Div. joint record low)
and only 19 points (4th Div. record low).

The biggest match in Workington's history. A few weeks later, and the Munich Air disaster decimated the United team

It took Workington F.C. 67 years to gain entry into the Football League; yet their stay remained for only the comparitively short period of 26 years. For this far North–East outpost of the country, the local supporters were to see their Club not only enter the Football League in the post–Second World War era, but also to depart from it during this period – the only Club to achieve this dubious distinction.

Football became a reportable sport in Cumberland at the relatively late time of the early 1880's. Whilst the North – overall – enjoyed varying degrees of journalistic coverage ten years or more earlier, the first mention of a Workington team did not appear until January 1884. The team in question, possibly the forerunner of Workington F.C., were referred to as Workington (Dronfield). It was some months later, in October, that a more specific reference to the Club was made, when it was announced that a new Association Football Club had been formed – principally for the men of the Westfield district – with a ground in the upper part of the town. In the absence of more definite evidence, this has been accepted as the formation of Workington F.C.

Workington can be truly considered as the birthplace of serious Association Football in Cumberland, for whilst Wigton could also lay claim to this title, it was the stimulation of the Reds presence that set the scene for the years to come. The steelworks company of Charles Cammell from Sheffield set up business in the town and it was the influence of their workers that played a large part in establishing a club, coupled with the enthusiasm of Frederick J.Hayes.

The early days saw the Club playing local friendly fixtures with Clubs such as Barrow–in–Furness, Newcastleton, Distington and Wigton Athletic. However with the introduction of the Cumberland Cup in the 1885/86 season, when five Clubs entered, games of a more competitive nature were able to be undertaken. In the final of this competition, the Reds met Carlisle – not the latter day United, since they were not formed until 18 years later. The match was played at Highmoor Park, Wigton, and was lost by two unopposed goals. One year later however the same opponents were met, again in the final, at Workington Cricket Field (at this time the Reds home ground), and revenge was more than sweet with an 8–0 victory.

It was not until 1890 that a suitable League competition was formed – the Cumberland Association – but the Club maintained it's prestige in the County with their continued successful wins in the County Cup competition. Locally the Club's dominance was undisputed with several championships of the Association League and later the Senior League, as well as more County Cup Final appearances, right up to the dawn of the twentieth century. The Cumberland County Cup Final of 1897, which was won with a victory over Carlisle City (their third successive defeat in the final), was seriously marred as the joyful victors made their way from the ground. The players were set upon by stone throwing hooligan 'supporters' of the losers and the Reds half back, John Fisher, was hit on the head. The twenty year old became paralysed, never recovering from the injury, for he died nineteen weeks later.

Entry into the F.A.Cup commenced in 1887, and their capability in this wider sphere was more questionable. It was not until five years later that the Club recorded even their first goal in the Competition – that in their 1–9 defeat at Fleetwood Rangers! The early seasons produced defeats at Bootle (Liverpool) – forerunner of the eventual second Division Football League Club – by 0–6 in the 1887/88 season, a three goal defeat at Liverpool Stanley twelve months later, and a 0–10 demolition at Blackpool South Shore – later to become the redoubtable Blackpool F.C. The first successes in the F.A.Cup came during the 1894/95 season with a commendable 4th qualifying round appearance – and defeat only in a replay. The first ever win in the Cup was achieved by 2–1 at home to Oswaldthwistle Rovers, followed by four goals to nil over Heywood Central, and a 'walkover' in the third qualifying round when Rossendale scratched. Defeat eventually came by five goals at Southport Central, after two goals were shared at Workington Cricket Field – the original drawn game also coincided with the use of goal nets for the first time at Workington.

The Reds dominance of the County League was underlined with such victories as that over Cockermouth Crusaders with a 17–1 scoreline (the Club's all time record victory) in the 1900/01 season, a game in which even the goalkeeper – Dawson – scored! Natural progression followed with their entry into the highly regarded Lancashire League the following season – together with neighbours Barrow soon after their formation. The Club's stay in this League lasted only two seasons, not due to their inabilities but caused by the League's closure after only 14 seasons. Workington, along with most of their previous opponents were absorbed into the rival Lancashire Combination in 1904. Based as the Club are in their somewhat barren (in football terms) location and amidst a rapidly developing Rugby League stronghold, it was an economic struggle, despite their promotion to the First Division at the end of the 1906/07 season. On the 23rd of January 1909, a 0–3 home defeat to Manchester United Reserves riled the local fans, and their anger was taken out on the referee who managed to obtain a lift, in secret, to the railway station on a milk float! The Football Association were not amused and fined the Club £15, as well as closing the Workington ground for one month; the following two 'home' matches were played at the Recreation Ground, Whitehaven.

The added boost in prestige of the Lancashire Combination did not prove to be a financial uplift, and a move to the more local North-Eastern League was made for the 1910/11 season. During this season, the longest time for a definite match result occurred in a Cumberland County cup-tie versus Lowca. A scoreless draw was followed with a two goals shared game (after 'double' extra time of thirty minutes plus twenty). The third game ended up 2-2, and finally in the third replay the Reds lost by 0-2 - a total of six hours and fifty minutes having been played!

During these early years of the twentieth season, the Club's ability in the F.A.Cup gradually improved, and the 1908/09 sortie produced their first ever appearance in the first round proper. The run produced some high scoring games - 9-0 versus Barrow Novacastrians, 11-0 over Hindpool Athletic, by eight unopposed goals versus Lancaster, and two 4-1 wins when high status opponents South Shields Adelaide and Crewe Alexandra were defeated. All the games had been played at the Workington Cricket Ground, but the end came at Football League First Division opponents Bradford City, with a nonetheless very creditable 0-2 defeat following an abandoned match - caused by blizzards during the game. One year later the first round was also reached, once more with some high scoring qualifying rounds, and on this occasion the end came at Second Division Champions-elect Manchester City, with a close 1-2 scoreline.

Despite the Reds progress, the financial situation grew worse, and on the 29th of April 1911, the team played their last match - a two nil league defeat at Hartlepools United. At a shareholders meeting three months later a resolution was passed for the Club to go into voluntary liquidation. Despite the emergence of Workington Central F.C. for three seasons plus the United and Athletic teams from Workington, the slumber of Workington F.C. was not awakened until a few years after the completion of the Great War, in 1921.

GRAND CHARITY MATCHES:

WORKINGTON v. FRIZINGTON ATHLETIC	WORKINGTON v. CLEATOR MOOR CELTIC
Lonsdale Park, Workington.	Lonsdale Park, Workington,
Monday, May 16th, 1921.	Thursday. May 19th.
Kick-off at 6 p.m.	Kick-off at 6 p.m.

ADMISSION TO GROUND (INCLUDING TAX)

8d. Boys, 4d. Side Stands, 1/3. Grand Stand, 2/-

Total Proceeds of both games to go to Miners' Kiddies' Fund and to the Children's Clog and Clothing Fund.

John Varty & Co., Ltd., Printers and Bookbinders, Workington.

At a public meeting in the MasonicHall on Thursday the 20th of January 1921 a number of football enthusiasts met to discuss the possibility of reforming Workington F.C. A further meeting on the 19th March at the Jane Street Co-operative Hall saw the re-birth of the Club, when a Committee was formed.

Dan Richardson was elected Chairman, a position he was to initially fill for nine years.

In order to 'test the water' three friendly games were played in May, versus Barrow, Preston North End and Frizington Athletic, when mostly local players composed the Workington team. A new 'home' was utilised, that of Lonsdale Park, a venue that was to be used for many years.

Despite being only a fledgling Club, their past record, plus available places in the North–Eastern League – due to the 'defection' of four members to the newly formed Third Division North of the Football League – ensured the Club's election to this Competition.

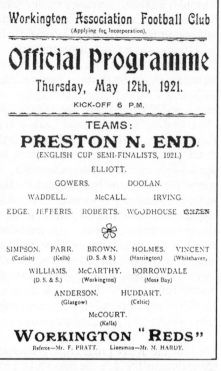

Darlington Reserves, Preston Colliery and Seaton Delavel were also admitted to the League. The Club's isolated location caused problems, not only for themselves, but also for their opponents, in view of the travelling distances that had to be undertaken. The extra cost of guaranteeing the opposition's travelling expenses from Newcastle – the locality where the majority of the teams were located – was insisted upon by the League.

The first competitive game, was played on the 27th of August 1921 at South Shields Reserves, an inauspicious start with a 1–2 defeat. Workington were represented by:

Hanna, Huddart, Taylor, Sykes, King, McArthy, Harvey, Henderson, Kirkpatrick, Holmes and Hayhurst

and it fell to Chic Harvey, the honour of scoring the first goal for the new Club. The return with the Geordie team was played at Lonsdale Park one week later, when a scoreless draw ensued. There were to be no sensations in these early days, and it was not until the fourth league match that the first win – 2–1 over Preston Colliery – was recorded. On Boxing Day the first of many local derbys was staged, with the visit of neighbours Carlisle United, and although a 1–3 reverse was the result, the best attendance of the season – 9,000 – at least kept the Club's Treasurer happy! The return at Carlisle was also lost, before an attendance of 11,815. A satisfactory start had been made on the field, for at the season's end a final placing of ninth (of twenty teams) was achieved with 17 wins, 8 draws and 13 defeats; of more concern was the later announced loss on the season of £922, a worrying figure for a non–league Club.

One year later however the deficit had been turned into a profit of over £162, and a rise in the final League table to seventh position. The ensuing years produced healthy final league placings, in fact the lowest position up to the last before the Second World War – except for the 1926/27 season (an uncharacteristic 16th) – was 9th. Although the team was undoubtably one of the consistently better outfits, the league title always eluded the Club and the runners–up place, in 1938/39, was the sole honour in this competition for the Reds. The North–Eastern League was however a very strong combination and was dominated by the reserve teams of several Football League Clubs, notably Newcastle United and Sunderland – it was rare for either of these teams to not feature in the end of season honours. Due to this dominance, a 'Non–reserve' Medal was awarded to the highest placed 'first team' Club each season, and this was won by the Reds in the 1930/31, 1931/32 and 1938/39 seasons.

Throughout the 1920's and 30's, the Reds proved themselves a goal scoring machine, and over the years produced some high scoring victories – the exception to the rule being the last four games of the 1926/27 campaign when each match ended as a no score draw! The 1923/24 season became the real start to 'goals galore', when league wins included the 8–1 thrashing at Bedlington United, the Club's first double figure score of 11–1 when they hosted the Jarrow match, and a 9–1 thrashing of Wigton Harriers in the F.A.Cup.

It was in this season that Jack Thom came to the fore, scoring 3, 4 and 5 goals in separate matches. There was a gap of some four years before his prolific scoring was witnessed again, but in the 1928/29 season both he and the Club surpassed themselves when it came to winning margins. Thom scored no fewer than ten hat–tricks that season (including two five and three four goal efforts), these goal avalanches included 9–2 wins over Scotswood (away) and Washington in the league, plus a 10–1 demolition of Egremont in the Cumberland Cup. This prolific rate of scoring continued into the next season when in six League and three F.A.Cup games, five or more goals were scored. Once again Thom was the main feature in this his last of three seasons, during which he had endeared himself to the local supporters. During these years, on twenty–one occasions he had scored a minimum of three goals in separate matches, and his total for the season in 1928/29 of sixty-nine (including four in friendly matches) stands as an all match Clubman record. Thom's 'missing' years were spent at Nottingham Forest who paid Workington £400 for his transfer, he then had a spell at Bristol Rovers before returning to the North West.

The top marksman personality then fell to Billy Charlton – transferred from Tranmere Rovers – for the next three seasons; during those years he also managed on twenty-one occasions, to find the back of the net three times or more in separate games, with one game of five goals (a 7–2 home win over Ashington in their first season out of the Football League) and a Club all time (joint) record six goals in the match versus Annfield Plain, which produced a 9–3 win. To Charlton goes the record number of League goals – 57, during the Club's fourth final runners-up place in the 1931/32 season; his second of three succeeding top goalscorer campaigns. To add to his achievements he remains as the most prolific marksmen, overall, for the Club having netted 193 in league and Cup games for the Reds, and these included a remarkable sequence in the 1931/32 season when he notched up 25 goals in eleven consecutive scoring games.

The high-scorers were by no means restricted to just Thom and Charlton in the pre-war period, for in the last half of the 1930's Billy Boyd recorded hat-tricks on thirteen occasions, Fisher five times and Sewell four. Billy Boyd's four hat-tricks during the 1935/36 season were all the more remarkable as they were confined to a four month period! Arriving in September 1935 from Manchester United his potential with the Reds were soon noted and he departed for Luton Town in December. Due to an injury he was unable to play in the Luton match versus Bristol Rovers on April the 13th, and an unknown replacement by the name of Joe Payne took his place; Payne proceeded to score ten goals in a 12–0 victory, a Football League individual goalscoring record! Boyd however returned to the Reds in April 1938 and went on to record a total of 92 goals for the Club.

In the period 1923/24 to 1938/39 – in just sixteen seasons – there were in excess of 120 competitive games which featured hat-trick heroes – if the custom of presenting the ball to the goal hero was customary at this time, it would surely have been stretching the Club's financial resources! An all-time second highest record score by the Club, and the highest ever in any North-Eastern league game, was played in the 1933/34 season at home to Chopwell Institute (significantly their last season in the league) when an astounding 16–1 win (6–0 at half-time) was achieved, a match in which Miller, Walker and Stanger scored three goals apiece; the earlier away fixture produced a 7–4 victory. During the same season a 15–1 rout of Walker Celtic was also recorded, with Andy Lincoln providing the other joint record score of six goals in a match.

By May 1934 the final record showed a goal score of 147 in 38 league games (an average of nearly four per match), a Club all time record, far and away higher than the next best in the 1938/39 campaign which produced 'only' 121 successes! The latter period however produced it's own record for the Club with an 18 unbeaten game sequence which stretched over three months. During the 1935/36 season the Club put in a somewhat spectacular bid for the services of Scottish International Hughie Gallacher, but a move by the Derby centre–forward never materialised.

After the long serving Chairman, Dan Richardson stepped down, Tom Mounsey took the chair, but he was soon superseded by William Henderson (1931–1934), followed by the return of Dan Richardson again until 1950. In 1929, the Club decided to offer themselves for admission to the Football League but at the election meeting, they received no votes (along with Chester and Rhyl) and this emphatic rejection did not encourage a further application for many years.

The Club's fortunes in the F.A.Cup competition varied, and produced games against long forgotten names in Non–league football; Whitehaven Recreation in 1921/22 – a 0–1 defeat – followed one year later with an away victory after a home draw versus Wath Brow. A seven goal victory over Windermere, plus successes over Cleator Moor Celtic, and the Whitehaven outfit. A final defeat in the 4th qualifying round was inflicted at the more familiar club Barrow, and it was to be some years before the 1st round proper was reached. More unfamiliar teams were later met including Wigton Harriers (a 9–1 victory in 1923), Whitehaven Athletic, and Ulverston Town, together with others that have stood the test of time including Southport, Carlisle United (in two successive seasons), Penrith and Lancaster Town. The 1927/28 season saw an appearance with the League Clubs for the first time, when seven games took the Reds to the 1st round proper. Although some impressive wins had been recorded en–route (8–0 over Cleator Moor Celtic after a four goals shared draw, and 7–1 versus Barrow Y.M.C.A.). But the Club met their match at Valley Parade when they were crushed by six unopposed goals by Bradford City.

In 1929 it took three matches before the team bowed out to Lancaster Town, but the most bizarre series of games occurred three years later. After a 6–1 home victory over Netherfield, followed by a 7–0 away win at Kells United, the next opponents were Whitehaven Athletic. After taking a somewhat commanding lead at Lonsdale Park to the tune of 10–0, the match was abandoned! The game had been played in atrocious weather, and the cold decimated the visiting team as the players progressively left the field suffering from exposure; with just one player left after 70 minutes play, the referee had little alternative but to abandon the match – the Reds appeared to be made of sterner stuff as none of their team had succumbed to the weather! The replay resulted in a more moderate 5–2 victory after, extra time, but yet again the tie was not resolved due to a protest from Whitehaven that only twenty minutes of extra time over the ninety had been played instead of the required thirty. The match was ordered to be replayed this time at Whitehaven where at last an undisputed result, a 4–1 Reds win ensued. This protracted match was followed with victories over South Kirby Colliery (3–0) and fellow non–leaguers Scunthorpe United in the 1st round proper. The Club's longest run – to the second round – was ended at Halifax by the narrowest of margins, 1–2.

This excellent progress was rewarded the next season when the Club entered at the 4th qualifying round stage, and Manchester Northern were dispensed with after a 6–3 win following six goals having been shared in Lancashire. Some unexpected wins over Third Division visitors followed – Southport, Newport County and Gateshead – which took the team to the fourth round and a home game versus the redoubtable Second Division Club, Preston North End (eventual runners–up in their League). This game was unquestionably the biggest, to that time, in the Club's history and a new record attendance of over 16,000 spectators crammed into the Lonsdale Park ground. They were by no means disgraced with the 1–2 defeat that resulted.

From this season up to the war period, Workington only failed to reach the 1st round proper on one occasion – in 1936/37 – whilst the third round had been reached one year earlier (victories over Northwich Victoria, New Brighton and Kidderminster Harriers) before eventual defeat at Bradford Park Avenue in a closely fought 2–3 match. The 1938/39 season was to be the last in the Cup for seven years, and the Club bowed out gracefully with a 1–2 defeat, after a home draw, to Mansfield Town.

The 1939/40 season rapidly came to an end after only three games. The end also came to the career with the Club of Tommy Carruthers, when he departed after fourteen years service. It had taken many years to become a prominent force in the Non–league world but with the Second World War looming, it was to be another decade before Workington F.C. could make a serious challenge for Football League Membership. In view of their repeated record of high scoring wins, the goalscoring personalities of that era and their progress within the F.A Cup Competition, this period could arguably be considered the heydays of Workington F.C., despite the Club's later entry into the Football League.

Come the peace, and the Reds were eager to carry on where they left off – a leading team in the North–Eastern League. This competition started for the clubs one year earlier than their Football League counterparts.

But Workington's hopes were soon dashed with a dismal 17th league placing in a league of twenty clubs, their worst ever position in 19 attempts since their re–formation in 1921. No solace came in the F.A.Cup either, for a 1–2 home defeat to Chorley, the Lancashire Combination team, in their first game was their reward.

The following three seasons were much the same with final placings of 13th, 16th and 18th. The 1946/47 season with the enforced abandoned games during a terribly harsh winter brought about a bizarre situation when at the season's end, the Reds played two league matches in one day! On the 31st of May they travelled to the Horden Colliery Welfare Ground, where they were beaten 0–2; with only time for a quick bath, the players immediately changed into a second team strip and moved on to Stockton. That hot afternoon they managed a 1–1 draw, with Stockton also playing their second match of the day! The commencement of the next season saw the Club's first ever Player/Manager – Sam Barkas. Despite the overall lack of league match successes, the F.A.Cup exploits during these years gave hope for the future.

Exempted on each occasion until the 4th qualifying round, the 1st round was reached on two occasions whilst in 1948 one step further was obtained, and included a giant killing. Netherfield were first beaten by 2–1 at Borough Park followed by the daunting prospect of a visit to 3rd Division North leaders Lincoln City. A minor sensation occurred when the Reds returned with a well merited 2–0 win. But this victory was not repeated in the second round when the comparatively easier task of beating Crewe Alexandra at home was not accomplished, and the Club lost by the odd goal in three. The 1948/49 season produced four F.A.Cup games, but only one win! It first took three attempts to defeat Lancaster City, before somewhat lamely succumbing to Stockport by three goals at Borough Park. A change in the Club's fortunes followed and two far more encouraging final placings of 9th and finally 5th in 1951.

Yet another prolific goalscorer was found in the form of Jackie Oakes. He joined the Club from Maryport Athletic, and soon made his mark by scoring 42 league goals from the total of 80, in the 1947/48 season – a surprising feat since the team finished in 16th place that year! Oakes continued to dominate the goal scoring charts, becoming the Club's leading marksman for four years running. By now the Club's eyes were on the Football League and an application was made at the Football League meeting in June 1950. It had been decided that both Third Divisions would be increased by two clubs, which gave the Reds some hope, although their overall post–war form hardly made them front–runners. Their application was unsuccessful, but only in the strangest and most controversial of circumstances.

The voting figures confidently gave Shrewsbury Town high marks (30), whilst Workington and Wigan Athletic polled 19 each and Scunthorpe 17; the 'also rans' – Nelson, South Liverpool, Northwich Victoria, Ashington and North Shields (three ex–league teams amongst them) were well down the list. To accompany the Shropshire team it was logically assumed that a straight second poll between the Reds and Wigan would be taken, however in their wisdom, the 'powers that be' decreed that all eight teams would be included in this second poll.

On this occasion a remarkable result put Workington in third place behind Scunthorpe and Wigan, each of whom received 15 votes. A third poll was taken, this time just between the top two, and Scunthorpe romped home. Despite the protests and dismay of both the Wigan and Workington representatives the decision remained. One year later, with, in theory less of a chance since the Club had to go 'into the hat' with the bottom two League members, the Club were successful. Accrington had no trouble in retaining their place, but the hapless New Brighton team only received 18 votes of confidence whilst the Reds received ten more. There were no doubts on this occasion – for Wigan received only a paltry 4 votes – Workington F.C. had made it!

Saturday the 18th of August 1951 drew eleven thousand spectators to Halifax to see their locals compete against the newcomers – Workington F.C. John Maxfield went down in the history books as the scorer of the first ever goal in the Football League for the Club; but it was no dream debut for the team for they lost 1–3. The team that day consisted of:
McIndewar, Wallace, Hainsworth, Rooney, McAlone, Andrews,
Hepburn, McDowall, Simmonds, Maxfield and Mullen.

The next match was at Borough Park and 7,000 fans went away happy following their favourites 3–1 victory over Chesterfield; McDowall scoring twice and one by Cushin, who had replaced Hepburn in the team from the first match. Victories were hard to come by in the ensuing nine months although a 6–1 thrashing was dished out to Southport, but this did not compensate for the 1–5, 0–5 and 0–7 reverses at York, Grimsby and Lincoln respectively.

By the season's end only 11 wins had been recorded, plus 7 drawn matches and 28 defeats; worst of all the Club finished bottom of the League, and had to go cap in hand to the re–election meeting – this time hopefully to retain their membership rather than gain it! As hoped for they were given another chance and although receiving five votes less than the 23rd placed Darlington, their 40 votes were well in excess of those constant triers Wigan Athletic's nine.

The post-war football support was still present, and despite their debut with the football elite being such a disappointment a reasonable average attendance at home matches of 6,720 was the outcome. A third round appearance in the F.A.Cup provided some welcome money for the coffers. Non-league opponents in the first two rounds were fairly easily overcome – 5-2 at Blackhall Colliery and 1-0 over Witton before 7,240 fans at Borough Park, which followed the earlier 3-3 draw. The third round tie was a 'plumb', a visit to Anfield, Liverpool. The First Division Club could always guarantee good support, and the Workington Reds were well represented in the huge 52,581 crowd – by far the biggest attendance ever to watch a Workington game. The result was as expected, but only by a solitary goal. Twenty-five players had been used in League matches, with Simmonds missing just one game and McDowall heading the scorers with 14 successes.

The first season in the League could be put down to experience and consolidation, and it was hoped that a vast improvement was to come in the next – but it wasn't to be! The next campaign started with a 'reversal' of a year earlier, i.e. the Reds at home (rather than away) to Halifax, and this time a win ensued, by two unopposed goals; it was a different story in the return some time later however – a 2-5 defeat. The next match, away to Southport, indicated that things would not be so rosy, as a 0-2 defeat resulted. However, a few days later on August the 30th, a single goal win at Accrington restored the fans hopes, which were again shaken when the return with Southport was lost 2-4 – the first 'double' achieved over the Reds, and at such an early stage in the campaign. The home derby with Carlisle occurred on the 6th of September and two goals were shared, followed by a scoreless draw at Mansfield.

A start of six games in which there were two of each – wins, draws and defeats, was perhaps not so bad, and definitely an overall improvement on the previous season. The two Christmas games resulted in honours even on points, winning at home and losing away, to neighbours Barrow, but as the season wore on it was apparent that it was going to be a poor second 'innings'. Although there were no terrible defeats – the 1-6 reverse at Bradford Park Avenue excepted – there was little improvement on a year earlier when the final tables showed Workington in 23rd place, five points and one place above the tail-ender, the hapless Accrington Stanley. There had been a three points improvement over a year earlier, but it was obviously insufficient to avoid the embarrassment of another re-election application.

Once again the League members kept faith with the newcomers, and they retained their Football League membership, but with nine less votes than

Accrington who had finished below them! Wigan's standard application to join – this time with no others – received a healthy, but insufficient, 17 votes. Earlier the Reds F.A.Cup run finished at the first hurdle, a single goal exit at Chesterfield. Attendances meanwhile were slightly up on the season by around 500 per match, even though the 'top' game – at home to Carlisle – showed a significant drop to 14,114, an encounter that had attracted a near record 17,187 in the previous campaign. With only 55 League goals scored, it was a poor top–scorer total, in fact Simmonds and Dick achieved only low double figures, of eleven each. In trying to get a winning combination no less than 33 players were called up for League matches.

The third season was entered with some trepidation and hope that the Club's fortunes would change, whilst another poor showing and re–election application may very easily have seen the Reds voted out. The end result was a very near thing with a finish in 20th position – one above the re–election zone. With 40 points, they were only two points clear of 21st placed Darlington. Surprisingly the aggregate League attendances totalled 194,882 or an average of 8,473 per home match – a figure that was later to prove to be the Reds best ever in the Football League. Champions Port Vale attracted the highest number of spectators to Borough Park, 14,000, whilst the match at Vale Park was the highest Workington away game crowd of 16,787.

It came as a welcome surprise for the Club, when the final place in the table for the 1954/55 season produced a healthy 8th. In a generally successful side, a settled line–up was the outcome and only 21 players were required for League duty, with Dailey (who led the marksmen with 19 goals), Dunlop, Stokoe and Vitty all being ever–presents. The third round of the F.A.Cup was reached after victories over Hyde United and Leyton Orient, but a five goal defeat at high–flying Luton put paid to any glory in this direction. The following season could be was one of consolidation, for a final placing in the League of tenth was the outcome. It was an unremarkable season – save for two games in which Dailey scored hat tricks of goals – although there were some high scoring home wins; 6-1 versus both Barrow and Gateshead, 5-1 when Harlepools were the visitors, and an exciting odd goal in seven victory over Oldham. The F.A.Cup run ended in the second round at Park Avenue, Bradford. Only twenty different players were required in League games, with the aforementioned Dailey being only one of two ever presents, and he also headed the goal scorers (his second of three consecutive seasons) with 22 on target.

One novel event early in the season occurred on the 24th of September, when the home game with York City, before a 5,895 crowd, was featured for the afternoon's live radio commentary; despite a scoreless draw, the general opinion was that of the game being one of the best seen at Borough Park.

The 1956/57 season started on the 18th of August, with the Reds visiting Tranmere, the start of what proved to be not only the teams best season to date, but also one of the highest they were ever to reach in the Football League. With 24 wins, only half that number of defeats and ten drawn games, the final outcome was a placing of fourth in the Third Division North. With only one team being promoted (Derby County), and four points behind those Champions it was not a very close finish, but only goal difference separated the Club from third placed Accrington, and one point from runners–up Hartlepools. Whilst the League games gave the fans cause for satisfaction, this joy was not repeated in the team's displays in the F.A.Cup. The first round match produced a 2–1 win to the Reds, in a replay, after two goals were shared at Mansfield Town. The next round should have caused few problems, when Workington were destined to visit Midland League side Goole Town. The 2–2 draw was followed by a home replay, which was expected to be a mere formality, but the high flying Reds ended the game red faced as the Non–leaguers triumphed with the only goal of the game; this in the final event proved to be the only occasion when Workington, as a Football League team, lost in the competition to a Non–league outfit.

This disappointment was soon forgotten however as the Reds continued to hover around the top of the table, and although there were no honours at the season's end, they did score 93 Football League goals – far and away the most either before or after this season – and Dailey's twenty–five League goals was to become the highest in the Club's 26 seasons residence in top flight football. With an average attendance at home games of a shade under 9,000 (the second best ever) – the highest being 13,919 for Derby's visit – things looked good for the future. Football is an unpredictable game, and just when the Reds appeared to have got it right, their fortunes dipped. The 1957/58 season was doubly disappointing since this was the last of the regionalised Third Divisions and a top half placing would have guaranteed membership of the new single Third Division; in the event a slip backwards resulted to 19th place and the dubious honour of becoming a founder–member of the Fourth Division.

1957 heralded a new dimension for the Club, when in line with the new vogue, floodlights – at a cost of £12,000 – were first installed at Borough Park. The 'switch–on' occurred on the 20th of November, and the Reds triumphed by 6–1 over Hamilton Academicals. This match was followed by a visit from Blackpool, complete with Stanley Matthews, and an emphatic 4–1 victory before a crowd of 16,181. The following two seasons provided little to enthuse over with similar final positions in the League. The latter of these periods – 1959/60 – however produced some good wins that made a nonsense of their lowly 16th placing in the League; 5–0 at home to both Chester and Crewe, 5–1 versus Northampton and 5–1 over visiting Millwall. Conversely there were no heavy defeats, the worst being a 0–3 Borough Park reverse to Walsall, and the same scoreline at – ironically – Millwall. Economically worrying were the attendances at home matches which had slumped to an average of 4,300, virtually a 50% drop from just three years earlier. The season saw the last appearance of D.Jones who had given six years first team service to the Reds and had played in 210 League games for them; although only 25 players had been utilized over the previous 10 months, there was only one ever–present – Tennant – who by 1962 had made 151 appearances in League matches.

Following the embarrassing defeat in the F.A.Cup to Goole in 1957, the Club celebrated their most exciting run one year later. Crook Town were disposed of in the first round by no less than 8–1 followed by an amazing 5–1 victory at fellow Leaguers, Oldham Athletic. The third round draw however set the town buzzing with anticipation when the Reds were drawn at home to the mighty Manchester United. The game without doubt was the biggest in the Club's history, and fittingly an all time record attendance of 21,000 was present. The match also had it's poignancy since it was one of the last matches of the 'Busby Babes' who included in their line–up the likes of Harry Gregg, Eddie Colman, Duncan Edwards, Bobby Charlton and Tommy Taylor – a team that was to lose so many of its members in the Munich air disaster, just one month later. After only six minutes from the kick–off, the Reds shook the United and amazed their own followers when they took the lead through Clive Colbridge. The lead was held until the 55th minute when the United drew level through Dennis Violet. There were no more sensations and within nine minutes, Violet had scored two more goals, and completed a hat–trick which enabled the 'other' Reds to progress on (eventually as losing finalists) with a 3–1 win. One year later Workington departed from the competition in the first round, and in 1960 reached the third round again only to lose 0–2 at Crewe.

The early 1960's restored the supporters faith in the Club, as they gradually rose in the table to a final 3rd position in the 1963/64 season. This campaign had started reasonably well, although it was not until the third home match that the first home win was recorded, despite two victories having been won on foreign soil. After a 0–5 defeat at Rochdale – this first away defeat was hardly reassuring – only 3,753 turned up for the next game – a home victory over Oxford United. A week later another heavy loss (by four goals at Aldershot) hardly looked like promotion material.

But a run of nine games without defeat restored the fans faith. By Christmas things were looking very hopeful, and on Boxing Day a record League game attendance of 18,628 was present for the promotion battle – a 2–2 draw – with neighbours Carlisle. This was followed by a dent in the club's hopes two days later when the return match watched by another large crowd, saw Workington go down 1–3. From the start of 1964 to the end of the season just four defeats occured, and so for the first time in their League history, Workington had achieved a promotion by claiming the third place in the table.

It was a very close run finish, with just two points separating the top and fourth placed teams; Bradford City in sixth trailed by another two points, but undoubtably 'blew' their chance in the penultimate game when they lost to the Reds by two goals at Valley Parade before a 15,545 crowd. With such an indifferent start it took some time for the locals to get behind the team, and the largest attendance (apart from the Carlisle game) was only 8,600 for the last battle – versus Exeter – a disappointing scoreless draw, but none the less sufficient for both teams to secure promotion. Dave Carr, who went on to appear in the Workington colours on League duty in 121 games, led the scorers with 21 goals. The numbers at home gates nearly doubled over a year earlier to reach a figure of virtually 5,000 average, but apart from the next season when a slight rise followed, it was an almost regular decrease from then on in to the end.

Promotion came under the capable hands of Player/Manager, Ken Furphy, a man destined to move on to to Watford in November 1964. After the most rewarding season (on the pitch) in the Club's history the 1964/65 campaign was something of an anti–climax. It started with a bright 4–1 victory over Port Vale – which turned out to be the best result of the season – but dimmed with such defeats as those meted out at Shrewsbury, Bristol City and Gillingham – 1–6, 0–5 and 1–5 respectively, plus the 1–5 home defeat to Mansfield. None the less the Club survived and finished in 15th place in the Third Division. When all things were considered it was not so bad after all.

After a career with the Reds that stretched to eight years and 295 Football League appearances, Keith Burkinshaw was transferred to Scunthorpe, but it was later in his Managerial capacity that he came to prominence.

The 1965/66 season was something of a shock, for although a struggle seemed on the cards, the period turned out very successfully, and the Reds by finishing in fifth place (their highest ever in the Football League) were only five points behind promoted Q.P.R. The highlights were the three unopposed goals win over Champions–elect Hull – although a six goal defeat was later in store at Boothferry Park – plus a 7–0 and two 6–1 victories. In each of the three high scoring games, Kit Napier recorded hat–tricks, including four goals in the Swansea match. His stay with the Reds only lasted until November 1965, when he was transferred to Newcastle United for £20,000, the third highest fee received in the Club's history. Workington were at this time involved in one of the first relayed close circuit television matches, the occasion being for Millwall's visit to Borough Park, on the 28th of January 1966, when the match was seen 'live' at the Den.

One inexplicable fact was a near 40% drop in home gates from the previous year, which represented average attendances of 3,263, a terrible disappointment in the circumstances. The struggle to make ends meet had become a perennial problem, and it was necessary to sell players for the Club to remain solvent. Apart from the departure of Napier, Lowes and Chapman were also transferred, to the dismay of the supporters who accused the Directors of not wanting success!

The first game of the new season coincided with the first League match in which a substitute was allowable, and on the 21st of August Tony Geidmintis went down in the Workington record books for the second time when he was the nominated twelfth man; his earlier record being that of the youngest player to appear for the Reds. This period also saw the scoring of the Red's 1,000th Football League goal, by Dave Butler, who during his stint with the Club appeared in 195 League games but found the net on only eight occasions!

Any thoughts of promotion to the Second Division in the 1966/67 season were soon shattered, and the months proved to be one long desparate struggle in which the Club lost their status. They forfeited their rights to Third Division membership, an elevation that they were never to encounter again, when they finished in the wooden spoon position. Only twenty different players had been used for League matches, bought about more from financial restraints rather than consistancy! Despite their final lowly position, there were few bad results, the worst being a 1–5 reverse at Torquay, and this was balanced with the 4–0 home win dished out to visiting Walsall. For the visit of Reading to Borough Park a lamentable 856 crowd were present, the lowest to that date for a Football League match.

Little mention has been made reference the F.A.Cup, but equally little success came the Club's way during the mid to late '60's, as the third round was only reached once, which ended with a 1–4 defeat at high flying Second Division Bolton Wanderers in 1964.

The heady days of success, albeit limited, were now behind the Club, and they were now on a downward course in the Football League from which they were never to recover. The first period back in the Fourth Division was a disaster, for the decline continued with a vengeance, leaving the Club in bottom but one position in the Fourth Division. Along with three other Clubs, the Reds had to go cap in hand for re-election, and their 38 votes were well in excess of the nearest non-elected Club – Chelmsford City – with three. No fewer than fifteen teams sought election, and ironically of these Romford, Bedford Town, Guildford City, and New Brighton have now become defunct; of the remaining ten, four of those applying have since obtained their objective. It was somewhat ominous that although this was Workington's first re-election application for fifteen years (and only one year earlier they had been members of the Third Division), Bradford, who finished bottom of the League, nine points below the Reds and also had need to be re-elected the previous May, gained six votes more! A second round replay defeat to Doncaster put paid to the Club's hopes in the F.A.Cup, this after the seventh consecutive away match in the Competition.

1968 also saw the Club's all time faithfull stalwart 'hang up his boots' with the Reds, Bobby Brown, who had played for ten years with the Club and recorded 419 Football League appearances.

The next five seasons produced no real hopes for a recovery with around middle of the table final positions, except in the last of these campaigns, that of the 1971/72, when a very encouraging 6th place was obtained. In all this time the uninspiring record in the F.A.Cup continued, with one solitary appearance in the third round, when the Club were hosts to Brentford in 1971; the game encouraged a crowd of 5,953 – the best for some years – but all to no avail as a single goal defeat resulted.

The real problem on the field tended to be, unlike earlier years, that of scoring goals, whilst the defence had over the previous few years kept the goals against down to very reasonable proportions (64 being the worst, in 1969/70). The 'goals for' column was very lean with only 50 finding the back of the net in the highly placed 1971/72 season. Spratt was top scorer with a measly ten, a position he also attained a year earlier when along with Martin he scored eight.

Since 1960, Workington along with the bulk of the Football League teams had entered the Football League Cup. This competition which in the early days held little prestige saw the Reds reach the fifth round – the quarter final stage – on two occasions. In the 1963/64 season after beating Oldham, Southport, Huddersfield and Colchester, the end came at Upton Park with an uncompromising 0-6 defeat to West Ham.

Following this run of successes, the Reds repeated their performances one year later with a high scoring series. The first round saw a thumping 9-1 win over Barrow, followed by victory over Scunthorpe and then Blackburn – the latter via a 5-1 successful replay. Second Division Norwich were the next victims, which produced a surprising 3-0 home win before an 11,300 crowd. The fifth round required a visit from high-flying First Division Chelsea to Borough Park, when despite going two goals down after only 35 minutes, the under-dogs managed to pull back and earn a well merited 2-2 draw before 18,000 excited fans; a shock win nearly became a reality, but a 'goal' was ruled offside. The end of the run came with a respectable 0-2 defeat in the replay. At other times the third round was reached on a few occasions, but the 'norm', particularly in the latter years meant defeat in the first round!

The high placing in the League could not be maintained and the 1972/73 season saw a mid-table 13th position, but from then on things went from bad to worse. With the ever increasing worry of poor gate receipts, the best players were inevitably transferred in order to balance the books, notably David Irving to Everton in January 1973 for £28,000 and the record fee received, when Ian MacDonald moved to Liverpool one year later for £33,000.

For four consecutive seasons the Reds had to apply for re-election, during which time the bottom but one place was first occupied for two years, followed by the wooden spoon position for the next two. During this period the goal-scoring had become an even more acute problem, with 43 in the first of these re-election years being the best; Murray was the top goal scorer for the seasons ending in 1974 to 1976, but with totals of only 9,7 and 6 goals it was hardly a notable achievement! Efforts by the Club to save it's existence in the Football League became harder, for inevitably support dwindled, with an all time low of 1,170 average at home in the 1973/74 season. During that period there were sub-1,000 crowds on six occasions with an all time minimum Football League gate for Exeter's visit, of just 693. Ironically the next three seasons saw a reasonable improvement, in fact the last League campaign of 1976/77 produced the best attendances for five years – an average of 1,500 – but clearly well below the break even figure.

The last Football League season for the Club was an outright disaster with only four victories in total, Crewe and Scunthorpe – 1-0, Huddersfield – 3-2 – all at home – and the Reds last ever win at this level on the 19th of March 1977 when a solitary win away from Borough Park was achieved at Rochdale. The finale came at Newport County on Tuesday the 17th of May watched by a surprisingly large attendance of 8,313 – swelled no doubt by the fact that the Welshman needed a victory to ensure that they too would not need to apply for re-election. The Workington team consisted of:

Laisby, Leng, Wallace, Honour, Johnston, Scholes, Harris, Kisby, Ashworth, McDonald, Williamson and substitute Higgins.

A most remarkable coincidence, probably unique in Football League history, occurred in the team line-up for Ken Wallace at number three, superseded his namesake who had appeared in the first ever Workington League match twenty six years earlier – the 'first' Ken Wallace was in fact the father of the latter day player! The single goal defeat at Somerton Park completed an unusual double victory for Newport, for they had beaten the Reds at Borough Park by the same score just three days earlier. Defeat had also come in the first round of the League Cup – after two drawn games – at the hands of Stockport County.

The second replay was played at Preston's Ground, and it was coincidentally the North End team that succumbed to the Reds last ever victory in this competition, which had occurred some four years earlier. The F.A.Cup attempt was even worse than the League Cup, when the Club were defeated at the same stage by a crushing 0–6 scoreline at Bury.

In view of the Clubs immediate preceding record, it would have taken only a supreme optimist to expect a successful re-election application yet again. The three previous applications had seen Workington accepted back into the fold, but with an alarming lack of confidence when compared to their contemporaries; 21 votes in 1974 compared with the 16 for nearest non-leaguers, Kettering Town – 28 votes one year later, only eight more than Kettering again – and 21 in 1976, this time a bare three votes more than Yeovil Town. With such an awful 1976/77 record, six points below their nearest rivals in the League and a goals against total of 102, there was obviously very little hope.

Club Secretary Mary Laurie, who was one of only two females in the Football League when she took on the post a few years earlier, departed after the Club's rejection, following twenty-four years with the Reds.

For several years the enthusiasm and dedication of the playing staff, so necessary for a home-spun, small town Club, was missing from that short period in the 1960's when everybody had pulled together. The League meeting on the 17th of June 1977 put the Reds in 5th place, once again with 21 votes (only two Non-league teams attempting recognition on this occasion). But with Wimbledon gaining 27, the end had come; Workington F.C. were no longer a Member of the Football League.

The Club's previous six successful 'cap in hand' applications had resulted on each occasion with them obtaining the least points of the re-elected Clubs! It was no more than a formality that the Reds should be accepted into the premier Non-league in the North of England, that of the Northern Premier League. However, any assumptions that the Club's recent Football League status would mean success at a lower level would be a formality were soon dispelled. In many ways the task to produce a successful team at a lower level was rendered even harder. Despite the new competition being of a regionalised nature, virtually isolated in their North-west pocket, the Club were still faced with long journeys and the problem of recruiting suitable players - but in both cases with more limited resources. Whilst a fully professional squad previously lived locally and regularly trained together, the team now came from various directions and being part-time saw little of each other except at the games themselves.

Gordon Livsey was initially appointed player/manager but with a poor start to the season he departed just six months later in December 1977, being replaced by David Wilson who remained for an even shorter period - until the end of the 1977/78 season.

The fixtures in the Non-league circle commenced with a home game versus Stafford Rangers, and the attendance of 970 was very encouraging, but a three goal defeat was followed with further indifferent results. This crowd figure subsequently became not only the first, but also the best, home Northern Premier League match attendance to date. Performances were so bad that it was not until the fifth match that a goal was scored and even longer before the first victory. The end of the season saw the Reds in a poor 19th league position of 24 teams.

The following few years were little better with final placings respectively of 14th, 21st (of twenty-two teams), 10th and 11th. There was also no stability in the managership with no less than seven occupants of the hot seat in the first four years! The 1982/83 season however produced a big improvement, when a very respectable seventh in the league was the outcome, and the Club's nineteen wins included a club record score in the competition, of 7-1, over Morecambe. But attendances had dropped to a point until they were nearly non-existent, with regular dips in the averages to a lamentable low of 242 in the 1983/84 season. Even the best results on the field of one year earlier produced an average of only 283 (nearly forty less than the previous season), which was a great disappointment. A strange coincidence happened during this campaign, when on two Saturdays in succession the Club's goalkeepers had to be substituted - due to injuries - and on both occasions the incidents happened within ten minutes start of the matches.

Whilst the early 1980's produced, in general, a countrywide reduction of interest at the gate, the Reds had become one of the poorest supported teams in the their league, never matching the occasional 1000 plus crowds that they played in front of, on their travels. The F.A.Cup sorties since the Football League days have produced little of note, for despite frequent appearances in the first round (at first entry being required at the fourth qualifying stage), this round has not been passed. The only really notable achievements have been two home drawn games against Football League opponents – Carlisle and Huddersfield – in 1980/81 and a year later. The first of these two games attracted an interest in the town which had not been present for many years, and the attendance of 7,362 produced all–time record receipts of £8,909. Ironically the replay at Brunton Park (which was lost 1–4) saw a crowd of only 5,477. The following sortie in the competition, but without the 'derby' element in the game, attracted only 3,244 spectators for the Yorkshire visitors; after a 1–1 draw, the Reds were thrashed by five unopposed goals at Leeds Road.

With their reduced status, the Club have had the chance of success in the F.A.Trophy competition, but despite facing opposition of the same, or less, theoretical 'quality', results in this competition can be considered even worse than the F.A.Cup. On only one occasion have the team won the last two qualifying rounds to reach the first round proper – during the 1983/84 season – when the end came in a replayed game at Southport. In the 1980/81 season, when the Club had the ignominy of starting their cup matches in the preliminary round, the first game resulted in a single goal victory at Kirkby Town, with an official attendance of just 39, the lowest crowd in a competitive match that the Club have ever played before.

With goalscoring that had become a rare commodity during the latter non–league days, it comes as no surprise to find that few players have scored hat–tricks, however on three occasions four goals were scored in separate matches; twice by Walter Gillott (in the 8–1 thrashing of Thirlmere and the 5–1 victory over Keswick, both at home and in the Cumbria Cup during the 1978/79 season), plus Graham Gill's tally in a 5–2 away victory over North Shields in the F.A.Trophy game of 1980/81.

The Club's Centenary season of 1983/84 did not produce a hoped for happy time, for a final placing of 15th in the Northern Premier was the outcome, but at least for the first time in forty seven years a major Trophy was won!

By finishing in the top eight in the league a year earlier, the Reds qualified for entry into the League President's Cup. Victories over Chorley (two legs) and Burton Albion ensured a place in the two legged final with Marine. At Rossett Park two goals were shared, and despite extra time – in the return –

the match finished goalless. With the away goals counting double, the Reds captured the trophy to the delight of the 1,125 supporters present at Borough Park.

When Workington F.C. were elected to the Football League, the population of the town was less than 30,000. With the added problem of being located in a Rugby enclave, the organisation has always been a 'Cinderella Club', never having the degree of support and hence finance to raise themselves above the 'also-runs'. Conversely in view of these limited resources, and desperate situations that have faced the Club in the 1980's, it is obvious that a dedicated – albeit small – band of enthusiasts still exist that have managed to keep the Reds going at a high status.

Their unequal battle with the 'other' football can be best illustrated with a situation that occurred in 1952, at which time both the Football and the Rugby Clubs were using Borough Park – on alternate Saturdays. With the Football team due to play a home match with Oldham on the 15th of March and the Rugby contingent drawn at home in their league cup, there was no alternative but for both games to be played on the one Saturday, with the Reds kicking off at 2.00 p.m., followed by the 'Town's' match at 4.15 p.m., the Ground between times having been cleared of all spectators. A 'par for the course' five and a half thousand watched the Reds, whilst nearly four times that number were present for the later Rugby match!

THE GROUNDS.

The Club's home ground since 1937, could never be considered anything grander than a 'typical' Third or Fourth Division Football League venue, however with a one time capacity of 21,000, it could certainly hold it's own amongst many of the Reds contemporaries in their Non-league circles.

The first properly enclosed Ground at Lonsdale Park, immediately adjacent to Borough Park, was made up from an oval playing arena with a narrow flat area at the top of an embankment around the perimeter. On the North side there was a Pavilion and ancillary buildings set back from the pitch, whilst opposite a small seated Stand was sited. Before the Second World War, after the Reds had moved to Borough Park, the Pavilion and other buildings were replaced with a longer covered enclosure adjacent to the later greyhound track – which by now surrounded the grassed area – and alongside, other new buildings. The seated stand was also removed. The Ground remains much the same today – but just! Any spectator at a Greyhound meeting today would be well advised to ensure that his life Insurance has been paid, for seldom can there be seen a more dilapidated structure! With rust being the principal remaining building material, the whole arena presents a picture of decay and desolation.

The initial development of Borough Park which the Reds moved to in 1937, consisted of a brick and timber seated stand with a covered terraced area each side, and slightly extending around both ends of the pitch. Elsewhere were open terraces. The post-war years produced developments which included extensions to the end enclosures, large step concrete terracing all round and a covered enclosure opposite the Stand. But running a team on a shoestring has resulted in inevitable neglect, without the money to repair or replace. Whilst in many respects the facilities at the ground are still perfectly useable, the floodlight pylons were considered unsafe – they have now been reduced to half their former height – and the Stand was all but condemned. In November 1986, it was necessary for a few games to be played at Lonsdale Park – which can scarcely be considered any better! The start of the 1987/88 season saw a return to Borough Park, however without the use of the Grandstand, and an estimated £60,000 required to carry out repair works, most of the structure had to removed, to leave a truncated building, with single story offices, as the only remains. The future for the Club will be to say the least, an uphill struggle.

PROGRAMMES.

Since the Club were still members of the Football League well into the 1970's, their programmes are quite easy to obtain – except for selected difficult matches. However, despite the apparent relative abundance of Pre–War (non–League) programmes, these have become very much Collectors' items, and fetch high prices. Programmes were issued by the Club from their re–formation in 1921 up to the present.

(Right) The 'first', and 'last' in the Football League.

(Photo: Dave Twydell) (Below) 1987 – just before the upper structure of the Stand was removed.

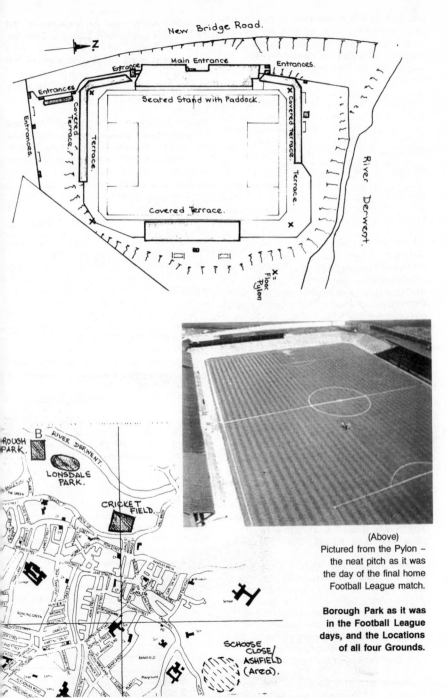

New Bridge Road.

N

Entrances

Entrance

Main Entrance

Entrances.

Entrances

Covered Terrace.

Terrace.

Seated Stand with Paddock.

Covered Terrace.

Terrace.

River Derwent.

Covered Terrace.

Floac Pylon

ROUGH PARK.

B

RIVER DERWENT.

LONSDALE PARK.

CRICKET FIELD.

SCHOOSE CLOSE/ ASHFIELD (Area).

(Above)
Pictured from the Pylon –
the neat pitch as it was
the day of the final home
Football League match.

**Borough Park as it was
in the Football League
days, and the Locations
of all four Grounds.**

Yore Publications was established in May 1991, and specialise in the Publishing of Football Books with historic 'themes' – those written by Dave Twydell and other Authors.

....

**YORE PUBLICATIONS
12 The Furrows,
Harefield,
Middx. UB9 6AT**

Previous books (by Dave Twydell) include:
'Defunct F.C.' – histories of five notable non–League Clubs that no longer exist (Now out of print and reprint unlikely)
'Rejected F.C. – Volume 1 was first published in 1988 and soon sold out, as did Volume 2 (Published in 1989) – a reformatted second edition is envisaged in late 1992/early 1992.
'More Defunct F.C.' – The detailed histories of six more defunct non–League clubs. A limited number of copies are still available – no reprint is envisaged.
Price £6–75 plus £1–00 U.K. P/P.
'Football League Grounds For A Change' – Published in July 1991. It is anticipated that this title too will soon be out of print. This hardback book of 424 pages contains a comprehensive study of **all** the Grounds on which all the relevant Football League Clubs once played. 'Potted' histories are included within the context of the Grounds, with around 250 illustrations.
Price £13–95 plus U.K. P/P £1–80.

'Rejected F.C. of Scotland Volume 1 (Edinburgh and The South).' Published in April 1992. The Scottish equivalent of the successful 'Rejected F.C.' books. A collection of intriguing former Scottish League Clubs (ten in this first volume include; St.Bernards, Solway Star, Nithsdale Wanderers, etc.). Details of these ten Clubs have been largely overlooked by Football Historians – you don't have to be a Scottish football fan to be fascinated with this well illustrated, 288 p. hardback book. Price £12–95 plus U.K. P/P £1–15.

'Rejected F.C. The Video' (Out of This League Productions: Trans Video Productions in conjunction with Yore Publications) You wouldn't have read this book if the ex–League Clubs didn't fascinate you! A 90 minute video includes amazing archive footage from six Clubs playing during their League days (e.g. Ashington in 1924 and New Brighton), Club personalities interviews, and a 'tour' of the Grounds.
Providing a visual history of the books. (Number 1 bestseller in *Sportspages*; 'Video rack list – The Guardian 14/3/92).
Price £12–99 plus U.K. P/P £1–00.

Titles published by Yore publications and written by other Authors currently include:
'The Ironsides. A Lifetime in the League. Who's Who of Newport County' (By Tony Ambrosen). Every player who played for the Club in the Football League is given a potted football and personal history, with detailed sections on the Trainers and Managers, plus the non–League periods.
Price £8–95 plus U.K. P/P £1–00.

*'Cardiff City Football Club:
The Official History of the Bluebirds.*
(By John Crooks). A well illustrated large format 320 page book by the acknowledged Cardiff City 'expert'. Detailed sections on the history of the Club, an abbreviated but complete 'Who's Who', the Club as seen from the players viewpoint over the decades, Ninian Park, and the full statistics of all the Clubs first team matches since 1910. (" *A masterly hardback... definitely in the super–league of soccer histories*" – South Wales Argus)
Price £16–95 plus U.K. P/P £3–50.

.... And in the future:
'Through the Turnstiles'. (By Brian Tabner). A book that will inevitably become a statisticians 'handbook', plus a good read for the average fan. An amazing book in which nearly **every** Football League attendance of every Club since 1888 has been traced! The figures are summarised in various ways, including seasonal averages of each Club, and a detailed well written history of the game with respect to the crowds is included.
Available September 1992.

*'History of the Lancashire F.A.:
1878 – 1928'.* A reprint of this rare and fascinating book. Well illustrated, the book includes sections on the 'early' Clubs, Lancashire cup competitions, biographies etc.
Available Autumn 1992.

Other titles are planned for the future, and a free Newsletter is issued every four months.
A S.A.E. will provide you with the current issue.